Assessing Ethnolinguistic Vitality: Theory and Practice

Selected Papers from the Third International Language Assessment Conference

SIL International
Publications in Sociolinguistics

Publication 3

Publications in Sociolinguistics is a serial publication of SIL International. The series is a venue for works covering a broad range of topics in sociolinguistics. While most volumes are authored by members of SIL, suitable works by others will also form part of the series.

Series Editor

M. Paul Lewis

Associate Editor

Gloria E. Kindell

Editoral Assistant

June Austing

Production Staff

Bonnie Brown, Managing Editor
Laurie Nelson, Production Manager
Judy Benjamin, Compositor
Hazel Shorey, Graphic Artist

Assessing Ethnolinguistic Vitality: Theory and Practice

Selected Papers from the Third International Language Assessment Conference

Edited by Gloria Kindell and M. Paul Lewis

A Publication of
SIL International
Dallas, Texas

© 2000 SIL International
Library of Congress Catalog No: 99-67495
ISBN: 1-55671-087-9
ISSN: 1091-9074

Printed in the United States of America

All Rights Reserved

10 09 08 07 06 05 04 03 02 01   10 9 8 7 6 5 4 3 2 1

No part of this publication may be reproduced, stored in a retrieval system, or transmitted in any form or by any means—electronic, mechanical, photocopy, recording, or otherwise—without the express permission of SIL International, with the exception of brief excerpts in journal articles or reviews.

Copies of this and other publications of SIL International may be obtained from

International Academic Bookstore
SIL International
7500 W. Camp Wisdom Road
Dallas, TX 75236-5699

Voice: 972-708-7404
Fax: 972-708-7433
Email: academic_books@SIL.org
Internet: http://www.SIL.org

Contents

Introduction vii
Contributors xiii

Theory

Reversing Language Shift: RLS Theory and Practice Revisited
    Joshua A. Fishman 1

Ethnicity, Ethnic Movements, and Language Maintenance
    Christina Bratt Paulston 27

Language Contact, Evolution, and Death: How Ecology Rolls the Dice
    Salikoko S. Mufwene 39

Motivations: Language Vitality Assessments Using The Perceived Benefit Model of Language Shift
    Mark E. Karan 65

Power and Solidarity as Metrics in Language Survey Data Analysis
    M. Paul Lewis 79

Practice

Towards Predicting and Planning for Ethnolinguistic Vitality: An Application of Grid/Group Analysis
    Sue Harris Russell 103

Social Network Analysis: More Toward an Application to
  Sociolinguistic Research and Language Development
  Assessment
   Steve Graham 131
Modifying Language Beliefs: A Role for Mother-Tongue Advocates?
   Carolyn P. Miller 167
Assessing Motivations: Techniques for Researching the Motivations
  behind Language Choice
   Mark E. Karan and Jürg Stalder 189

Introduction

This volume is a collection of selected papers presented at the Third International Language Assessment Conference, sponsored by the International Sociolinguistics Department of SIL International, held at Horsleys Green, High Wycombe, England in June of 1997. The conference brought together SIL's language survey specialists from around the world and provided them with an opportunity to interact with each other as well as with leading scholars in the area of the conference theme, *Assessing Ethnolinguistic Vitality: Theory and Practice*. In selecting these papers, we are attempting to explore, by no means for the first time, some of the ways in which language functions as a marker of ethnolinguistic identity and to supply some methodological insights into the collection of data regarding the vitality of that identity.

We have attempted to divide the papers in this volume between those that are primarily theoretical in nature and those that focus more on the practical aspects of ethnolinguistic vitality assessment. This has proven to be a difficult task. You will find that even those papers that are in the first section of the book, which ostensibly focus on theory, are quite practical and methodologically rich, and that those which we have placed in the practical section are equally theory-rich. We suggest that, no matter your primary interest, you neglect neither section.

The study of the phenomena relating to contact between different social and ethnic groups is a rich and complex endeavor. Since social and cultural identity markers are varied, there can be a variety of approaches to this study. Anthropologists, for example, might trace such contact through its effects on cultural patterns. Differences in patterns of dress, food, housing, or subsistence patterns over time might be seen as evidence of contact or responses to contact with another group. Psychologists, on the other hand, might look at the contact between these groups and consider what beliefs and attitudes are developed and how those are realized in observable behaviors. A sociologist, looking at the same data, would want to know about how the groups of people in contact develop and maintain their sense of group identity, and how that identity affects intergroup relations.

What is obviously missing from this collection of approaches is the consideration of language and how it both affects and is affected by the coming together of more-or-less disparate groups of people. Obviously, groups of people in contact have a number of means by which they can demonstrate their in-group unity and their separateness from the out-group (Garvin and Mathiot 1956), and language figures prominently among the resources that they have at their disposal.

Ross (1979) distinguished two approaches to this question. One, the objectivist view, says that group identity is a function of external, objective behaviors, "a sense of group identity deriving from real or perceived common bonds such as language, race or religion" (Edwards 1977:254, cited in Edwards 1985:6). The other position, the subjectivist view, claims that group identity is not so much a function of unifying and separating behaviors as it is a function of an underlying (subjective) sense of belonging. This sense of "groupness" is then manifested through overt behaviors which express that unity and separateness and in turn reinforce it.

Without taking a strong position with those who take the objectivist view of group identity, it does seem quite evident that the external markers of identity, such as language, are important for us to consider when looking at how strongly a group identity is held by individuals within that group and perceived by those outside of the group. Indeed, if we are to assess ethnolinguistic vitality, the most obvious data for us to consider is the actual behavior of those who are members of a given group.

On the other hand (you won't find the objectivist/subjectivist debate resolved here!), it also seems quite evident that groups of people who perceive themselves as being unified and separate from other groups, are quite willing to exchange the external identity markers that they use for others. Most frequently, this is done incrementally, with gradual changes and shifts taking place over a long period of time. In such situations, a simple analysis of the discontinuities between earlier objective behaviors and current behaviors may not reveal very clearly the level of group cohesion that is being maintained in spite of the obvious differences.

To further complicate the assessment of ethnolinguistic vitality, lines of subjective group cohesion may not be entirely coterminous with any of the objective markers of identity. Patterns of dress, food, housing, or subsistence may or may not be shared by groups that, at some level, do or do not see themselves as essentially unified. Similarly, linguistic patterns of lexicon, phonology, and syntax may or may not relate in a simple one-to-one fashion with the perceptions of social and ethnic groupings that are held by those who use the linguistic varieties. Thus, to speak of ethnolinguistic vitality is quite similar to speaking of ethnovestimentary vitality, or ethnoculinary vitality. The concept is interdisciplinary, sociolinguistic, and requires the ability to hold in one's mind simultaneously at least two conceptual frameworks, the sociocultural and the linguistic, and to reconcile the multiplex relationships that exist between them. The papers collected in this volume present such an interdisciplinary approach to the topic.

No scholar has more ably maintained this interdisciplinary perspective than Joshua Fishman, whose monumental work *Reversing Language Shift* (RLS) (Fishman 1991) clarified the interconnectedness of language, culture, society, religion, economy, and politics in efforts to retain and rebuild ethnolinguistic vitality and reverse language shift. Fishman's contribution to this volume is a new look at the issues related to RLS and highlights once again for us what is important and what is not, what can practically be done, and what is feasible. He does this by clarifying the theoretical underpinnings of ethnolinguistic vitality. Fishman focuses in on Stage 6 of his GIDS (graded intergenerational dislocation scale), which is "this crucial stage where intergenerational mother tongue transmission occurs and where its most crucial problems are located" (this volume, p. 4). He notes that the domains of intergenerational language (and ethnolinguistic vitality) transmission are the realm of intimacy, not the realms of power, and yet it is the latter, "...the world of jobs, statuses, recognitions, reputations, and opportunities..." (this volume, p. 4) which are most frequently the foci of language and culture revitalization efforts. This focus sets the tone for the rest of the volume and reflects the translation from theory into practice of the objectivist/subjectivist divide. Language status planning has tended to focus more on the objective external (and power-related) domains of language use, while the core of ethnolinguistic vitality issues is located in the subjective realm of intimate interactions.

A good example of how theory and practice are, and must be, inextricably linked is Sue Harris Russell's paper in which she presents, coming at it as an anthropologist, the grid/group model and shows how it can be productively used in assessing ethnolinguistic vitality and how that analysis can effectively shape language development activities. The grid/group conceptual model is another representation of the formal/informal, power/solidarity motif that runs through all of the papers.

Graham's paper looks at social network theory and suggests that a socially based understanding of ethnolinguistic vitality might be more productive than the linguistically oriented approach which has characterized much of SIL's work to date. Karan looks at the motivations for ethnolinguistic vitality maintenance and in the second section of the volume co-authors a paper with Jürg Stalder that describes a methodology for identifying and assessing ethnolinguistic vitality based on his model. Lewis' paper raises the possibility of assessing ethnolinguistic vitality in terms of a group's power and solidarity orientations which, as it turns out, are but two of the motivational forces identified by Karan.

Mufwene discusses language development and death in contact situations in much the same way a geneticist would approach the evolution of species under particular ecological conditions. He presents the contact situation as one of the ecological factors affecting the evolution of a language, why it was restructured and in which specific ways, and why it was or is endangered.

Paulston's contribution is an application of her analysis of social mobilizations (ethnicity, ethnic movement, ethnic nationalism, and geographic nationalism) and their effect on language maintenance or shift. She notes the important role of common sense in assessing the ethnolinguistic vitality of any given group.

As a good example of the application of common sense, Carolyn Miller examines the role of beliefs about language, a kind of language attitude, in language maintenance and shift. She concludes, as does Fishman, that while there are many variables that have been identified as affecting ethnolinguistic vitality, there are relatively few that anyone can do anything about. Following Allard and Landry (1992), Miller shows how something can be done about language beliefs. They can be changed through the appropriate use of language development methods, and this can have a positive effect on the ethnolinguistic vitality of the group.

While this volume hardly pretends to present more than a glimpse at some of the issues related to ethnolinguistic vitality and its assessment, it does gather together a useful collection of interdisciplinary approaches to the topic and a handful of very practical methods for assessing ethnolinguistic vitality. Our hope is that it will be an encouragement to our colleagues around the world who are working among speakers of the less commonly known languages and that it will be helpful to those who are looking for information about a wider range of language situations.

Gloria Kindell
M. Paul Lewis
April 1999

References

Allard, Réal, and Rodrigue Landry. 1992. Ethnolinguistic vitality beliefs and language maintenance and loss. In Willem Fase, Koen Jaspaert, and Sjaak Kroon (eds.), Maintenance and loss of minority languages, 171–95. Amsterdam: John Benjamins.
Edwards, John. 1977. Ethnic identity and bilingual education. In Howard Giles (ed.), Language, ethnicity and intergroup relations, 253–82. London: Academic Press.
———. 1985. Language, society and identity. Oxford: Basil Blackwell.
Fishman, Joshua A. 1991. Reversing language shift: Theoretical and empirical foundations of assistance to threatened languages. Clevedon: Multilingual Matters.
Garvin, Paul L., and Madeleine Mathiot. 1956. The urbanization of the Guarani language. In Anthony F. C. Wallace (ed.), Men and cultures: Selected papers from the Fifth International Congress of Anthropological and Ethnological Sciences, 783–90. Philadelphia, Penn.: University of Pennsylvania Press. Also in Joshua A. Fishman (ed.), 1968, Readings in the sociology of language, 365–74. The Hague: Mouton.
Ross, J. A. 1979. Language and the mobilization of ethnic identity. In Howard Giles and Bernard Saint-Jacque (eds.), Language and ethnic relations, 1–13. Oxford: Pergamon Press.

Contributors

Joshua A. Fishman is Distinguished University Research Professor, Social Sciences, Emeritus, at Yeshiva University, New York, New York, and Visiting Scholar/Visiting Professor, Linguistics, at Stanford University, Stanford, California. He is General Editor of the *International Journal of the Sociology of Language* and of the book series *Contributions to the Sociology of Language*.

Steve Graham has been a member of SIL International since 1983. He has participated in language development assessment in the West African countries of The Gambia, Guinea-Bissau, and Sénégal. Steve and his wife, Trina, are currently working on a sociolinguistic study of the "Portuguese-based" creoles spoken in West Africa. They have recently completed data collection on the Cape Verde Islands, off the coast of Sénégal, and the Islands of São Tomé, Príncipe, Annobón, and Bioko, in the Gulf of Guinea.

Mark E. Karan has been a member of SIL International since 1976. He worked in West and Central Africa in the areas of survey, linguistics, and translation and is currently the Director of Academics and Language Programs for the Central African Republic Branch of SIL.

M. Paul Lewis has been the International Sociolinguistics Coordinator for SIL International in Dallas, Texas since 1996. He began fieldwork in Guatemala in 1975, joining SIL International in 1981. He has worked among the K'iche', Uspanteko, and Ixil peoples in Guatemala.

Carolyn P. Miller has served with SIL since 1962. In Vietnam, she and her husband, John, were part of the Highland Education project, conducting teacher training for Bru literacy teachers. In Malaysia they participated in the Kadazan Children's Literature workshop and served as consultants on the Kadazan-Dusun Dictionary Project. In Thailand they conducted a sociolinguistic survey of Mon-Khmer groups in Northeast Thailand and helped with language development projects for six of these groups. Currently they serve as co-directors of the Mainland Southeast Asia Group. Since 1988 Carolyn has served on the International Board of SIL and in June 1999 was elected President of SIL International.

Salikoko S. Mufwene is Professor and Chair at the Department of Linguistics at the University of Chicago. His current research is on the development of creoles and on language evolution from the perspective of population genetics.

Christina Bratt Paulston is professor of linguistics, director of the English Language Institute, and former chair (1974–1989) of the Department of Linguistics, University of Pittsburgh. She has lectured and done fieldwork in such places as Azerbaijan, India, Peru, Tanzania, and Spain, among others. She has published in the fields of language teaching, teacher training, language planning, bilingual education, and sociolinguistics. She was President of International TESOL (Teachers of English to Speakers of Other Languages) in 1976 and trustee of the Center for Applied Linguistics from 1976 to 1981.

Sue Harris Russell was formerly a member of SIL International (1983–1997) and worked in the areas of linguistics, literacy, anthropology, sociolinguistics, and language planning. She is currently adjunct faculty at Biola University and continues to serve as an anthropology consultant.

Jürg Stalder has done extensive survey work in Cameroon and in the Central African Republic. He is now the Director of the Central African Republic Branch of SIL.

Reversing Language Shift: RLS Theory and Practice Revisited

Joshua A. Fishman

It is now ten years since I first began working on my *Reversing Language Shift*, a book which is very close to my heart. It deals with a problem that I have lived, intensely, consciously, and constantly for the nearly seventy years that I can remember. No scene from my childhood epitomizes it as much as the daily family "evening conference meal". During this meal each of us attempted to address the ever-present question, "What have you done for the language today?" What letters were written, what journals contributed to or edited, what meetings attended or conducted, which authors assisted, which schools supported, youth clubs attended or conducted, choruses encouraged or participated in, theater groups supported? These questions constituted the constant implicit or explicit agenda of the family's evening meal. It was here in my childhood home, as well as in the home that Gella and I subsequently established for ourselves and our children, that *Reversing Language Shift* was conceived, as were *Language Loyalty in the United States*, *Language and Nationalism*, *Rise and Fall of the Ethnic Revival*, and, most recently, *In Praise of the Beloved Language*. They are all (but *Reversing Language Shift* even more so than the others) a byproduct of the sanctity of the parental home, a home in which Yiddish was (and is even today) the "holy tongue". Of course, my *Never Say Die! A Thousand Years of Yiddish in Jewish Life and Letters* and *Yiddish: Turning Toward Life* are also in this category.

Nevertheless, as a sociolinguistic researcher and theoretician, I realize that reversing language shift's basic theory and data must be constantly revised and rethought, critiqued, and improved. I am now beginning to prepare a volume in which a dozen scholars from round the world will help me do exactly that, and I want to thank SIL for enabling me today to engage in this very process. From the very outset I have tried to focus upon manipulable variables (i.e., upon efforts and interactions that a threatened language, community could engage in and control or substantially influence by itself). I have set aside such obviously important variables as the size of the community of speakers and their proximity to larger languages, not because these are not important but because they can hardly be changed by any community that attempts to foster its own threatened language. When considering real estate issues, location is one of the three most important considerations: the other two are location and location also. So I do not claim that a language group's size or location is not important, but there is nothing you can do about that. I have discouraged such popular solutions, which people fly by me frequently, as buying TV time to advertise your language or taking out ads in the *New York Times*. These are all derived from product-marketing models. If you only market your language better, there would be more people who would buy it. However, from my point of view, it is not only too expensive to follow this model, but its results or impact are too ephemeral and too distant from the actual nexus of the problem—the intergenerational mother tongue transmission nexus. Frankly, I have not even advocated relying on outside support, extensive consciousness raising, or ideological arousing. Because language consciousness too, it seems to me, is a very rare phenomenon and a sometimes thing. Most members (most rank and file members) can call their language to consciousness, but they cannot be expected to keep it in consciousness all day long, day after day, or devote their daily evening meal to it, in the midst of life's many trials and tribulations. So that is my basic desideratum. What can the ordinary rank and file member do for the language daily, but even with very low consciousness, just as an expression of daily life (even though fostering that way of life consciously may very well be the responsibility of some subgroup in the community). I have come to view reversing language shift (RLS) as a subfield of status planning. It focuses on status *expansion*, as a subfield of language maintenance which focuses on status *protection*. So, for me, reversing language shift—please understand these are all highly overlapping but somewhat different circles—focuses on restarting a system of functional linkages, a system that will then feed back to and accumulate in the function which focuses on intergenerational mother tongue transmission. Reversing language shift tries to focus in on that particularly crucial issue, although it also can focus in on other functions.

I don't propose to spend much time today justifying reversing language shift philosophically. First of all, it has been done wonderfully by previous speakers at this conference. In each RLS setting, there will be adherents and detractors; there may even be, at this conference, differences between people as to the advisability of reversing language shift, each with their own particular justifications. For me, RLS activity represents a value of those convinced of the vital contribution of their language to the enrichment of their personal and collective lives. Their justification is in the realm of seeing a value in the lifestyle associated with the language. This is not a universal value, obviously, but I think it is an honorable and widely shared one. And even affirming or subscribing to the value is not the same as intergenerational mother tongue transmission per se. Many people are in favor of it in the abstract, but they just do not do it themselves in their own families. And, therefore, the one—the attitudinal, the ideological, even the value formulation—is not the same, either on an individual or societal basis, as the RLS process per se. An attitude is a predisposition to behavior, behavior in a certain way. Behavior itself is what reversing language shift is about. Attitudes and behaviors are differently constrained and, therefore, although they may both be important, they may not be important in the same social networks to the same extent. And it is the language behavior universe which finally will need to be turned around.

Let me return to another thing which I've already mentioned. Reversing language shift may focus on returning not only to the mother tongue, but returning the language to other functions that were once implemented in that language and that were subsequently lost to it (e.g., regaining lingua franca functions, regaining religious functions, or regaining governmental functions). I have focused on regaining mother tongue functions because of their rock bottom role in any vernacular transmission sense. I have tried to devise an approach to the analysis of regaining intergenerational mother tongue transmission that would lend itself to comparative study, at the same time being both diagnostic of what the dysfunction is, where the problem is, and prescriptive of amelioration, that is, what needs to be reconnected.

Some of you may be familiar with that little grid that I have called GIDS (graded intergenerational dislocation scale). I'm going to try to discuss it without assuming that you have read the book, so some of you will have read it and you will nod your head, but some of you will be hearing it for the first time, and I'm particularly concerned about the latter, that it will be understandable to them. So I will not review the entire 8-stage model, but merely remind you or make you sensitive to the fact that, first of all, the GID scale separates those languages in which most speakers are already beyond childbearing age (and they require special treatment) from those in which young adults are still available as mother tongue speakers, albeit diminishingly so. And now in the latter group, where there are still young mother-tongue speakers of childbearing age, although less available, it sets apart efforts that immediately feed back, or more immediately focus on the intergenerational mother tongue transmission nexus (or, in other words, focus upon home-family-neighborhood life, the sphere of intimacy and authenticity) in what I call Xish—where X is whatever language we are talking about at any particular moment. It differentiates between crucial intergenerational functions that must be under Xish community control because they impinge on the very young at the very time when the language is being intergenerationally transmitted, often quite unconsciously, from functions that are further away from that transitional point and perhaps more under Yish control—Y being the contrastive contextual language. So that distinction is an important one for me.

Clearly, what I have called Stage 6, is this crucial stage where intergenerational mother tongue transmission occurs and where its most crucial problems are located. That set of daily processes and interactions must be protected, if it is to be influenced at all by the institutions and relationships of face-to-face informal life. These constitute the realm of intimacy—home, family, neighborhood, friendship, and immediate community—a realm which is difficult to engineer, and easy to overlook, since higher functions easily elicit more attention because they are more obviously power related, functions to which individuals graduate as they leave the home and go out into life, into the world of jobs, statuses, recognitions, reputations, and opportunities, which are all post-mother-tongue transmission in the developmental sequence. The defense of Stage 6 is most crucially dependent on cultural conventions, on a cultural stance, which, whether consciously or unconsciously on the part of the community member, requires a careful compartmentalization or protection of the language. This must be protected primarily in its intergenerational transmission nexus as opposed to the language(s) of developmentally later, less intimate spheres of life. In other words, I assume that Xish speakers will ultimately be bilingual, and that Yish may dominate other than Stage 6 functions. Therefore, it is crucial that Xish be safeguarded somewhere in a safe harbor, somewhere that is all its own, or as much its own as possible, where it is the appropriate vehicle for the statuses and roles, the discourse styles and interactions of Stage 6. There is a long, at least one- to two-decade-long, hiatus between finishing school, for example, and beginning one's own family or procreation. Even if Xish is appropriately present in school, which is not always the case, it is often diminishingly present at all subsequent, less popularly, informally, vernacularly controlled stages of life, and these stages, therefore, tend to undercut the likelihood of the intergenerational mother tongue transmission. People who speak a language don't necessarily transmit it, and that is *the* problem, because of all the events and influences of the post-transmission life experience. Thus, it is up to the home, family, neighborhood, and immediate community to hold the fort virtually alone, through its own institutions, if the intergenerational mother tongue cycle is to be renewed and continued.

So, obviously, a question poses itself here. Would it not be preferable for the higher, later power stages also to be Xish dominant? But as one comedian said years ago, "They don't hardly make that kind no more." If that were the situation, then it would not be a reversing language shift issue. Yes, it would be desirable, but this is hardly ever the case, due to power problems, fiscal problems, legal problems, and just human resources problems. These other higher functions are usually, almost always, Yish-dominated. And any Xish presence in them is frequently tokenistic and cannot serve as a safe or strong support for Stage 6. More formal power-related functions can come into play in fostering Xish mother tongue transmission only as and if they do feed back to Stage 6, and that's the rub. If there are ethnolinguistic groups out there who could buy ads in the *New York Times* advocating the use of their language—and lots of readers of the little languages read the *New York Times* much more than they read their own languages—the problem is how would that feed back to the intergenerational mother tongue transmission stage? How would that happen, other than via some amorphous atmosphere effect, such that maybe it would and maybe it wouldn't? These subsequent stages are definite pluses for reversing language shift, only if they, on balance, relative to pro-Yish media, for example, really foster pro-Xish intergenerational transmission attitudes and behaviors among young adults. Attitudes are important only if and when they foster pro-Xish intergenerational transmission behaviors with the very young. And this is often improbable because these later stages, where we encounter the *New York Times* and the media and the bulk of the schools, are normally under Yish control or Yish domination.

As I see it, reversing language shift is a struggle to find solutions to four major recurring problems of threatened or weakened languages. And it could be that I better understand the problems than the solutions to them. Recognizing a good problem and struggling for a good solution is very worthwhile. So I would illustrate these problems and possible solutions, usually by using Xish schools as the common all-purpose solution that they are too often taken to be. Frequently, when one asks someone what can be done about a social problem they say, "Well, we'll teach it in school," as if that would take care of everything. Other all-purpose solutions also suffer from the same deficit—there are no all-purpose solutions. One has to have an explicit purpose in mind. Typically, schools in recessive languages, and, even more so, schools in the higher-power languages suffer from a double feedback failure vis-à-vis the Xish.

First of all, schools often do not reinforce or feed back significantly to problems of normal, ongoing, out-of-school daily life. Frequently, the more modern they are, the more Western they are, the less they do feed back to the ongoing daily life of the home, family, community, and neighborhood. Language acquisition and use becomes situationally overspecific, and later, mobility oriented. John Macnamara, a fine Irish psycholinguist and philosopher of language who died recently, tells how he and his sister grew up in a family somewhat like mine (only they were staunch Catholics, so there were some differences), and their parents sent them to all-Irish schools. (There were options, and if you were really into the language you could go to an all-Irish school.) After school they walked into a candy shop to spend their few pennies, and the lady that ran the store scolded them for speaking only English to each other right there in front of her in the store. She said, "You should be ashamed of yourselves, to be talking English after what your parents are going through." And they were quite polite children and didn't say anything, but when they left the store, John turned to his sister and asked, "Is Irish for talking?" It had never occurred to him that Irish was any different from algebra or some other school-based rigamarole that youngsters have to go through on their way to escaping from the school. So this is a *within-stage lapse*. The school itself is frequently not oriented so as to feed back to foster the ongoing community use, family use, daily use, informal use, or familiar use of any language outside of school. Children are often very shocked to see the teacher walking around outside of school. The teacher, like everything else in school, belongs in school, and frequently, that is where the language belongs, with the schoolteachers. For recessive languages, the school language rarely influences home or community language use.

Every stage can be looked at from the point of view of how it itself, admirable though it may be, does or does not feed back to daily life, does or does not connect with the nexus of transmission. Subsequently, once school in regressive languages is over, the school's impact is not sufficiently reinforced by post-school institutions, because the latter have their own rewards, rewards that are even further from the parenting, informality context. Therefore, the Xish school is very rarely an influential agency by the time former students become parents and they need to implant a mother tongue in their own offspring. I call this the *between-stage lapse*, a lapse which follows after the within-stage lapse. As a result of both of these lapses, the next generation in most recessive languages starts in the Xish school, if there is one, without Xish as its mother tongue, even if its parents *had* acquired Xish in school. Therefore, schools, major occupational opportunities, major mass media, armed forces experiences, and higher governmental services—to mention just a few out of home-family-neighborhood functions with their own reward systems—are most often not only not mother-tongue rewarding, not Xish-rewarding, but are Xish-counteractive even if Xish-using to some small extent. That is, they do not or cannot feed back to or foster the intergenerational mother tongue system because their focus of control is primarily Yish, and therefore, they do, intentionally or unintentionally, subtly penetrate the realm of intimacy in favor of Yish, even if they have some Xish there, as I say, for "ornamental purposes".

So, unless schools are carefully controlled to be pro-Xish, which may be a null set, or carefully linked back to the home-family-neighborhood nexus of intergenerational mother tongue transmission, so that they support it and thereby help carry the young during the period between the end of schooling and the beginning of new families—which is a very rare orientation indeed for schools—we are left with an overriding problem, the third problem, the need for and the danger of diglossia. Parents must be fully immersed in a culture of Xish, home-family-neighborhood life, in order to transmit Xish as a mother tongue. That is, Xish must have its protected functions, to a large extent compartmentalized from other functions. Effective diglossia norms are necessary to keep Yish out of this sector, so that Xish may have a safe institutional haven, notwithstanding Yish's admittedly greater power payoff in the surrounding outside world. Such compartmentalization is hard enough whenever the weak confront the strong, but to make things worse and even more Xish-improbable, effective Yish skills are crucially needed, at least by the influential segment of the Xish community, since Xish economic and political viability often depends upon such skills. Only last week I read quite a touching plea in an ultra-orthodox Yiddish newspaper—I am not of that group myself, but I try to keep abreast of their press. It was a plea for parents to realize that the children do need English, this in a New York newspaper. And that if they are to be effective economically and politically (upon which the fate of the community depends), they must learn effective control of English. This is something that parents have to do; there has to be a plea to parents to recognize this. Now, obviously, that community has no intergenerational mother tongue transmission problem. It does have, however, a problem of excessive compartmentalization, in my view. Therefore, there is a difficult, tense balancing act that is called for between safeguarding against insufficient diglossia (insufficient compartmentalization of home, family, neighborhood, the intimacy realm, "our own life", so that the realm of intimacy can be fully Xish, protected and sheltered as such), on the one hand, while avoiding excessive compartmentalization, leading to possibly anachronistic traditionalism, and excessive social distance, which might alienate some, endanger the total community, and lead to hostile actions from the Yish side. Of course, the easiest way of maintaining diglossia is the ultra-orthodox way of fostering minimally interactive cultural norms, such that only the work sphere, for example, which usually involves males in the communities that I know, has contact with Yish. So the old order phenomenon among the Amish, the old order phenomenon among the Mennonites, is an effective one, but this is not an attractive model for many and it also is not as simple as it appears to be on the surface. Note, for example, the Quebecois' inability to stem the influx of English via the media, and they are not a recessive community. They are linked to the world system largely dominated by English, and they don't want to sever that link. Nevertheless, it poses a problem because once admitted in, English can spread. So there is a difficult issue of cultural balance among weaker languages, where there is a foregone conclusion that the co-presence of the other language cannot be denied. This is a problem of just how many people need to know the outside language, how well, and in what functions.

And finally, there is fourth problem, that of planning spontaneity. Can home-family-neighborhood life really be planned or fostered, let alone protected? For those who have lost it, seeking to find a way back—is there a way back? Essentially, building Stage 6 is not merely, or even chiefly, a language enterprise, and we, above all, are most guilty of overdefining it as such. It is a kind of managed culture-care enterprise in the realm of daily life (its norms, behavioral interactions, and realms), in terms of persons, places, and situations that undergird that life. Reversing language shift must serve a larger surrounding common purpose, common lifestyle, and common norms. This larger purpose is not only greater than reversing language shift alone but, in fact, it may not be an exercise in which most ordinary people can constantly engage, because it is tantamount to pursuing goals not derived from power but from internal authenticity notions. RLS involves a self-removal from many established ways of living associated with the greater Yish reward, advantage, and gratification sphere. Such self-removal is a punitive experience for many who are not operating under the counterbalancing internal authenticity reward system.

The above mentioned four great problems of reversing language shift have resulted in a record of RLS success that is quite underwhelming. The problems are often overwhelming although pro-reversing language shift efforts continue on all continents. They have increased in incidence during the past two or three decades. They may well continue to increase for decades to come, and they also have very definite gratifications.

So, having sketched this minitheory in terms of the problems that it poses for those who pursue it, I recognize that it needs to be tied much more closely to sociological, anthropological, political science, and economic theory than to sociolinguistics alone.

I propose now to switch gears and look at some concrete cases. If you have looked at the *Reversing Language Shift* volume, you realize that it covers thirteen cases, a baker's dozen. I always talk about three or four of those, although with all thirteen I am constantly trying to update my own contact.

I want to start with languages that have not been much discussed in this group, but are increasingly important on the world scene. These are the immigrant languages. And here I want to look at the Australian record. Australia is perhaps the only predominantly English mother tongue country with a national language policy. Most major English contexts, Britain and the United States, have preferred to foster English through thousands of informal conventions, rather than through an official English only policy.

Australia, in its national language policy, has declared that one child's heritage language (which is the way immigrant languages are looked upon) is another child's foreign language and vice versa, and, therefore, the heritage languages, too, should be fostered on behalf of the total Australian commercial and political relationship with the world. One can see behind this the sense of Australian isolation. They are out there, all by themselves, far from the rest of the world, and they need these other languages. Now that is a wonderful situation for immigrant languages, to be declared to be something in the national interest, because usually immigrant languages are low man on the totem pole. Whatever other small indigenous languages may deserve because of *primum mobile*, immigrant languages deserve less, if anything at all. So Australians, in the most recent report that I have seen of the Language Policy Institute Agency (now called Language and Literacy Policy Agency), take pride in the fact that a growing proportion of elementary students are now in language courses. Since the policy has been instituted, the percentage has gone up from ten to nineteen percent. Japanese classes have more of an enrollment in Australia than French classes do in many states. In Australia children get credit in school for their mastery of heritage languages, even if those heritage languages are studied after school, out of school, in the afternoons, or on Saturdays or Sundays. This policy has now made a transition from being initiated by the labor government to being continued by a conservative government which came into power just a few years ago. Heritage language schools are now called "complementary providers" to public schools, making it possible for all public schools to offer eight languages in every year of study. That is their goal. And heritage language schools also, therefore, receive direct state funding, certificates for their teachers as being pedagogically up to date, and professional curriculum development assistance; similarly, there is publicly funded heritage language radio broadcasting, TV, and now cable broadcasting. One can constantly get the news or the best films or opera or other exemplary programs in Italian, Chinese, Indonesian, Greek, Spanish, and so forth. There are now novel recommendations for immersion language villages. Initially, these are going to be just short-term (summer-long, for example), also briefer exposures including sports and hobbies, and total immersion with adults co-participating in recreational activities so that the language is really living rather than just school related. That, to me, comes closest to attempting to innovatively reverse language shift for the heritage languages. Frankly, the immigrant languages are still weakening, as the newest census figures have shown, despite all efforts, because they are primarily not reversing language shift but are oriented by state language policy. That is, Australia needs a certain number of people who can sell computers somewhere using each heritage language. Another minus is, of course, that being concerned with little languages, Australia has started off with "the white ones". They have generally done very little for the aboriginal languages, most of which are continuing to weaken (although some of them have stemmed that tide) due to self-preferred isolation which may ultimately come back to bite them. So, there is one setting from which you in Britain and we in the USA have a lot to learn.

Let me mention another context, Basque. Here again, there is good news and there is bad news. Let us start with the good news—because good news is so rare—the functional and even the geographic spread that Basque has accomplished. By geographic spread I mean the official attention to Basque in Navarre, which is not part of the Autonomous Basque Community, and the very begrudging but nevertheless greater attention to Basque in the southern part of France neighboring on the Autonomous Basque Community. It is really unprecedented in the annals of Basque and in the annals of small peoples and besieged languages. There are many institutional indications of reversal of language shift; for example, the A-type schools have practically disappeared. These were the schools that were teaching Basque just a very few hours per week, sometimes only one or two hours per week. And then there were two other kinds of schools: there were all-Basque schools, some of which were previously *ikastolas* 'illegal Basque schools' that had gone underground in the Franco years, and now have been made part of the public school system. They were all-Basque. And then there are balanced-Basque schools in which there is both Spanish and Basque as equal media. Even in the all-Basque schools, of course, Spanish is taught as a subject, in Spanish. There are no monolingual Basques or so few that it doesn't pay to mention them; it is a null set. The number of local services and local and governmental communications with the public in Basque keeps growing. That was the initial area in which they began, and it keeps growing constantly. I want to give you more details about that later. There is more adult learning of Basque, appreciation of Basque, and Basque understanding, than ever before.

But the bad news is that it is still an uncommon principal and informal language outside of atypical circles, while more common as a kind of decorative flourish during major informal activities of everyday life, which are more often in Spanish. So there has been little progress for Basque as sole mother tongue or co-mother tongue. The Basques keep that record too. They report one-mother-tongue Basque speakers and two-mother-tongue Basque speakers in their statistics. Certainly, the proportion of Basquephones is growing among the very young, but it is still rather low. However, Basque is much better off today than it would be had the government's new policies of the past decade not been initiated. On the other hand, it is still dependent on these policies rather than on the natural flow of daily life. In many respects it is still a hot-house plant—living, thanks to an artificial environment. Currently, after almost two generations of this policy, people who have kept quiet about their opposition to it are now speaking up. So there is more polarization of views. Spanish statists, who are sick and tired of this Autonomous Basque Community, want the whole thing scrapped. On the other hand, Basque ultranationalists and a good proportion of the moderate nationalists (what I call bilingual, bicultural nationalists) are all now more upset with each other, with the middle being upset with both extremes and not going along with either of them. By this time there have been several phases of what the Basques insist on calling normalization, but, as one can see, much of it is not entirely normal.

There was the first stage of intra-administrative use of Basque at governmental insistence. This meant that every civil servant, including university professors, had to be able to pass an examination in Basque, and therefore the "Basque teaching industry" mushroomed. Then those people had to be retested periodically to make sure that they did not slip back after they had passed the test. Since, if people do not know Basque, no other language that they might know could be of any conceivable help, this intra-governmental insistence on Basquization was a major problem (particularly for middle-aged and older people who are quite past the stages where they could acquire even cognate languages well, let alone

Basque). The amount of Basque humor about the mistakes made by Spanish speakers in speaking Basque increased more rapidly than did Basque fluency among the Spanish speakers. Perhaps, it saw them over the roughest stage to be able to laugh at those mistakes.

Then a second stage took off and soon went into high gear, when administrative use in services to the public was insisted upon (in the late '80s and early '90s) and now assistance to the public includes Basque public schools for adults and children as well.

And now the third stage, since the mid '90s, involves things like the following: year-round as well as periodic, camps, clubs, sports groups, choruses, and hobby groups for children, so that children in any kind of school can be taken to a Basque village—and there still are Basque-speaking villages—and spend their time there. Hopefully, this has better results than taking children to the Gaeltacht in Ireland (where the local Gaeltacht children usually learn English from all these English-speaking children who came there to learn Irish). There is also the establishment in all urban centers of *casas culturales*. One such in every neighborhood in urban centers is the goal, and they are getting close to that. These are centers for adults, particularly for young adults, offering activities such as painting, ceramics, film, theater, lecture groups, cooking courses, popular weeklies, monthlies, and local radio broadcasting right from the *casas culturales*, so that young people have daily fun-places where they can go to speak Basque, or to learn how to really be Basque speaking, even after they have officially passed their courses. At the moment, the latest statistics show that 22 percent of the population in the Autonomous Basque Community can now use Basque informally. One has to go back to those born before 1932 for a higher rate of Basque mother tongue acquisition and use than there is today. It was thirty-one percent then, so it has been attriting for a long time. Eighty percent of those families in which both parents are Basque speaking, however, now transmit Basque to their children. In the Autonomous Basque Community alone (i.e., not counting Navarre, which was lost a long time ago, and not counting the French provinces), it is now up to 94 percent. So that means that they are beginning to keep people whose parents are Basque speakers. Most modern nationalists also believe the language is getting ever more normalized, which to me means intergenerational transmission as first informal language, and therefore, to them it stands head and shoulders above where Irish or Frisian are. They describe themselves as *sosegados y optimistas* 'relaxed and optimistic' about the future and about the stability of the language, although the growing internal political polarization between the middle and the extremes is worrying them nevertheless.

Now, let us compare the above activities to those included in a recent report from the Frisian academy. This is the headquarters for all Frisian-fostering activities, whether they are carried out by moderates or by people who call themselves *Djip Friezen* ('deep Frisians'; the designation is a play on words to evoke an association with the expression "deep freeze"). These activities are 100 percent Frisian in orientation. They are now focused on the next volume of the great unabridged historical Frisian dictionary (which will ultimately be twelve volumes), a better bilingual Frisian-Dutch dictionary, a better Frisian-English dictionary, a spell checker for Frisian on the computer, Frisianization of place names, and daily TV in Frisian. (Actually, that is available only one hour per day, and even that is on working days when most people can't listen to it. Note the tokenization when you're financed by the central administration.) There are also new, obligatory, one-year courses in Frisian in high school and a new department of Frisian at the University of Amsterdam. You can see the qualitative difference between these efforts and the efforts at the *casas culturales*. Frisian is now the second official language of The Netherlands. The government ratified the European charter for regional minority languages, and that gives a national status to the Frisian Language Academy, which will always be supervising the efforts on behalf of Frisian and will make periodic reports that will go to "Europe", not just to The Hague. But I would say, all in all, there is very little of this which is reversing language shift. Much of it is lexicographic and legalistic in nature.

Lest you think that such tokenism is just a European way out, I want to turn now to something that I have kept in touch with for a long time, and that is the Maori situation in New Zealand. Here you have a success story that the world does not know enough about, the *kohanga reos* 'language nests', which are preschool, nursery, childcare centers, conducted by elderly speakers of Maori. Initially, they were all mother tongue speakers but now, as there are more of such childcare centers for the little ones, more and more of the staff are not necessarily mother-tongue speaking, and not even necessarily competently Maori speaking. It has had some noteworthy success at that level, but it has had little elementary school follow-through—perhaps some 15,000 children are now attending elementary schools in which Maori also is used as a language of instruction—and there has been even less secondary school follow-through. At the moment only about a thousand of the initial *kohanga reo* pupils are attending secondary schools with Maori instructors. So you see that by the time those secondary school children then go on to start their own families, they really would need much more than the school exposure. Within-family use is still falling and there is almost no chance of influencing intergenerational mother tongue transmission.

Maori is an official language of New Zealand. The attitudes toward it are more positive than they were. I remember the first time there was a TV broadcast in Maori, even just a few greetings during "Maori appreciation week" or something tokenistic like that. The number of scurrilous telephone calls to the TV station was absolutely appalling. Attitudes now seem to be more positive, but informal home and community use is still only at the 10 percent level and falling. And when they think of new things to do, there is a major push on the legal front. The courts have granted the right, and the government has therefore implemented it, of Maori to be required in court if a Maori defendant or plaintiff wants it. More importantly, the courts have ruled that the government has a treaty obligation to support Maori, since, in the initial treaty with the Maoris, the government (the treaty power, Britain, having now passed on its rights and obligations to the New Zealand government) committed itself to protect the treasures of the Maori people. The court ruled that the Maori language was a treasure of the Maori people, and, therefore, the government is obligated to protect it. There is a growing use of Maori in tourism, where touristic authorities recognize that when tourists come to New Zealand they want to hear the Maoris talking Maori, they do not want to hear them talking English. There is a lot of government symbolism: there are Maori letterheads for government agencies, government agencies have Maori names (as of course they have Irish names in Ireland), but the daily-life use of Maori is fading and may never be retrieved, and therefore I leave again this rapid review with the question, "Can daily-life use be returned to Stage 6 when it is already at Stage 7 and 8?"

Finally, I want to summarize the main points and reflect upon them. Positive evidence with respect to reversing language shift comes only from atypical speech networks. Where it has been accomplished, they are atypical in atypical settings. Ultra-orthodox everyday Yiddish is atypical for the American Jewish community or the Israeli community or the Jewish community in Amsterdam. As a whole, they are atypical. Everyday revivalist Irish is atypical. Activist Frisian is atypical. As far as Maori and Basque are concerned, they are exceptional in their own settings. But it seems to me that what can be atypically attained might be an indication of what might be more generally attainable (even if perhaps not universally attainable) if sufficiently understood as a lesson in reversing language shift.

Reversing language shift is basically not about language, certainly not *just* about language; it is about adhering to a notion of a complete, not necessarily unchanging, self-defining way of life. The fact that some can attain or retain this pattern is a sign that it is not a will-of-the-wisp or a waste of time and money. It is something that we can learn from. One of the rewards of such efforts is that they invariably accomplish more RLS than would obtain with no efforts at all. Under similarly situated circumstances, all the RLS groups are at a better stage than comparable groups that did not undertake any such efforts, although the latter are still not at the stage that they would or should like to be. Not only do such efforts build bonds of solidarity and identity with kindred spirits—they also foster commitment to a common good that transcends purely individual interests or self-interest of a material kind. And the activism that they entail is a great social cement for those folks that are involved. Such efforts transform lives through a compelling vision of community counter to dominant views. Being counter to dominant views is energizing; that is, if you can stand the tension, it is also energizing. *Angst* is a very creative force if kept within limits. The resistance is also linked to practice. It is not only a declaration of good intentions. Such efforts foster a quasi-spiritual sense of belonging, in addition to the physical and social sense of belonging. There is a glimpse or an image of sanctity in reversing language shift efforts which is ennobling and inspiring, even as RLS attainments themselves are meager. Not having gotten as far as one would like to get is a common experience of people who recognize a spiritual component to their lives. They commonly feel that they would like to have gotten more of this or have gotten further with that. These are all the joys of collective struggle against overwhelming odds, often focused or conceptualized in terms of language goals, but fruitful in ever so many other ways besides language, at least for the hardy band of RLSers.

In my view, reversing language shift efforts should be self-financed and, therefore, not dependent on prolonged feeding from outside, if only because subsidy from outside is usually related to control from the outside. Such efforts should mostly involve community volunteers, and as many people as possible should be activated to face the daily question, "What did you do today for the language?" They should constantly stress feedback to Stage 6 goals, regardless of whatever stage one may be attending to at any moment. If one is working on the mass media, one has to face that question, "How does that help feedback to Stage 6?" If one is working in the schools for one's language, one has to face the questions, "What are you preparing the students to do after school, when they leave school that day? After their schooling period is over entirely, what are you preparing them to do? How are you extending the school's contact with them in that direction?" There are community-building schools, community-involved schools. And finally RLS should involve as much community planning, that is, home-family-neighborhood planning, as language-stressing activity.

Let me give you a quotation from Blaže Koneski, who died just a few years ago. He was one of the preeminent Slavic specialists of our generation and could have held down a chair in Slavic studies in any of the great Slavic universities and had been invited to do so, but he spent his time working on behalf of the Macedonian language, writing its grammar, its dictionary, establishing its norms, and insisting on the norms which were then established in the written language. One of his statements which I particularly like is as follows:

> ...someone who knows better than all of us how the world should be arranged obviously decided that apart from the big peoples and languages there should be small peoples and languages. (Koneski 1994:216)

That is how he explained why he was willing to devote his life to that particular small language, the very existence of which is not only doubted today but counteracted today in two neighboring countries. It is a service to this Someone for me to work on behalf of small languages and peoples and a pleasure for me to be in the company of those who are also dedicated to that service and to its improvement.

Questions and Answers

Q: You state that schools do not usually feed back to everyday life in Stage 6, and yet in each of the cases you mentioned, school was one of the primary things you commented on.

A: Well, if you ask people what can be done for their threatened language, they tell you "school" right away. There are obvious reasons for that. There are government budgets for schools. Like the clergy, schools have personnel which are going to be there, and therefore language- and culture-focused people think of them right away. In the United States there is also a practice, which is very regrettable, that whatever unsolvable problem there is, whether it is teenage pregnancy or drug use, everyone decides that the schools should teach about it. Schools are the all-purpose, available agencies, maybe because teachers are a professional group which is not in control of itself. They have to do whatever they are told to do. They are there. And there is some underlying notion that if they were competent they would be doing something else. So there are a number of reasons why all problems are passed along to the school.

Now let's look at it in terms of social process. Schools are at the continental divide between the intimate familiar *gemeinschaft* of the home, family, neighborhood, and friendship on the one hand, and the totally

Upper Domains which take you away from that and require that you know how to interact in a formal way with formal people not of your own kind, those who are in Yish control. No matter what they say about helping Xish, that is not their major function. So school is in the middle; it is fed from below and it feeds to above, and therefore, if you look at reversing language shift, there are three different kinds of school patterns. With all my conviction that you cannot leave it to the school, I do recognize three different kinds of schools, and the difference is related to the extent to which they are community-regulated. Even the old order orthodox recognize they have obligations to prepare students to function in English. All the Old Order Amish schools teach in English half the day and there are no monolingual Old Order Amish, and this is accomplished even though the teacher may not have state certification. (In Pennsylvania the state has more or less decided to let them do whatever they want at school. "We do not want any bad publicity about arresting Amish parents and children. It is not worth it.")

So the only time the state is really rough on them is when they do not inoculate the children against contagious childhood diseases. Most teachers are young ladies whose only credential for teaching the school is, first of all, she is acceptable to the elders, and, secondly, she has been to such a school herself, and therefore, she can conduct the school. They bought up all the one room schoolhouses that the state abandoned. And they regularly buy up the textbooks that the state abandons, provided that the textbooks are something on the order of forty years old, because newer textbooks, even though abandoned, have pictures of all sorts of things that they do not want the children to be interested in. Nevertheless, all the children play with one another in the playground speaking in Pennsylvania German. The teacher will speak English to them in that part of the day that they are supposed to teach in English, and the texts are in Luther German; they do not teach Pennsylvania German, they just live Pennsylvania German. The teacher will speak informally to a child ("Behave!" or "Sit straight!"). You don't say that in Luther German, but otherwise the Luther German text is one that the elders approve of. So there are schools which are fully under local control, and they have decided on the degree of Yish that is necessary in the school. The Amish don't want the children to go to high school. A school that would prepare students to go to high school would be considered a destructive force in the community, so you have to make sure you don't get too much of this. So English is like an inoculation. You have to have enough of it, but not too much of it, because too much of it will lead you away from the community. *That's* a community which is in control of its schools.

And then there are school types which have increasingly more Yish control. So, you have to realize the pivotal functions of schools. A community somehow has to have an image of its self-defined purpose for the school. If you have a self-defined purpose which the state will not permit, you have to be willing to support and run the school yourself. Of course, that's a terrible problem for many groups not accustomed to running their own schools, but to having the state run the schools for them. They just can't conceive of running their own schools. I remember expressing the idea to Navajos that they could run their own schools which would not be in lieu of public education. They could run supplementary schools of their own and teach only what the elders wanted, and it was a startling idea because it had never come to their attention that you could do anything like that. But I said, "You know, that would be of some help only if you are not depending on it. You can't shift your responsibility to that kind of unit, which is supplementary, and then depend on it to do whatever you need for the language." So we have to talk about school, because there *is* a disproportional amount of attention given to it. If you want to really control it, then you are going to have to fund it yourself. And there may be therefore some kind of division of labor between the school that children attend in lieu of public education and the school that children attend which is cheaper and fully controllable. But that doesn't mean that you can rely on it alone.

You have to learn how to think beyond school, even if you are thinking about school. If you are thinking *about* school, then think of *beyond* school and link the two.

Q: How do we have a Stage 6 in Hebrew language in Israel? Was there always an ongoing face-to-face intimacy with the Hebrew language, or was there a conscious decision that reversed the language shift? My Hebrew friends, when I was growing up in Baltimore, had to go to Hebrew school, but that was not the same as what you are talking about.

A: There is a chapter in the book which is on intergenerational transmission of second languages. That involves languages which are not family-transmitted, and how, therefore, you can focus on some other level and work out the same puzzle. That is, how do you foster *that* kind of transmission? Now let's take these two very different Hebrew cases, the Baltimore one and the Israeli one. The Baltimore one tended to foster intergenerational transmission of reading competence and prayer competence from a written text or a printed text, not necessarily understanding it. As the whole way of life that supported that transmission Americanized, and as its significance in the lives of the students decreased, there was also a lot of rejection of that kind of transmission and, therefore, other interpretations of the tradition arose which didn't even require Hebrew-reading prayer, let alone Hebrew speaking, which even the people doing the praying didn't emphasize. So, Hebrew instruction never led to Hebrew speaking (not even in the Eastern European Diaspora, where the school was totally one under community control). So Hebrew had to be vernacularized by people who were "non-pray-ers". They did not have either the conviction or the facility of praying in the language. *They* revived the language. The praying function, just like the school functions, is a self-contained function. There are always stories about some Jew from Fez winding up in a market or great fair in Vilna, Lithuania being able to interact either in Judeo-Arabic or in Yiddish with the local population and trying to interact in Hebrew, but those are just examples of what the problem is. That is, the fact that you know how to pray in the language doesn't mean you can formulate a sentence such as, "What's in the soup today?"

As far as reviving the language as a vernacular, of course, that's a revival story, not just a reversing language shift. Remember, reversing language shift starts off with a small, diminishing number of young mother tongue speakers. In revivals, you start off with *no* mother tongue speakers. That's a different scenario. (Those self-defined nonbelievers—secular, nationalist individuals—revived the language with the nationalistic conviction that this had to be done, to unify all the people that were going to be brought together in the new country.) But even in that scenario it didn't fully work out that way. They could force themselves to stammer greetings to each other in modern Hebrew, but for the children they established the children's house where the children were raised by special individuals. There are always some adults who can acquire a second language flawlessly, although only a few can do that. So those adults, the *mitapelet*, were preoccupied; they were concerned (that's what the word means) with the children. The children lived with those people, not with their parents, and were rendered Hebrew-mother-tongue children by those special individuals, selected for that purpose, because the parents couldn't do it. The parents involved themselves in a self-denying reward system. They didn't have the usual rewards of raising their children; in fact, the children came home to the parents only one hour a day.

My sister lived in a kibbutz like that, and as recently as the late sixties, the children came home once a day for an hour, even though by then Hebrew had been fully re-vernacularized. So, that's a different scenario, but they did have to substitute for the home-neighborhood- community a special context and function of "the revivers". If you look at the minutes of that time of all the kibbutzim, they had "a reviver" writing the minutes because the discussion was not conducted in Hebrew. It was in Yiddish, by and large, and sometimes in Russian, German, or Polish. And the cities were the last to be vernacularized, because they had huge immigrant groups all in their own neighborhoods and, therefore, even when the second war came along they were not vernacularized.

Then after the second war, new immigrants came and the cities were again rendered multiethnic and multilingual. So, in the cities it is not unusual today to find neighborhoods which are not Hebrew speaking, although you can't fully get that from the census because the census follows the Basque practice, or if you like, the Basque follow the Israeli practice of listing people who speak Hebrew as their first language of 1, as their second language of 2, as their third language of 3—all the possible combinations, down to the fifth language. In this way they squeeze every ounce of Hebrew out of that population and they report that 98 percent of the population is Hebrew speaking, but not necessarily as a first language, particularly for the ultra-orthodox, who largely remain Yiddish speaking. Those small, ultra-orthodox parties usually have the balance of power after elections. And nothing terrified a minister in the previous government more than the fact, as she once said in a talk in the Knesset, "that the fate of our country is in the hands of people who speak Yiddish." So there are sizable, both Jewish and non-Jewish, linguistic minorities in Israel. That is a lengthy answer, but it is clear that the revival was not school dependent.

Q: I like to think of language in terms of cost and benefit. In your examples you can't help but notice an economic and ideological infrastructure. In the places where reversing language shift has not worked, there is no infrastructure. When the countries in Africa were becoming independent, there was an enthusiasm for the native African languages. I don't think much came out of that. My question for you is, Are there languages in conflict or are we coming to reconcilement? Where are we headed?

A: Thank you very much for a troubling observation. But look, my friends. We all, I mean you and I, but I definitely mean you, are involved in a struggle which has its ultimate justification in something other than economic reward. And if you think there is any sense to it, then, you must admit that people can also pursue goals that have other than economic reward. I have not in the least indicated any conviction that Yish should not be seriously pursued. In fact, I carefully pointed out that that is a fact of life. Yish stands for greater economic reward than Xish. And it is true, as I said, that if the Xish folks could only control the economy, they wouldn't have their current problems. But now, having said that, I fully agree with you that that is a problem; you now still have to ask yourself, "So what can we do nevertheless?" Doctors have to cure people who are sick, not people who are well. Of course, it would be nice to have preventive health, but no one is really working on preventive health for languages. It may be that some of the currently threatened languages will be so successful that they will cross the continental divide, and they will be on the other side of it, and, therefore, they will try to undercut the diglossia which they originally tried to establish.

Like the Catalans, having attained greater security as to their ability to have a Catalan-speaking society, are now trying to undercut Spanish where possible. That's hard to do because they don't want to offend the Spanish state, on the one hand, or the Spanish-speaking population there, so it is a hard balancing act for them, but they can think of accomplishing it. For them, "normalization" is overcoming diglossia, whereas for smaller groups "normalization" involves building diglossia. So, yes, you have to reconcile yourself.

Small languages need something other than economic reward systems, at least other than economics of the highest order. There is always the local economy, and the language should have a lower economy that it can appropriately be used in, at least on one side of the counter—it depends on whether there is an intergroup economy or in-group economy. There are many stories about New York where one language is spoken between sales persons, and another language is spoken across the counter; meanwhile, those people on the other side of the counter are also speaking their own language, which may not be the language they are using across the counter. These are all economic considerations.

Now, as far as language and the economy, there are some very thrilling new publications that I would like to mention to you, since it is an important topic. Although I basically am not in agreement with a cost-benefit analysis of language, in the usual cost-benefit terms, I do want to mention books by Florian Coulmas on the economy of language. Also, issue 121 of IJSL, the *International Journal of the Sociology of Language*, on economics and language, edited by François Grin, has a cost-benefit article, and sometimes, you know, we have to use cost-benefit as part of our own justification to others.

What benefit will there be from the use of threatened languages? Frequently, literacy is more easily attained first in your own language before you can attain it in another language. That's why literacy is now part of the Australian national language policy. They try to foster both language and literacy, because opponents of the national language policy said that we shouldn't be concerned with literacy in "all these little languages"; we should be concerned with literacy in English. So they were answered, "Oh yes, but there is bi-literacy, there is multi-literacy, and if you can acquire literacy more easily in your own language, then you should do that first and then transfer your literacy to English and other languages." That's a common bilingual education argument. So, I don't feel ashamed, and I'm sure you don't feel ashamed, about the fact that we are involved in a pursuit that has more than economic, or other than economic, rationales. As long as you then don't bar them, the Xish community, from any economic prospects whatsoever via Xish, because that would be self-liquidating. So you have to compromise, you have to balance.

Q: I'd like to go back to schools and other institutional support types of issues. Do you despair that the relationship between schools and hearth and home can be established, if we are aware ahead of time that the two must be coordinated?

A: One thing that doesn't characterize me, even as I get old, is despair, something I never feel.

Yes, there are schools and school programs that try to link to after-school life *while* the children are in school, and even *after* they have left school. There is certainly a kind of linkage, a kind of joint planning as part of overall community planning, with the school as a part of community planning. The Basques are doing some of that; even the Irish are doing some of that. The question is, "What proportion of your school effort is related to total community planning?" I would say that more and more schools realize that they cannot succeed even with the things that they already feel responsible for, unless some real out-of-school reality for these subjects exists for the children. Why is it that children forget so much of the history and mathematics that they are taught? If you read the letters parents send to school with their children as to why Johnny didn't come to school yesterday, you will find they, themselves, cannot put together a sentence in writing, even though they have gone to school. And it's because many of the things that the schools teach do not have community validity, real life validity. But people can live without remembering who is the senator now, what the law is, or how you solve a quadratic equation. They live without that.

The thing to recognize is that language is basically not a school subject like math or history. Language is not a subject like geography or algebra. Language is the way you live. That is what language is. Therefore, if you're not teaching language that way, you're not really even teaching language and, therefore, of course, it will not be useful when you get out of school. So, this immersion in a community—the clubs, the teams, the home visits—must increase for other subjects as well.

In large cities, where both parents are working, there is no one home when a child comes home, and there is no one to help with the homework; there is no one to see if the homework gets done. There is going to have to be school-sponsored after-school homework sessions, including snacks of cookies and milk, all the things you used to get at home and a teacher that will play games with you. There is no limit to the school day, although the teachers' union may demand double pay, and they deserve double pay even without the extension of the day. Yes, the school must be an attribute of the home just as much as the home must be linked to the school if the school is to succeed. In a reversing language shift setting, the school must realize that language is not a subject; it is the very socializing vehicle of life.

The language constitutes a certain expression of life, a certain style of life, a certain definition of what makes life worth living, an expression of ethic community identity that we want to build. The language is what has to follow students outside of the school, more so than the quadratic equation, more so even than history or literature. Of course, you know, you can't just be teaching grammar out of school. It is no more transferable out of school than in school. You have to be giving children out of school something that they really want. You see we're a funny species; we really want to talk. We want to talk about something that interests us. That is what has to be done with children after school—homework sure, but games and sports and hobbies and visiting the poor, too.

I know that in my neighborhood the school requires children to sign up for after-school visits to the sick and to the poor, who are by and large not speaking English. That provides a validity for the language that the children can't find in school and may not even have in their own homes. So you have to think of things that link the child to the community. The school alone doesn't have to do that, but the school should too, and the child will learn more language out of school than in school. It may be embarrassing to the teachers once in a while when a child says, "But when I visit so and so, she doesn't say it that way." That is another problem. That is the school standard as a substitute for the real language. The school should come to grips with that problem too. But that is not necessarily a reversing language shift problem.

Q: One of the things that interests me is the way languages change. In Africa, language contact among African languages (as well as English or French) often causes a generational gap in the spoken language. The parents know one variety of the language, their children are speaking another variety of the language, and, presumably, when the latter have children, the language will have changed further. There is a problem knowing which variety it is that you are going to pass on.

A: Languages are always changing. All languages are changing all the time. Nevertheless, it is not always a problem of the kind you describe. Even though English is changing all the time, English-speaking parents in Great Britain do not have the problem of trying to maintain the language per se; they think of it in terms of maybe improving or influencing the children's language. Should we hold out for the standards of the previous generation? Should we realize that there may be a new standard now, that the standard may be age-graded, with changes going on all the time?

So, if you consider South Africa and the kind of re-ethnification and re-linguafication that is going on there as populations shift, remember that the language change will not necessarily have that tempo forever. There may be some stabilization, and some groups may want to, just as the Amerindian groups have done, return to reversing language shift at a much later stage. They may be at Stage 8 by then, or at Stage 7, and then have the problem of reintroducing some young people to the language that the older generation alone remembers. Among Amerindian languages you get the extreme of that now, where there are just very few people left that have the old language. I once met an Amerindian woman and she told me, "The only person I have left to talk to is a linguist, and talking to a linguist is no fun."

The California "master-apprentice program" in connection with Amerindian languages doesn't do it that way anymore. Instead of sending a linguist to be there working with an informant in the traditional question-and-answer way, they send a young interested person to live with that lady as a kind of aide. The apprentice lives there with the "master" for a year or more and learns the language as far as that master still remembers it, and then the apprentice has the obligation to try to teach it to others in some live way. Those are all additional complexities, and one of the possible complexities is that it may no longer be possible to find a speaker of the language.

I don't claim that it is always possible to do reversal of language shift. However, remember that 8 is a stage, which means reassembling the language and teaching it. There is no language for which something can't be done. The thing that can't be done may be re-vernacularizing it. But you can possibly reassemble it, and you can possibly even make use of the fact that there are still old people living a normal life and talking to each other, but they have no one young to talk to anymore, just a linguist. And you can work with that stage. So, sure, you can say it is no longer possible. In that case start working with the old people so that the language isn't lost.

If you are sure nothing is possible in terms of intergenerational transmission, because the new generation has gone off to other places or interests, then the language should at least be preserved. Actually, I tend to shudder when I hear "preservation", because that means putting it in a museum, and nothing is living in a museum. It is just there so you can look at it. I have this very fine citation from the Ainu (a people of Japan) that starts off with, "We will not be put into a museum." Because that was the next stage the Japanese government was in favor of. They would have an Ainu museum, where you would have recordings of the people still speaking the language. But even that is a stage that has some value, some kind of promissory note that you will save enough of it so that some future generation will want to learn it.

If you look at the list of the language courses that the Mercator Project course lists for Europe, there are two pages of language courses for Cornish. So a language that was "preserved" in some fashion is now being taught. That might later provide opportunity for other people to vernacularize it. RLS steps taken today can provide the foundation for other steps that will be taken tomorrow.

References

Koneski, Blaže. 1994. A situation and a personal viewpoint. International Journal of the Sociology of Language 108:216–18. (Translated from Macedonian by Ilija Čašule with Victor A. Friedman)

Ethnicity, Ethnic Movements, and Language Maintenance

Christina Bratt Paulston

A longish introduction

Some comments on my initial experiences which later came to influence my thoughts and reflections on ethnic groups in multilingual settings are worth repeating here. These were my two years in Morocco with Arab diglossia, Berber multilingualism, and French as an ex-colonial lingua franca, later to be studied and understood at a very different level of awareness than when I actually lived there. Later, I went to lecture for three months at the University of Chandigarh in the Punjab of northern India, a country where caste and class still prevent easy understanding and is often an exception to generalizations in sociolinguistics. Two years in Peru brought me, besides two babies, into contact with SIL. The people who introduced me to the *selva* 'jungle' were Rolland Rich and Millie Larson. Donald Burns first introduced me to the notion of bilingual education (BE), and its controversies, with his program in Spanish and Quechua in the Peruvian highlands.

It is naïve to think that any scholar works in a vacuum, and when I returned to the United States in 1968, these extended stays in three very different cultures were to have a formative influence on my thinking about ethnicity and language maintenance. (There were other influences as well, such as a year spent teaching foreign languages in the Swedish countryside, but I am focusing here only on my work with linguistic minorities.) Nineteen sixty-eight was the year of passage of the US Bilingual Education Act, and for the next ten years I spent a lot of scholarly energy—and passion—on writing about bilingual education. Eventually, I came to understand that any accounting for the success or failure of BE would have to be found in factors external to the particular program, an insight which in retrospect seems embarrassingly obvious. But I had been trained as an applied linguist with the importance of teaching methods and the like (training, besides skills, also easily provides blinders). And, of course, medium of instruction, the mother tongue of the children, was seen as the saving grace—and I am not using it flippantly—of those early programs, i.e., a variable internal to the program. That thirty-year search for the Holy Grail (dictionary definition 2: Object of prolonged endeavor), i.e., the school success of linguistic minority children, may come to an end with the passage, with strong *latino* support, of the Unz Initiative (which seeks to end BE) in California.[1] One conclusion we can draw from those 30 years of program and research efforts is the importance of L_1 maintenance or shift for school success. The more rapid the shift, the less need for BE; the slower the shift, the more important mother-tongue instruction becomes, but that is another topic for another time.

But these were the questions which led me to focus on the topic of language maintenance and shift, and that is what I will discuss for the rest of this chapter.[2]

The study of language maintenance and shift[3]

In the study of language maintenance and shift, we either know what the trends or results are in individual cases, or we know how to find out, but we have a poor understanding of the causal factors. Basically, the problem is a search for independent variable(s) which can be generalized to other situational contexts. Mostly ignored are the intervening or contextual variables, the answer to, Under what social conditions? which often profoundly influence the linguistic outcomes of ethnic groups in contact within a modern nation-state (see appendix 1).

---

[1] The Unz Initiative, Proposition 227, passed in June 1998.
[2] See also the chapters by Paul Lewis and Carolyn Miller in this volume which deal with the same topic.
[3] In the following pages, I am drawing on my *Linguistic Minorities in Multilingual Settings* (1994) to which the reader is referred for further discussion.

In an analysis of the causal relationship of language and social structure (social institutions), it is possible to see both language and social structures as determinants in a chain of interactions where social structure or behavior affects language which in turn affects social behavior. Such a perspective is probably the most accurate way to account for all phenomena in the process of language maintenance and shift. So, for example, structural power will lead to the selection, standardization, and literature of a language, which in turn will bestow literary prestige and language loyalty on a language, which in turn will contribute to language maintenance or a slower rate of shift.

In *Linguistic Minorities in Multilingual Settings,* I deal with generally recognized cases where the analysis may differ but the basic facts are well known. I acknowledge that SIL people, more than any other group I know, are likely to be familiar with a great number of the most unusual, divergent, and difficult-to-generalize conditions. Similarly, the point I have just made, about structural power leading to standardization leading to prestige and maintenance may not be an accurate generalization for many SIL cases, and the reader has to make such an allowance. Certainly, it remains true for any linguistic minority that to have its own written language is a source of pride and prestige. The Ottoman Empire, for instance, respected Christianity and Christians as *people of the book,* not just the teaching but the written word. You know better than I do that the same joy and prestige remains true for all of SIL's far-flung groups; what is harder to predict is the degree of language maintenance. The only sensible approach, then, for the SIL reader of this chapter, or indeed any chapter in these Proceedings, is (because of the nature of so many isolated cases that SIL deals with) to pick and choose what applies and seems appropriate to you. Common sense may not always be highly prized in Academia but it should not be rated less than theoretical speculations.

Because a linked perspective as suggested above may easily contribute to confusion rather than clarification, I shall for the rest of this chapter consider social structure, specifically the types of social group mobilization, as the determinant variables and the differential linguistic outcomes as the resultant variables.

The guiding hypothesis I propose for explaining and predicting the language behavior of ethnic groups in contact within a contemporary (nation) state is the following: Linguistic groups can form four distinct types of social mobilization—ethnicity, ethnic movement, ethnic nationalism, and geographic nationalism—which under certain specified[4] social conditions result

---

[4]For specified social conditions, see my chapter 2, also Lewis and Miller in this volume.

in differential linguistic outcomes of language maintenance or shift (see appendix 2).

Some shortish comments on conditions for shift

The major point about multilingualism, which is not widely recognized in the literature, is that maintained group bilingualism is unusual. The norm is that subordinate groups in prolonged contact within a nation-state shift to the language of the dominant group, whether over three generations or several hundred years. Where shift does not take place, there are identifiable reasons of which lack of incentive—usually economic—and lack of access to the dominant language are the two major ones. Another one is that the political unit may not be a nation-state, as was the case with the Federated Soviets.

The mechanism for language shift is bilingualism, often with exogamy, that is, intermarriage between ethnic groups. Groups will vary in their degree of ethnic maintenance and in their rate of shift. One major influence on rate is the origin of the contact situation. Voluntary migration results in much faster shift than does annexation or colonization. Other factors affecting rate of shift are continued access to a mother tongue that is standardized and written and that has cultural prestige and tradition in contradistinction to a nonstandard nonwritten language of no prestige. Sacred languages, like Hebrew and Sanskrit, tend to be carefully maintained. Had Hebrew not been a sacred language, the revival of Hebrew would not have been possible, and Israel today would likely have been a German-speaking nation.

Ethnicity and nationalism

The past discussion has dealt exclusively with the linguistic consequences of ethnic minority groups in prolonged contact within one nation-state. But groups can find foci of social mobilization other than ethnicity, and I shall extend the discussion here to include ethnic movements and nationalism. I have long thought about the social mobilization of religious groups within this framework and eventually opted for considering religion as a social resource similar to language. Linguistic groups may choose a religious identity as the main base in strategies of competition, but they do so as preexisting ethnic or national groups. For purposes of explaining language behavior of groups, I doubt that religion needs to be considered a primary force of group cohesion.

Religious groups are also theoretically problematic because of the preponderance of "irrational" behavior, where it is difficult to predict behavior using the notion of "acting in their own best interest". Self-immolation in the name of *jihad* will serve as an example of what I have in mind.

Also not included is a discussion of social organizations of tribes and clans within a single ethnolinguistic group, spread over several states, such as Kurdistan. Nor do I discuss the role of pan-movements in language maintenance. The role of English and French in pan-Africanism, the role of classical and literary standard Arabic in pan-Arabism, and the role of the Chinese character writing system all share certain features, one of which is language maintenance beyond what might reasonably have been expected.

What follows is a consideration of four distinct types of social mobilization of linguistic groups within a modern nation-state. Under certain specified social conditions, I argue that these groups show differential linguistic outcomes of language maintenance and shift.

Ethnicity

Royce defines ethnic identity as "the sum total of feelings on the part of group members about those values, symbols, and common histories that identify them as a distinct group. 'Ethnicity' is simply ethnic-based action" (Royce 1982:18). Ethnicity by itself provides little power struggle and not much purpose, so the common course is assimilation and concomitant language shift. Ethnicity will not maintain a language in a multilingual setting if the dominant group allows assimilation and if incentive and opportunity of access to the national language are present. The immigrant groups in Sweden, with the exception of the Finns, are a very good example of this point. Voluntary migration, access to public schools and thus to the national language, and economic incentives in the form of available jobs all contribute to assimilation and language shift. Other factors influencing shift include low Swedish tolerance for culture differences. Under such circumstances, even the very liberal Swedish educational language policies concerning mother-tongue instruction will not succeed in bringing about mother-tongue maintenance and will, at most, contribute to a few generations of bilingualism before a complete shift to Swedish.

The indigenous groups of Peru provide another example of ethnicity and language shift within a nation-state. The shift is infinitely slower than in Sweden, and we can identify contributing factors such as colonization, much less economic incentive, and more difficulty in obtaining access to the national Spanish language because of geographic isolation. We also need to consider the stigmatized status of things "Indian" and the cultural definition of race. The rewards clearly lie within Hispanic culture, and under these conditions General Velasco's language policies of bilingual education and Quechua as an official language clearly failed to stir up national consciousness to bring about a sense of nationalism with Quechua as its symbol.

Ethnic movements

The major difference between ethnicity and ethnic movements is seen when ethnicity as an unconscious source of identity turns into a conscious strategy, usually in a situation of competition for scarce resources. An ethnic movement is ethnicity turned militant, consisting of ethnic discontents who perceive the world as against them, an adversity drawn along ethnic boundaries. While ethnicity stresses the content of the culture, ethnic movements are concerned with *boundary maintenance*, in Barth's terms (1969:35), with us against them. It is very much a conscious, cognitive ethnicity in a power struggle with the dominant group for social and economic advantage, a struggle that frequently leads to violence and social upheaval. Many ethnic movements have charismatic leaders, probably always born members of the ethnic group, but the movements need not have an intellectual elite or a significant middle class.

Ethnic movements by themselves probably cannot maintain a language but will affect the rate of shift so that the shift is much slower and spans many more generations.

Nationalism

Boyd C. Shafer (1976) concludes that it is impossible to fit nationalism into a short definition, but I will attempt to identify some salient features. Cottam insists that nationalism is best interpreted as the manifestation of nationalistic behavior; a nationalist is defined as "an individual who sees himself as a member of a political community, a nation, that is entitled to independent statehood, and is willing to grant that community a primary and terminal loyalty" (Cottam 1964:3). Group cohesion to the end, a goal orientation of self-determination, a perceived threat of opposing forces, and access to or hope of territory are characteristics of all national movements.

The improvement of one's own lot in life or at least of one's children's is probably a common goal of all national movements; the motivation is one of perceived self-interest, a self-chosen state. Very often nationalism happens as a protest against oppression, against the common enemy, whether it be against a (dominant) group within the same nation or against another state.

Goals in national movements, besides general independence, tend to be quite definite and specific. These goals are often legitimized by or based on historical events or conditions. During the Finnish school strike in Stockholm during February of 1984, when Finnish parents kept their children out of school in support of their demand for Finnish medium schooling in kindergarten through university level courses, the reason given was that Finland is bilingual in Swedish and Finnish and that Sweden should reciprocate. This demand was legitimized and based on the national law in Finland and on the ethnic immigrant group's past history and is much more characteristic of nationalism than of ethnic movements, which tend to base their claims on a rationale of equity with others within the nation-state.

A national movement also differs from ethnic movements in that it must have a well-developed middle class. Victor Alba's (1975) anecdote of the Catalan workers who considered issues of language immaterial is representative. "We don't care if we are exploited in Castilian or Catalan," was their rejoinder, and they aligned themselves with the workers' unions and the socialist party rather than mobilize themselves along national lines. Without a stake in property, nationalism is not perceived to further one's self-interest.

Ethnic nationalism and geographic nationalism share many features, and the major difference is probably the same as that which Hans Kohn (1968) outlines for *open* and *closed* nationalism. In ethnic, or closed, nationalism, the ethnic group is isomorphic with the nation-state. The emphasis is on the nation's autochthonous character, on the common origin and ancestral roots.

Kohn calls open nationalism a more modern form; it is territorially based—hence geographic nationalism—and features a political society, constituting a nation of fellow citizens regardless of ethnic descent.

Language is a prime symbol of the nation in ethnic nationalism but not necessarily in geographic nationalism. Although one cannot change one's genes, one can learn a new language. In a nation that uses language to define membership, as does Catalonia, learning the new language obviously held both practical and symbolic significance: knowing the national language became the hallmark of membership and in-group status within the Catalan nation.

A final caution

It remains an open question how applicable this model of language shift and maintenance is for SIL. Most of the groups with which SIL works are likely to fall in the category of "ethnicity" and so be a potential target for shift. On the other hand, neither are they likely to be a target of national economic rewards, and frequently poverty and geographic isolation will hinder easy access to the national language. As I have said before, the reader will have to use common sense in sorting out appropriate features.

Appendix 1: Language maintenance and language shift: Conditioning factors

Factors at societal level

Political—legal conditions
The ideology of the dominant group
Language legislation
Implementation
Economic Factors
    Industrialization—urbanization
    Occupation (esp. dominant group)
    Communications
    Labor market
Sociocultural norms
Education

Factors at group level

Demography
    Size
    Nucleus
    Migration
    Age and gender spread
    Marriage patterns (endogamy-exogamy)

Language conditions
    Official language
    Official language in another country
    Spoken in more than one country
    Dialect or language split
    Standardized and modernized
    Relationships between speech and writing
    Bilingualism
    Language proficiency
    Language attitudes
Hetero-homogeneity within the ethnic group
Types of occupations
Type of ethnicity
Organization—internal
Institutions
    Educational
    Religious
    Status and corpus language planning
    Research and culture
Media
Cultural expressions

Factors at the individual level

Language choice
Socialization—acquisition

Source: adapted from Hyltenstam and Stroud (1991)

Appendix 2: Linguistic consequences of social mobilization in multilingual settings

(1) Defining characteristics	Ethnicity	Ethnic Movement	Ethnic Nationalism	Geographic Nationalism
	As identity	As strategy in competition for scarce resources	Territory	
			Closed nationalism (Kohn) — Exclusive	Open nationalism
	Unconscious learning behavior			
		Goal: socioeconomic advantage	Intellectual leaders Middle class Loyalty (important)	
	Shared ancestors: roots			
	Taken for granted Not goal oriented No violence	Cognitive Self-chosen Militant Violent	Common enemy Taught behaviors	
		Charismatic leader Language as rallying point Boundary maintenance Glorious Past	Goal: independence, political self-determination	
	Common values and beliefs Survives language shift		External distinction Internal cohesion (Haugen)	
		Cultural self-determination	as identity	

Less ←——— Legislation Involved ———→ More

(2) Facilitating or constraining factors	? Under what social conditions question
	e.g., participation in social institutions, schooling, exogamy, military service, religious institutions; mass-media; roads and transportation; travel, trade, commerce, war, evangelism; occupations; in-migration, back-migration, urbanization, demographic factors, etc.

(3) Linguistic consequences Also: Language reformation Language spread Language death	Language shift	Language shift but slower rate	Maintenance	Maintenance
		Religious factors with maintenance of sacred language	National language as powerful symbol Language planning-academies Strong language attitudes Standardization Modernization Literacy-teacher training Language problems: Choice of national language	National language

Source: Paulston (1994:110)

References

Alba, Victor. 1975. Catalonia: A profile. New York: Praeger.
Barth, Fredrick, ed. 1969. Ethnic groups and boundaries: The social organization of culture differences. Boston, Mass.: Little, Brown and Co.
Cottam, Richard W. 1964. Nationalism in Iran. Pittsburgh, Penn.: University of Pittsburgh Press.
Hyltenstam, Kenneth, and Christopher Stroud. 1991. Språkbyte och språkbevarande. (Translation by Christina Bratt Paulston.)
Kohn, Hans. 1986. International encyclopedia of the social sciences, 11:63–70. New York, N.Y.: Crowell, Collier, and Macmillan.
Paulston, Christina Bratt. 1994. Linguistic minorities in multilingual settings. Amsterdam: John Benjamins.
Royce, Anya Peterson. 1982. Ethnic identity: Strategies of diversity. Bloomington, In.: Indiana University Press.
Shafer, Boyd C. 1976. Nationalism: Its nature and interpreters. Bloomington, In.: Indiana University Press.

Language Contact, Evolution, and Death: How Ecology Rolls the Dice

Salikoko S. Mufwene

Introduction

This paper is about what can be characterized, borrowing a term from population genetics, as language *evolution*. I mean by this phrase no more than the long-term change that a language qua species undergoes in isolation or under contact conditions. The change may amount to different ways of expressing things (phonologically, morphosyntactically, lexically, or pragmatically), more, or less, complexity (in any structural or pragmatic respect), diversification into other varieties (regardless of whether these are identified as dialects or separate languages), to erosion of the vitality and/or structures of a language variety (also known as *attrition*), or its *death*. Not all language varieties have had a life marked by all such changes, nor have they all followed identical evolutionary paths if they underwent combinations of such changes. To account for both differences and similarities in these diverse evolutions, it will be necessary to understand, as in population genetics, the respective *ecologies* of the developments.[1]

Johanna Nichols (1994:276–77) distinguishes between different senses of *evolution*, including "progressive change toward increasing complexity" and "Darwinian evolution, that is, change brought about by natural selection of existing variation." I assume in this essay that evolution has no purpose or defined goals; it should not be interpreted as progress (Gould 1993:323), although it is often characterized in terms of adaptations to changing ecology, which actually explains why at least some evolutionary paths are reversible (as acknowledged by Nichols). Linguistic systems may evolve as much toward more structural complexity as toward more simplicity, just as they may be *restructured* (i.e., reorganized, Mufwene 1996a) without becoming more complex or simpler. Unlike Johanna Nichols, I show that natural selection (out of competing alternatives) plays an important role in language evolution, a natural consequence of analogizing language with population (Nichols 1994:12) at the mercy of ecology. The latter may sustain variation, but sometimes it favors some variants over others, often also prompting the advantageous ones to adapt.

Language as species

Since the nineteenth century, language has been claimed to have life. It has also been analogized with *organism* in biology. While the species metaphor will underlie much of the following discussion, I reject the organism alternative as inaccurate, for a number of reasons.

First of all, the language-as-organism metaphor does capture variation within language, thus making it more difficult to think of language internal variation as what makes internally motivated change possible.[2]

Second, the analogy makes it also difficult to account for partial or differential change in a language where some speakers may participate in the change whereas others may not or do so in a different way. This phenomenon can be illustrated by, for instance, the fact that English has undergone divergent kinds of changes in England and in North America since the seventeenth century and is spoken differently in the two

---

[1] I do not want to suggest that language evolution is in all, or most, respects like species evolution (see below). There are, however, some similarities between the concepts of *language* and *species*, which I find informative and would like to use cautiously to shed light on the process of language evolution.

[2] As much as genetic linguistics has been influenced by biological taxonomies (Mufwene 1998), it is curious that language-internal variation has not been made as critical to theories of language change as species-internal variation to evolutionary theories. Much of the substance of the latter presupposes variation.

polities.³ A notion of organism that accounts for such a differential evolution would be tantamount to that of population.

Third, the metaphor cannot account for variable speeds in the way long-term change takes place in a language, proceeding not only faster among some speakers than among others (hence differentially in a communal system), but also faster in some dialects than in others. This may be illustrated with statistical variation in the usage of *aller* in French and *(be) going to* > *(be$_{contracted}$) gon(na)* in English as *future* auxiliary verbs.⁴ A notion of organism that captures such facts would not in essence be different from that of population.

Fourth, the same language may thrive in one territory and yet fall into attrition or die in another (Hoeningswald 1989). This was the case of several immigrant languages in the New World which continue to be spoken in their homelands. Only a notion of organism which is tantamount to that of population can capture such differential processes in the life of a language.

Fifth, as Jerry Sadock (personal communication, May 1998) observed, language and dialect boundaries are fuzzy; there is no question of fuzziness in the boundaries of organisms as individuals. The closest analog to an organism may be an idiolect. Just as one needs more than one organism to speak of a population qua species, a language is a projection over idiolects which are governed by similar structural and pragmatic principles or which may be traced to the same ancestor.⁵

---

³ The phenomenon has been characterized as *speciation* in evolutionary theories. It occurs when a species splits into two or more kinds under conditions of separation in which its members develop different self-reproducing patterns or behavioral characteristics. This often happens when such subgroups evolve in separate geographical locations, at the mercy of different ecological factors. *Geographic specialization* is another term used to describe such adaptations (Thompson 1994).

⁴ There are also cases where, regardless of whether it is truly a change, a phenomenon is contained within one particular segment of the population, without affecting (seriously) other members of the community. Such appears to be the case with usage of *like* as a discourse marker to introduce what may be interpreted as a quotation (albeit an unfaithful one) but especially to signal change of speakers or points of view in a narrative. It seems to be associated with a particular generation (the young) and speakers outgrow it, consistent with age-grading. The language qua organism metaphor fails to capture this, especially because speakers do not graduate from age-groups all at the same time nor at the same rate. Members of a community are not all born the same day, month, or year. The life of a community depends on an uneven and quite variable staggering of several individual lives.

⁵O'Hara (1994) provides an informative discussion of the different ways *species* has been defined in biology.

I thus break with the tradition, as in Mufwene (1996a), and I submit that species, not organism, is a more adequate analog for language.[6] Consistent with Hagège (1993), with Keller (1994), and with practitioners of accommodation theory (e.g., Giles and Smith 1979) and of network theory (James Milroy 1992, Milroy and Milroy 1985), I also submit that the agents of language are individual speakers. The variation that matters to evolution starts really at that inter-idiolectal level, before reaching the next higher level of cross-dialect and/or cross-language differences. As in population genetics, changes start taking place by selection at the level of individuals who, while interacting with each other, cause their varying features to compete with each other. That is, when individual speakers communicate with and accommodate each other, some alternatives among the competing structural options may be selected out of a dialect or a language, or at least their significance may be decreased. If Labov (1998) is correct in observing that there is not as much inter-idiolectal variation as I suggest is possible, this state of affairs would be the result of the kinds and extents of accommodations that speakers make to each other in particular communicative networks or speech communities, as discussed below. However, those of us teaching syntax classes have witnessed several instances where one construction is (un)acceptable to some native speakers but not to others, e.g., *Larry may be sick and Bill may too.*

One important caveat is in order here regarding how fast changes spread in a speech community: typically faster than in a species in which change is effected through vertical transmission of genes from one generation to another. However, linguistic features are transmitted primarily horizontally (Mufwene 1997a), more or less on the pattern of features of parasites, through speakers' interactions with members of the same communicative network or of the same speech community. This peculiarity makes it possible for a new feature to spread fairly rapidly. If such a feature leads to some restructuring qua system reorganization, such as the vowel shifts in North American white varieties of English (Labov 1994, Bailey and Thomas 1998), the process need not wait for generations to

---

[6]The reason why, unlike in Mufwene (1996a), I will capitalize here on the notion/term species rather than population is that no justification need be provided for lumping several individuals together as a population. One is needed for grouping them as a species, for example, if the individuals descend from the same ancestor and/or share genes. Such is also the case for people who are said to speak the same language. They need not understand each other, as long as one may show some genetic and/or structural connection among their idiolects or dialects. Things are more complicated with language, since native speakers may claim or deny such a connection on ideological grounds, such as in the Balkans, where language boundaries have often been redefined (Friedman 1996). For the purposes of academic classifications, however, the above explanation stands.

become evident, although there is generational variation in the way it takes place in different idiolects.[7]

Like species, language is an aggregating construct, a projection over individual idiolects assumed to share common ancestry and several structural features through the interaction of their speakers with each other. Membership in a species is predicated on a family resemblance model, though there is a range within which variation is considered normal and outside which one is considered not speaking a particular language natively or fluently. From this perspective, evolution consists of changes within the structure of the acceptable range of variation within a species.

A central question in the approach outlined here is why language boundaries are not more random and why there is not more variation among speakers of the same language. The answer to this question lies in the notion of *contact*, which in linguistics has typically been considered at the level of languages or dialects. Weinreich (1953) states it correctly: contact takes place within the multilingual or multidialectal individual. Unfortunately, most of the literature on language contact, other than code switching and second-language acquisition/learning, has ignored individuals and focused on populations, making it more and more difficult to understand such matters as borrowing into, and substrate influence on, a particular language.

I submit that there is one basic form of contact, that between idiolects of individuals who interact and communicate with each other. This is a basic factor that accounts for what Le Page and Tabouret-Keller (1985) identify as *focusing*, a process whereby members of the same speech community communicate more like each other than like nonmembers. Through the accommodation process discussed above and below, some features gain selective advantage over other competitors which are selected out.[8] In some cases, a network starts using a feature which is more typical of a different network even when most of the members of the two networks do not interact with each other. Individuals commuting between such networks are the agents of transmission (Milroy and Milroy

---

[7] Consistent with variation theory in linguistics, one may assume such variability in a speech community to be the counterpart of the distribution of advantageous and disadvantageous genes among the members of a changing species. The only difference is that in a species where the selective advantage of some genes depends primarily on their vertical transmission, it takes many generations before the disadvantageous genes become latent and the change at the level of the species conspicuous.

[8] There are, of course, several situations in which no particular competing feature prevails over others, such as when more than one pronunciation is accepted for the same word, e.g., [dayrɛkt] versus [dIrɛkt] for *direct*, or when more than one strategy can be used for the same function, e.g., *the person to whom you spoke* versus *the person who you spoke to* versus *the person (that) you spoke to*.

1985), hence, initial agents of the change as they transport linguistic features, like they would germs, from one community to another.

Nothing by way of focusing or change would take place without individuals who interact with each other, setting their respective features in competition with each other, and having to accommodate each other by dropping some features, or accepting some new ones, or even by modifying their respective individual systems. Little by little, thanks more to lateral than to vertical transmission, linguistic features spread in a community and affect a whole language, often leading to a minor or serious reorganization of its system. Speciation into separate subspecies (identified as dialects or separate languages, depending on the speakers' ideological inclinations) obtains when networks of communication have little contact with each other and make different selections even out of the same pools of features.[9]

Although I oversimplify things here, the above discussion accounts, at least partially, for differences that have developed, for instance, between British, American, and Australian Englishes, or between White and African-American nonstandard varieties of English. A similar explanation applies to the development of different regional and social dialects, based on which individuals interact with which other individuals the most, what features have competed with each other within their networks of communication, and which particular selections speakers have made to accommodate each other, thereby "focusing" their varieties in diverging directions.

Note that language is more of the parasitic, more specifically symbiotic, than of the autonomous kind of species. Parasitic populations are apparently a fairly adequate analog chiefly because a language does not exist without speakers, just like parasites do not exist without hosts. The life of a language is, to borrow from Brown, "closely tied to the distribution of [its] hosts, which provide many of the essential environmental conditions necessary to [its] survival and reproduction" (1995:191). Many of the ecological factors that affect a language are not necessarily physical features of its speakers but features of other parasitic systems that are hosted by the same individuals, such as culture (which brings along notions such as status, gender, and power) and other language varieties.[10]

---

[9] In some cases, it is not so clear-cut that different features have been selected into, or out of, the linguistic system. Differences between two varieties may lie in the weights accorded to the competing variants and/or to their conditioning factors, the kinds of things that have concerned quantitative sociolinguists over the distinctiveness of African-American vernacular English compared to other nonstandard varieties of English.

[10] Among other justifications for comparing language to parasitic/symbiotic species are the following: (1) a language vanishes if the population of its speakers is decimated; (2) a language falls into attrition and/or dies if things are done to its hosts which do not enable it to thrive, for instance, if its speakers are relocated to an environment where another

By the same token, knowledge of more than one language by the same speaker makes one linguistic system part of the ecology for the other, just as much as knowledge of competing structural features of the same language used by other speakers makes them part of the ecology for the speaker's own features. (The competing features may be phonological, morphological, syntactic, semantic, or pragmatic.) One speaker's features may affect another speaker's way of speaking, thereby setting conditions for long-term change in the overall structure of a language qua species. All this leads to two important questions regarding language evolution: (1) How can feature competition be articulated in an approach in which one feature becomes part of the ecology for another, assuming ecology to be both external and internal to the species? (2) How different is internally motivated change from externally motivated change? It will help to explain more explicitly what *ecology* stands for.

The ecology of language

Ecology has been invoked to account for language evolution for quite some time now, although less frequently than might be expected, despite progress in the ethnography of communication. Among the earliest instances are the Voegelins and Schutz (1967) and Haugen (1971), who use it basically in the sense of the social environment in which a language is spoken, for instance, in reference to whether socioeconomic conditions in a particular polity favor or disfavor usage of a particular language. This is also the sense in which Mühläusler (1996) uses it, as he puts the coexistence of Melanesian languages among themselves and with the invading European languages in perspective.[11] Like them, I am interested in how

---

language must be spoken as a vernacular; (3) whether or not a language thrives or falls into attrition depends very much on social habits of its speakers, e.g., whether, in a multilingual community, knowledge of a particular language provides some socioeconomic advantages or disadvantages (in ways similar to avoiding hosts of a particular parasite or to selecting individuals more resistant to it in interbreeding patterns); (4) parasites affect the behaviors of their hosts and adapt themselves to the hosts' behavioral responses (Thompson 1994:123); (5) different life histories of both parasites and hosts favor different patterns of specialization geographically and otherwise; and (6) parasitic populations are more likely to specialize, hence to diversify into related subspecies, than their hosts (Thompson 1994:132), as well illustrated by dialectal speciation. In the latter case, the development of separate dialects is not necessarily correlated to the development of different ethnic or biological groups.

[11] See also Robinson (1997). Dixon (1997) and Mazrui and Mazrui (1998) may be interpreted in this light, too, although they hardly use the term *ecology*. Manheim (1991:31) invokes ecology, also, characterizing it as "the ways in which linguistic differences are organized and set into a social landscape," including, among other things, "the ways in

the *ethnographic environment* affects language, in this particular case, how it may trigger or influence the restructuring of a language. However, I am also influenced by how the term is used in macroecology, a branch of population genetics in which *ecology* is treated as a cover term for diverse factors which are both external and internal to a species and bear on its evolution, for instance, "population size, habitat requirements, and genetic variation" (Brown 1995:5), as well as "differences in initial conditions, stochastic events, time lags, processes operating on different time scales, and spatial subdivisions" (Brown 1995:15–16).[12]

A practical way to approach this subject matter without making it too abstract is by discussing specific cases and showing how they justify invoking ecology to explain language evolution. I will select them from the experience of colonization and the fates of various languages in North America. I will often go beyond these geographical and linguistic delineations to compare language evolution in North America with changes elsewhere. I use *colonization* to characterize any case where a population migrates on its free will from a territory and settles in another in which it controls much of its fate. This justifies my observations on the earliest stages of the development of the English language from settlements of the Angles, the Jutes, and the Saxons in England. As I discuss colonial phenomena, I also cover all sorts of structural and ethnographic developments in a colonized territory which affect languages that are indigenous to it or were brought to it by third-party populations.

A species-external interpretation of ecology: An ethnographic perspective. The language contact literature of the New World has focused mostly on what European colonial languages have become, especially on the varieties spoken by descendants of non-Europeans and the extent to which they have been influenced by African languages. More has been written on the survival of African cultures than on the survival of African languages. Warner-Lewis's (1996) discussion of Trinidadian Yoruba is a rare case, compared to the vast literature on Haitian Voodoo, on Shango cults in several parts of the New World, and on Brazilian Orisa rites. To be sure, there have been some publications on African-based secret languages but not on the survival of African languages as vernaculars.

---

which language and dialect differences are institutionally channeled and used." I focus in this essay mostly on the variation aspect of ecology, which bears directly on competition and selection.

[12] Space constraints prevent me from discussing all these factors, some of which are dealt with in Mufwene (1996a) and in much of the literature on the development of creoles. I focus here on a subset that bears on the few language evolution topics that I discuss.

Warner-Lewis (1996) is exceptional because survivals of such vernaculars are also rare.

The American colonial socioeconomic settings were not hospitable ecologies to the survival of African languages, in part because the plantation populations were ethnolinguistically so mixed that a lot of Africans could not speak their native vernaculars with anybody else and knowledge of these must have fallen into attrition, an experience common among some Africans living in North America today. Even on plantations where a few Africans shared an African language, be it a vernacular or a lingua franca, this had to compete on every plantation or polity with the local European-lexicon vernacular. Typically, this colonial variety gained selective advantage from being associated with the dominant political and/or socioeconomic group, which everybody had to accommodate. It prevailed not only over African languages but also over other languages brought by Europeans of various nationalities.

Species and ecology become useful metaphors here in several ways. One of them is that only the parts of those languages which came to the New World were negatively affected by the competition with the local vernaculars. They died in the relevant colonies but not in their homelands. The case of European languages is doubly interesting, because they died in some colonies but not in others. For instance, French died in Maine but not in Quebec, and it has been belatedly endangered in Louisiana. Dutch survived in a new, colonial, but not extensively restructured form in the New Netherland (New Jersey and New York), identified as Negerhollands in the Virgin Islands and as Berbice Dutch in Guyana, but it apparently thrived (identified also as Dutch) in Suriname, where it was spoken by the Dutch rulers and the non-Dutch elite as the official language but not as a vernacular.[13]

These examples also illustrate how selection operates on and through individuals. The loss of both African and European languages did not take place concurrently in all its speakers. The fact that some African languages survived as ritual or secret languages in some communities likewise suggests that for a while these languages were also transmitted from one generation to another. However, in population genetics terms, there were fewer and fewer individuals who could successfully contribute as

---

[13] I discuss survival in, and development of, new forms for European languages below. The last speaker of Negerhollands, literally 'Negro Dutch', died a little over a decade ago (Smith 1995), and fluent speakers of Berbice Dutch must be dead or dying by now, based on Kouwenberg (1994). The vernaculars spoken by Surinamese of African descent are creoles lexified mostly by English, e.g., Sranan (also influenced by Dutch), and at least one of them, Saramaccan, partly also lexified by Portuguese.

agents or as hosts to the reproduction of the relevant species, and little by little the relevant languages died in the relevant territories.

Yoruba in Trinidad and French in Louisiana highlight an important aspect of the ecology of language which determines whether or not a language may thrive in a new setting. The Yoruba which survived in Trinidad up to the mid-twentieth century came over with post-Abolition indentured servants, virtually all who originated in the same part of Nigeria and lived in communities marginalized from the creole ones. Its death was an inverse reflection of its relative integration in the larger, creole community. In the case of French in the United States, the Louisiana Purchase in 1803 was resented by the French colonists, and the integration of the francophone and anglophone populations of European descent has been a gradual process. The endangerment of French in Louisiana, well marked by concerted efforts to promote French culture, is likewise an inverse reflection of the integration process.

The socioeconomic history of settlements in the New World suggests that integration within the economically or politically dominant group was a critical factor in the general disappearance of African languages and regionalized loss of European languages in the Americas. The plantation industry did not develop overnight and was generally preceded by small farming industry in which slaves were generally well integrated (although discriminated against) in homestead settlements. (Besides, the plantation industry never replaced the farming economy, although it often grew out of it.) Reasons of practicality led the Africans to speak the languages of their masters or the local colonial languages as their vernaculars. Their children acquired these local colonial languages as their native vernaculars.[14]

By the time segregation was instituted in the colonies, typically decades later than the institution of indenture and/or slavery on the large plantations, the creole, and, later, seasoned slaves became the agents of enculturation and of linguistic transmission. Despite the gradual basilectalization among some of them, every new installment of slaves brought from different parts of Africa aimed at speaking the local vernacular as they heard it spoken by the creole and seasoned slaves. Its appropriation as their primary means of communication also led to the attrition of the African languages in the New World, while these in turn influenced the second language acquisition process and the development of new language varieties. The explanation for the loss of African languages lies thus in a simple effort on the part of African

---

[14] This is a development observable even today in African urban centers, where the majority of children express more interest, or find it more practical, to speak only the city's lingua franca, which becomes their native vernacular. This is part of the trend that endangers some indigenous languages in Africa.

captives to survive in the new ecology by being practical and acquiring the vernacular that would enable them to function in it.

Colonial history also suggests that Native American languages must have been endangered in two ways and at different periods. In the earlier stages of colonization, Native Americans were driven away and not integrated in the colonial populations, despite trade and negotiations of all kinds with them. The Native American languages were endangered then mostly by the decreasing numbers of their speakers, due to wars with the immigrants, to diseases brought over from the Old World (Crosby 1992), and to their relocations (Patricia C. Nichols 1993). This trend actually continues to date in Latin America, where the physical ecology qua habitat of Native Americans who have remained marginal to the ever-changing world around them is being destroyed by modern industry (as evidenced by, for instance, the literature on deforestation). In all this history, we are reminded of the parasitic/symbiotic nature of language, whose fate depends very much on that of its hosts.

The second kind of endangerment is more recent in North America, concurrent with the absorption of Native Americans into the larger American populations that have already adopted English or French as their vernaculars or lingua francas, and with increased pressure on them since the late nineteenth century to shift to the same European languages in order to compete with the mainstream populations for jobs and feel integrated in them. Reservations in North America have lacked the socioeconomic vitality necessary to sustain their communities as autonomous and to keep them free from the lure of life in mainstream North American society or the pressures to acquire English or French.

Overall, general integration of populations of diverse backgrounds at the expense of Native American traditional ways of life, typically to the benefit of a capitalist socioeconomic system that originated in Europe, has entailed the erosion of the socioeconomic ecologies that supported Native American cultures. Hence, it has entailed the endangerment of Native American languages. No human intervention will stop the trend unless it recreates socioeconomic ecologies that may either grant them selective advantage or make them equally competitive with the European languages. A favorable ecology involves more than pride in one's cultural heritage. It involves more fundamentally the use that a speaker can make of such heritage to survive and thrive in the new way of life.

In Latin America, where the integration of Native Americans started earlier, as reflected by what may be identified as the Hispanicization of races, the one-sided restructuring of socioeconomic systems has favored the European cultures and languages. The only chance for the indigenous languages to survive and possibly thrive has lain in those Native Americans who did not participate in the physical hybridization of the people which was concurrent with the cultural assimilation of non-Europeans. Thus from the beginning of colonization, the Native American languages suffered from a numerical erosion of speakers, which was in inverse proportion to the people who shifted to Spanish or Portuguese, chose to acquire them as native languages, and showed little interest in their ancestral languages.[15]

A species-internal interpretation of ecology. This section presupposes that languages are *complex adaptive systems* (CAS). They share with CASs in population genetics the following properties articulated by Brown (1995:14):

1. They consist of numerous components of many different kinds which interface with each other—some linguists will argue that such systems are modular.
2. The components interact nonlinearly and on different temporal and spatial scales—thus, the phonological component, for instance, may undergo some changes while the syntactic component barely does, or the semantic component may be more extensively influenced by another language than the syntactic component is.
3. They organize themselves to produce complex structures and behaviors—this is precisely the case even if one considered only, from a simple mechanical perspective, the complexities of the phonological, morphological, and syntactic subsystems and tried to explain how they interface to produce speech.
4. Some inherent features of the smaller units allow the systems to respond adaptively to environmental change—this captures the traditional concern of historical linguistics, which should also include the development of new varieties such as creoles.
5. Because the direction and magnitude of change is affected by preexisting conditions, there is always a legacy of history in the current system—this is what Mufwene (1996a) attempts to capture by the *Founder Principle*. For instance, American varieties of English reflect to a large extent the kinds of language varieties that the earliest colonists spoke, including nautical and non-English influence in the original proletarian colonial communities. (Dillard 1985, 1995)

---

[15] Part of the attrition process followed from the intervention of European colonists in promoting some Native American languages, such as Quechua, as lingua francas (Calvet 1987). Mühlhäusler (1996) discusses consequences of similar European interventions in Melanesia.

From a structural point of view, language evolution is marked by *restructuring* qua system reorganization (Mufwene 1996a). This may consist of the redistribution of phonemic contrasts in a language if some phonemes are lost, such as /æ, ə, ʌ, θ, ð/ in several new varieties of English, or when a new sound is introduced, such as the flap (the word-medial [D] in *wri*ter and *ri*der) in American English. It may consist of new ways of introducing subordinate clauses, such as with the use of *se* < *say*, instead of *that*, to introduce object clauses but not relative clauses in Atlantic English creoles. The change may also consist in differing ways of weighting alternative markers of the same grammatical function, for instance, whether or not *going to/gonna/ gon/ga* (pronounced [gə] in Gullah), or *will* functions as the primary marker of *future* in a particular English variety.

When several such changes co-occur, a language may be restructured into a new variety that some speakers may doubt belongs in their language. This has typically been the case for creoles, which linguists like to disfranchise as separate languages, against the sentiments of most of their speakers. Mufwene (1996b, 1997b, 1998) argues that basically the same restructuring formula takes place in all cases of language evolution which result in new varieties; the main difference lies in the specific distinctions and principles that have been affected, in the overall extent of restructuring, and in the sources of influences that affected the restructuring. I argue here that part of the ecology that determines such system reorganization lies within the affected language itself. Below, like in the previous section, I will invoke some specific examples of new varieties that developed by restructuring, which reflect an important role of language-internal ecology.

It appears from Trudgill (1986) that even without the presence of Africans and continental Europeans in the New World, North American varieties of English would have wound up different from British varieties of English. Important indirect evidence validating his observation comes from the fact that Australian, New Zealand, and Falkland Islands Englishes all sound different, reflecting in part differences in the specific compositions of the pools of features that competed with each other in these colonies. Even if the same features were taken to all these territories, their preference strengths relative to their competitors sometimes varied from one pool to another, which led to the selection and/or dominance of different variants from one new variety to another.

It so happens also that English in England and the United Kingdom was undergoing changes during the colonization of the Americas, Africa, and Asia by western European nations. Assuming incorrectly that English was originally homogeneous in England, differences in the timing of migrations to different colonies would also have produced differences, for instance, between Australian and American Englishes. They would simply reflect the variation in the varieties that were taken to the colonies, regardless of influence from the other languages that English came in contact with. The fact that Australia was colonized over 150 years later than North America is significant and must be considered as one of the species- internal ecological factors that bore on the evolution of English in these territories. Theoretically, different British varieties and pools of features were exported to Australia than to North America, although the latter also received these later varieties as adstrate influence on the new vernaculars that were already evolving.

However, English has always been regionally and socially diverse in England, and different mixes in the colonies would also yield different outputs to restructuring. This is precisely part of what seems to have happened as we correlate the regional English origins of settlers in parts of North America with the relevant regional dialects. According to Bailyn (1986) and Fischer (1989), settlement patterns in the original North American English colonies were not identical. Most of the colonists in New England, for instance, were Puritan farmers who migrated in family units from East Anglia. They engaged in family-run subsistence farms that used limited indentured or slave labor. They continued to interact among themselves in much the same way as they did in the metropole. Despite influence from speakers of other languages (e.g., French) and dialects (e.g. maritime English) that they came in contact with, New England's English is said to have remained the closest to British English. This is a situation where English's internal ecology in the colony varied little from that in the metropole, which prevented the language from being restructured as extensively as it did in other colonies or too differently from the evolutionary path of English in England.

On the other hand, the Chesapeake colonies (Virginia and Maryland in particular) were settled from more diverse places and socioeconomic classes in the British Isles. There were the plantocrats, who descended largely from British aristocratic families and came in family units and mostly from southern England cities, notably the London area (Fischer 1989). A large proportion of the colonists—up to seventy-five percent by the mid-seventeenth century according to some estimates (Kulikoff 1986, Fischer 1989)—came mostly as singles not only from southern England (London, Bristol, and Liverpool) but also from northern England, and many others from Ireland and Scotland. Most of those who came from Ireland did not speak English natively either, as English in Ireland was used pretty much the way it is used today in former British exploitation colonies of Africa and Asia. That is, it was spoken by the educated and/or those who had to interact closely with the colonizers.

Such internal diversity among the English-speaking colonists set things up for restructuring. Several variants came to compete with each other in novel ways and the selections that were made were not always consistent with those made in metropolitan cities—those important contact settings where, as noted above, English was also being restructured as a consequence of the same population movements that extended to the colonies. Nor were the selections identical with those made in New England, where the population mix was relatively conservative, with a majority of founder colonists who spoke alike already.

The Appalachian Mountains received larger proportions of Scots-Irish, who also came in family units and brought with them some Gaelic influence. Their English has been claimed to share features with Irish English, which also developed concurrently with English in North America, as the Irish have gradually shifted to English as their vernacular only since the seventeenth century. (Before then, as observed by Lüdtke in 1995, English was typically an urban and elite second language variety.) All these facts show that variation in the internal ecology of the colonial language bore significantly on how it would be restructured during its adaptation to its new external ecology.

Another species-external interpretation of ecology: A structural perspective. Part of the external ecology of English in North America consisted of the other languages that it came in contact with. As it was being appropriated as a vernacular by adult speakers among Africans and continental Europeans, the latter's languages often availed their structures as alternatives to those of the target, especially when there was partial structural or functional similarity between the relevant languages. This seems to have been the case with the introduction of object clause with *say* or in omitting the copula before a nonverbal predicate, as it may not have been identified as significant where it is contracted, as in *he's shy/gone*.[16] In the case of *say*, the fact that it is often used in colloquial English to report speech quotatively is an important factor (Mufwene 1996c). Languages previously spoken by such new speakers of English influenced the restructuring that was independently in process with the change of its species-internal ecology, as explained above. In communities where the second-language speakers were either the majority or marginalized from the native speaking populations, knowledge of the

---

[16] The fact that it is semantically empty lexically, although it carries tense in finite clauses, may have been a more significant factor, as several languages around the world do without a copula in similar constructions.

other languages favored variants that were more consistent with their structures, causing some subsystems to evolve in directions that diverge from those of dialects that developed where either the native speakers were the majority or where the nonnative speakers were well integrated.

Focusing on the case of complementation with *say*, note that although colloquial and nonstandard English offers the alternative of quotative object clauses introduced by the verb *say*, its use as a subordinator in African-American English and Atlantic English creoles is much more extensive. In the latter variety it is used also for indirect reported speech and in combination with verbs other than *verba dicendi*, for instance, in *Uh hear say Robert gone* 'I heard that Robert is gone/has left' in Gullah. In African-American English, *say* also functions as a discourse marker used by the narrator to remind the listener that the speaker is still the same in a chunk of quotatively reported speech (Mufwene 1996c).[17]

The ethnographic ecology, as discussed above, definitely affected the role of the external structural ecology toward more, or less, influence, because it determined the particular conditions under which it was possible for a language to influence the restructuring of the target language. More examples will help articulate how all this works. The point here is to explain that when English came in contact with other languages, no particular restructuring process took place that was different in kind from what took place in situations in which mostly dialects of English came in contact with each other. In the vast majority of cases, English as a vernacular among descendants of Africans was restructured along parametric options that were available in the lexifier but were not equally weighted.

For instance, English has more than one kind of possessive construction, as in the *cover of the book* versus *the book cover* versus *the book's cover*. There is a semantic difference between the last two alternatives, but this may not have been so obvious to some nonnative speakers in colonial settings. Since several West African languages mark possession by word order only, on the pattern of *book cover*, it is not surprising that this pattern is so commonly the dominant one among Atlantic English creoles. In African-American English, it alternates freely with the Saxon genitive, as in *the book's cover*. The fact that in the relevant substrate languages the same possessive construction applies both to nominal and to pronominal possessor nouns accounts for constructions such as *me/we book* 'my/our

---

[17] On the other hand, recall that although in some contexts it can be interpreted as a substitute for *that*, it cannot be used to introduce a clause in complex noun phrases. This should make more explicit what is meant by the definition of *restructuring* as system reorganization. Not only are there new morphemes that replace, or alternate with, older ones, but also the functions of the new ones may not be identical with those of their alternates.

book' in several of these creoles. (Incidentally, there are nonstandard dialects of English in which *me book* is normal.)

The above example suggests that at least in most cases, the respects in which English creoles differ structurally from other English varieties today are developments from English itself where the external structural ecology favored options not selected by the others. In several cases, these options were, of course, generalized to some novel uses, a process not so unusual in language change. Parallels to such developments may be observed in Atlantic French creoles, formed by Africans from more or less the same ethnographic backgrounds. French has the following possessive construction: NP *de/à* NP_{poss} and Pro_{poss} + NP, as in *le livre de/à Jean/moi* 'John's/my book' (literally, 'the book of/for John/me') and *mon livre* 'my book'. Haitian Creole selected only the option the closest to the first, applying it universally to nouns and pronouns alike, as in *liv Jean/mwen*, under the partial influence of the same African languages in which possession is indicated only by word order, regardless of whether the possessor is nominal or pronominal. In French, only tonic pronouns are used as nouns, as in *le livre à moi*. Otherwise, a possessive pronoun, preceding the possessive noun phrase, is used, as in *mon livre*. (Interestingly, Haitian Creole pronouns developed from French tonic pronouns.)

Mufwene (1996a, 1998) discusses more such examples, which will not be repeated here, regarding serial predicate constructions, negation, individuation, and the role of the stative/nonstative distinction. They show that generally creoles have restructured options available in the lexifier according to patterns consistent with some of the languages that they came in contact with. There is evidence of such external ecological structural influence in the development of noncreole varieties of English in North America, too. One such influence is the *bring/take/come/go with* construction, as in *Mary bought a card to bring/take with*, which seems to have developed under German influence (Goodman 1993). Another comes from Trudgill's (1986) discussion of the alternation between infinitival and gerund object clauses in English, as in *(It was) nice to see/seeing you*. Trudgill observes that the infinitival construction is used more commonly in North America than in the United Kingdom. According to him, this change in the preference of the two alternants may reflect influence of continental European languages that came in contact with English in colonial North America: most of them do not have a gerund and use an infinitival construction in similar syntactic environments. The explanation is consistent with the fact that, since the founding of the North American colonies, part of the European colonists came from continental Europe.

These examples illustrate what has been evident all along in the literature on second language acquisition: The speech of nonnative speakers is typically influenced by features of their own native languages. More accurately, it is influenced by languages they have been speaking prior to the latest.[18] Let us identify such languages for convenience as substrates. What we are learning is that once such speakers are either marginalized by segregation or form a significant proportion of a new community, they are very likely to influence the restructuring of the new language they have appropriated as their vernacular, either by selecting options consistent with some of the substrate systems or by introducing in it features that it just did not have. Segregation and integration are matters of degree. Basically, the same explanation applies to the developments of ethnic varieties such as Jewish and Italian Englishes among European Americans.

In the competition-and-selection approach proposed in Mufwene (1996a), the language that prevails actually wins a pyrrhic victory, as it adapts itself to its new speakers, i.e., part of its changing ecology. This validates again approaching language as a parasitic/symbiotic species and seeing its evolution in terms of how it adapts itself to the responses of its new hosts while affecting, or eliminating, other linguistic symbionts that it comes in contact with. How natural selection, which operates at the basic level of individual speakers, spreads at the level of the society is, of course, part of what linguistics is expected to explain, taking into account processes such as accommodation, which leads to focusing in Le Page and Tabouret-Keller's (1985) sense, and ethnographic notions such as communication networks.

The strong version of my approach to language evolution is that the competition-and-selection process has been typical of language change in any community and at any time. Languages are generally osmotic and the traditional distinction between language-internal and language-external causes of change seems irrelevant. The main cause lies in the punctuation of equilibrium which affects the extant system.[19] Regarding restructuring, there seems to be no obvious processual difference in whether the features which compete with each other are inherent in the same language

---

[18] More and more creolists agree that creoles and the like have resulted from the restructuring of the lexifier not by children but by adult speakers. This explanation is also consistent with the socioeconomic histories of the territories where the new language varieties have developed (Mufwene 1996a).

[19] Also inspired by evolutionary biology, especially by the views of Steven Jay Gould (1993), Dixon (1997:73–84, 139–41) invokes punctuated equilibrium to account for language change, arguing that significant changes happen in shorter periods of time than historical linguistics has led us to believe. This suggests, contrary to his own position, that creoles are normal instances of punctuation of the equilibrium in a particular language qua species in a new ecology.

variety or in more than one, and whether the varieties in contact and in competition are assumed to be the same language or separate ones (Mufwene 1998).

In conclusion, how history repeats itself

The history of English in North America is largely reminiscent of what happened over one thousand years ago in England, and much of the same explanation proposed above applies to language evolution in different parts of the world. In the early Middle Ages, the Angles, Jutes, and Saxons, who spoke related Germanic language varieties but perhaps not the same language, migrated to England; their descendants have ruled it ever since. First they drove away or killed some of the indigenous Celts. Eventually, they assimilated the survivors through a government system that led to the attrition or extinction of the Celtic languages, of which Welsh and Gaelic are apparently the best known cases.

Up to the seventeenth century, very few Irish—typically in urban centers—appropriated English as a vernacular. It remained a foreign language. Although the integration process started earlier in Wales, the development of Old English, then confined as a vernacular to England, must be interpreted largely on account of contacts among the invaders/settlers themselves, as they accommodated each other. Explanations of subsequent changes all the way to Early Modern English must, however, factor in contacts of English with Old Norse, Latin, and Norman French. Explanations of why these languages died in England, or why they did not lead English to extinction but only influenced its structures, must be sought in English's external ecology, especially in the ethnographic symbiosis that obtained between it and these other languages.[20] On the other hand, English's internal ecology should explain why the influence of French is more significant in its educated varieties than in its nonstandard vernaculars.

The fact that English endangered the Celtic languages is actually quite informative, as we learn from its ethnographic history that political

---

[20]The deaths of Old Norse and Norman French in England illustrate again those situations in which part of a species is disfavored by one particular ecology, while the remainder is well sustained by another. Old Norse developed into Norwegian and Danish, and continental varieties of medieval French have developed into today's varieties of French in and outside France. Power may not be an important component of the explanation, because Old Norse and Norman French were associated with the powerful in England, unlike the African languages that died in the Americas and the Indian Ocean. Integration into the demographically dominant population in the case of England may be a more plausible explanation.

power is not as critical an explanation as it looks regarding language endangerment. These languages survived as long as their speakers were not assimilated to the Germanic rulers, just like the Native Americans who were not killed in the colonial invasion were able to preserve several of their languages up to the early twentieth century, and Africans and Asians in their homelands have preserved their indigenous languages.[21] In both cases, the indigenous populations were marginalized and continued to interact mostly among themselves and in their own languages. Gradual socioeconomic integration since the seventeenth century led the Irish to interact more and more and in less subservient terms with the rulers. In the process, more and more of them have shifted to English, just like the gradual socioeconomic demarginalization of Native Americans has been a catalyst in the endangerment of the indigenous languages. There are, of course, differences in the ecological structures of these integration processes, but we need not get into them here.

Irish and Scottish Englishes have developed from the appropriation of English by the Celts, more or less like indigenized varieties of English in Africa and Asia (see below and Mufwene 1997b), whereas Native American varieties of English (Mithun 1992) do not seem to have developed to the same extent, at least not in the same way or with the same vitality as, say, African-American English in the United States or English creoles in the Caribbean. The ecologies of the integration process have of course not been identical for the Africans and Native Americans. For instance, while marginalized and yet integrated to some extent (until the Jim Crow laws were passed in the late nineteenth century), the Africans in English North American colonies needed English to communicate among themselves; hence their usage of it as a vernacular among themselves, in gradually segregated communities, made more allowance for distinctive patterns of their own to develop.[22] Similar developments have taken place among immigrants who aggregated in communities of their own, more recently the Hispanic immigrants. On the other hand, at least during the colonial

---

[21] There are of course several African languages that are endangered today, however, because they are being driven out of competition by other African languages, especially the lingua francas which are becoming urban vernaculars, but not by the European colonial languages. (See Mazrui and Mazrui 1998 on this subject.)

[22] To elaborate the explanation provided above in *A species external interpretation of ecology: An ethnographic perspective,* an important reason for this rapid language shift among the Africans in the New World is societal multilingualism, which impeded routine communication. Even if, on large plantations, handfuls of slaves may have come from the same areas in Africa and may have shared one or another lingua franca, there was nothing in the colonial political and economic ecologies that sustained the transmission of these languages from generation to generation. As noted above, the preservation of Yoruba in Trinidad was exceptional, under post-Abolition ecological conditions.

period, the Native Americans needed English less to communicate among themselves than with the colonists and other immigrants. The endangerment of their languages in the twentieth century is largely the result of their relative integration into, or dependence on, the mainstream American socioeconomic ecology, which has eroded their language transmission from one generation to another. As with other ethnic groups, the restructuring of English among them has been inversely correlated to their relative integration in the dominant culture.

Integration accounts also inversely for why African-American English is still thriving as a distinct variety and may continue to do so for several generations to come: In the main, European and African-American communities form their own separate mega-networks of communication whose members do not have to accommodate each other but must learn the other network's variety if they want to participate in their social or economic activities. This trend has typically been in the direction of white middle-class varieties of English, with African Americans having to learn (white) educated English. At the same time, they are also under pressure of ethnic loyalty to preserve African-American features within "the community".[23]

I should clarify that no ecological factor alone accounts for everything. Lack of, or less, integration does not explain why African-American vernacular English is closer to white nonstandard varieties of English in North America than Gullah; its creole kin is. Gullah developed in colonial settings where the Africans were the majority, in the rice fields of coastal South Carolina and Georgia, in settings similar to the sugar cane plantations of the Caribbean, where similar English creoles have also developed. Rigid segregation was instituted within fifty years of the founding of South Carolina, thus enabling early divergence of African-American and European-American speech habits. On the other hand, African-American vernacular English developed on the tobacco and cotton plantations of the hinterlands, as well as on smaller farms, where the Africans were the minority. Although there has always been discrimination against them, they were not rigidly segregated until the last quarter of the nineteenth century, after the Jim Crow laws were passed. Although this fostered the divergence of African-American and European-American vernaculars, the preceding 250 years of common socioeconomic history, marked by regular interactions between the two groups, account for the large amount of

---

[23] This dual pressure may not be an African-American peculiarity. Note, for instance, that American white southern English is stigmatized but is far from being endangered in the southern states, despite equal pressure on white southerners to use the same educated English taught in the school system.

similarities among them, which are due to more than sharing the lexifier (see also Mufwene, in press).

We should note in the development of African-American varieties of English a phenomenon that is inversely reminiscent of the appropriation of English by the Celts in the British Isles and Native Americans. At first, the latter populations were marginalized by the English. Subsequent, gradual integration led them to shift to English and develop new varieties. The Africans were integrated early but marginalized after appropriating the language. In the case of Gullah, its greater divergence is due largely to later massive importations of servile labor under conditions of rapid population replacement in which fewer and fewer native speakers of the colonial English varieties among the slaves served as models (Mufwene 1996a). These conditions favored the basilectalization of the vernacular, i.e., its restructuring further away from the lexifier.

The indigenized varieties of English spoken by Native Americans could not thrive as long as their speakers were being absorbed by the general American populations outside the reservations. Irish and Scottish English thrive because they are spoken in their homelands, in which the speakers are the majority and use it to communicate among themselves.[24]

Getting back to the development of European-American varieties of English, the process also has more concomitants in the United Kingdom itself. According to Bailyn (1986), British emigrations to extra-European colonies in the seventeenth and eighteenth centuries were an extension of population movements that were taking place in the British Isles. People in search of jobs moved to different parts of the British Isles, which led to the restructuring of English, especially in urban centers such as London, Liverpool, and Bristol, to which northern populations migrated and from which a large proportion of the colonists also emigrated.

The fact that population movements in England in the seventeenth and eighteenth centuries caused English to restructure into diverse contemporary dialects is evidence that English in North America and in other former settlement colonies would have changed even if it did not come into contact with other languages. That more than one particular dialect emerged in England since then, some of them probably more conservative than others, is also evidence that extra-European varieties of English would still be different from British varieties, because neither the actual English variants in contact and competing with each other nor their strengths were identical from one contact setting to another. More recent evidence for my position may be found in the development of recent

---

[24] Although Native Americans are in their homelands, the socioeconomic ecology has changed to where external pressures seem to have disempowered them linguistically.

British dialects out of recent population movements such as reported by Kerswill and Williams (1994) and Britain (1997).

Overall, answers to diverse questions about language evolution, such as why a particular language was restructured and in which specific ways, or why a particular language was/is endangered, are to be found in its ecology, both internal and external, and both structural and nonstructural. Such considerations undermine the significance of the distinction between internally motivated and externally motivated linguistic change, except for sociological reasons. Linguistic systems seem to be rather osmotic; and no differences in kind of structural processes may be clearly associated exclusively with external or internal ecological factors. Approaching language as species makes it possible to capitalize on variation within a population, to highlight factors that govern the competition and selection processes when equilibrium is punctuated in a speech community, to pay particular attention to the linguistic behaviors of individual speakers, on whom selection operates, and thereby to understand language evolution better as we can make more explanatory uses of notions such as accommodation, networks of communication, and focusing.

References

Bailey, Guy, and Erik Thomas. 1998. Some aspects of African-American vernacular English phonology. In Salikoko S. Mufwene and John R. Rickford, et al. (eds.), African-American English: Structure, history, and use, 85–109. London: Routledge.

Bailyn, Bernard. 1986. The peopling of British North America: An introduction. New York: Random House.

Britain, David. 1997. Dialect contact and phonological reallocation: Canadian raising in the English fens. Language in Society 26:15–46.

Brown, James H. 1995. Macroecology. Chicago, Ill.: University of Chicago Press.

Calvet, Louis-Jean. 1987. La guerre des langues et politiques linguistiques. Paris: Payot.

Crosby, Alfred W. 1992. Ills. In Alan L. Karras and John Robert McNeill (eds.), Atlantic American societies: From Columbus through abolition 1492–1888, 19–39. London: Routledge.

Dillard, Joey Lee 1985. Toward a social history of American English. Berlin: Mouton.

———. 1995. American English in the English diaspora. In Zoltán Kövecses (ed.), New approaches to American English, 3–18. Budapest: Department of American Studies, Eötvös Loránd University.

Dixon, Robert M. W. 1997. The rise and fall of languages. Cambridge: Cambridge University Press.
Fischer, David Hackett. 1989. Albion's seed: Four British folkways in America. Oxford: Oxford University Press.
Friedman, Victor A. 1996. Observing the observers: Language, ethnicity, and power in the 1994 Macedonian census and beyond. In Barnett R. Rubin (ed.), Toward comprehensive peace in Southeast Europe: Conflict prevention in the South Balkans, 81–105. New York: The Twentieth Century Fund Press.
Giles, Howard, and Philip Smith. 1979. Accommodation theory: Optimal levels of convergence. In Howard Giles and Robert St Clair (eds.), Language and social psychology, 45–65. Oxford: Basil Blackwell.
Goodman, Morris. 1993. African substratum: Some cautionary words. In Salikoko S. Mufwene (ed.), Africanisms in Afro-American language varieties, 64–73. Athens, Ga.: University of Georgia Press.
Gould, Steven Jay. 1993. Eight little piggies: Reflections in natural history. New York: W. W. Norton and Co.
Hagège, Claude. 1993. The language builder: An essay on the human signature in linguistic morphogenesis. Amsterdam: John Benjamins.
Haugen, Einar. 1971. The ecology of language. The Linguistic Reporter 13, Supplement 25:19–25. Also in Anwar S. Dil (ed.), 1972, The ecology of language: Essays by Einar Haugen, 324–39. Stanford, Calif.: Stanford University Press.
Hoeningswald, Henry M. 1989. Language obsolescence and language history: Matters of linearity, leveling, loss, and the like. In Nancy C. Dorian (ed.), Investigating obsolescence: Studies in language contraction and death, 347–54. Cambridge: Cambridge University Press.
Keller, Rudi. 1994. On language change: The invisible hand in language. London: Routledge.
Kerswill, Paul, and Ann Williams. 1994. A new dialect in a new city: Children's and adults' speech in Milton Keynes. Final Report on a project funded by the Economic and Social Research Council.
Kouwenberg, SILvia. 1994. A grammar of Berbice Dutch Creole. Berlin: Mouton De Greuter.
Kulikoff, Allan. 1986. Tobacco and slaves: The development of southern cultures in the Chesapeake, 1680–1800. Chapel Hill, N.C.: University of North Carolina Press.
Labov, William. 1994. Principles of language change: Internal factors. Oxford: Basil Blackwell.

———. 1998. Co-existent systems in African-American vernacular English. In Salikoko S. Mufwene and John R. Rickford et al. (eds.), African-American English: Structure, history, and use, 110–53. London: Routledge.
Le Page, R. B., and Andrée Tabouret-Keller. 1985. Acts of identity: Creole-based approaches to language and identity. Cambridge: Cambridge University Press.
Lüdtke, Helmut. 1995. On the origin of Modern and Middle English. In Jacek Fisiak (ed.), Linguistic change under contact conditions, 51–53. Berlin: Mouton de Gruyter.
Manheim, Bruce. 1991. The language of the Inka since the European invasion. Austin: University of Texas Press.
Mazrui, Ali, and Alamin Mazrui. 1998. The power of Babel: Language in the African experience. Oxford: James Currey/Chicago: University of Chicago Press.
Milroy, James. 1992. Linguistic variation and change: On the historical sociolinguistics of English. Oxford: Blackwell.
———, and Lesley Milroy. 1985. Linguistic change, social network and speaker innovation. Journal of Linguistics 21:339–84.
Mithun, Marianne. 1992. The substratum in grammar and discourse. In Ernst Håkon Jahr (ed.), Language contact: Theoretical and empirical studies, 103–15. Berlin: Mouton de Gruyter.
Mufwene, Salikoko S. 1996a. The founder principle in creole genesis. Diachronica 13:83–134.
———. 1996b. The development of American Englishes: Some questions from a creole genesis perspective. In Edgar Schneider (ed.), Varieties of English around the world: Focus on the USA, 231–64. Amsterdam: John Benjamins.
———. 1996c. Creolization and grammaticization: What creolistics could contribute to research on grammaticization. In Philip Baker and Anand Syea (eds.), Changing meanings, changing functions, 5–28. Westminster: University of Westminster Press.
———. 1997a. Métissages des peuples et métissages des langues. In Marie-Christine Hazaël-Massieux and Didier de Robillard (eds.), Contacts de langues, contacts de cultures, créolisation, 51–70. Paris: L'Harmattan.
———. 1997b. The legitimate and illegitimate offspring of English. In Larry Smith and Michael L. Forman (eds.), World Englishes 2000, 182–203. Honolulu, Hawaii: College of Languages, Linguistics and Literature, University of Hawaii and the East-West Center.

———. 1998. What research on creole genesis can contribute to historical linguistics. In Dieter Stein and Monika Schmidt (eds.), Proceedings of the XIII International Conference on Historical Linguistics, 315–38. Amsterdam: John Benjamins.

———. in press. Accountability in descriptions of creoles. In John R. Rickford and Suzanne Romaine (eds.), Creole genesis, attitudes, and discourse: Studies celebrating Charlene J. Sato. Amsterdam: John Benjamins.

Mühlhäusler, Peter. 1996. Linguistic ecology: Language change and linguistic imperialism in the Pacific region. London: Routledge.

Nichols, Johanna. 1994. Linguistic diversity in space and time: Chicago, Ill.: University of Chicago Press.

Nichols, Patricia C. 1993. Language contact and shift in early South Carolina. Paper presented at the annual meeting of the Linguistic Society of America, Los Angeles, California.

O'Hara, Robert J. 1994. Evolutionary history and the species problem. American Zoology 34:12–22.

Robinson, Clinton D. W. 1997. Developing or destroying languages: What does intervention do to linguistic vitality? Notes on Sociolinguistics 2(3):109–26.

Smith, Norval. 1995. An annotated list of pidgins, creoles, and mixed languages. In Jacques Arends, Pieter Muysken, and Norval Smith (eds.), Pidgins and Creoles: An introduction, 331–74. Amsterdam: John Benjamins.

Thompson, John N. 1994. The coevolutionary process. Chicago, Ill.: University of Chicago Press.

Trudgill, Peter. 1986. Dialects in contact. New York: Basil Blackwell.

Voegelin, Charles F., Florence M. Voegelin, and Noel W. Schutz, Jr. 1967. The language situation in Arizona as part of the Southwest culture area. In Dell Hymes and William E. Bittle (eds.), Studies in Southwestern ethnolinguistics: Meaning and history in the languages of the American Southwest, 403–51. The Hague: Mouton.

Warner-Lewis, Maureen. 1996. Trinidad Yoruba: From mother tongue to memory. Tuscaloosa: University of Alabama Press.

Weinreich, Uriel. 1953. Languages in contact: Findings and problems. New York: Linguistic Circle of New York.

Motivations: Language Vitality Assessments Using The Perceived Benefit Model of Language Shift

Mark E. Karan

Introduction

Language vitality and language shift are intrinsically related. Where there is continuing, undiminished vitality, there is an absence of shift away from the language in question. When there is language shift in process, people are using one language more and more, and another less and less; the latter language is suffering challenges to its vitality. Prognoses of language vitality in a community can be justly interpreted as prognoses of language shift.

The most consistent indicator of any future change is present change. Thus, the most productive and accurate way to make predictions of future language vitality is to investigate the present language shift situation (Edwards 1985:67).

The *perceived benefit model* of language shift is a model designed to better describe and understand language shift dynamics and patterns. Its foundational element is that individuals with certain *language use motivations* modify and exploit their linguistic repertoires in such a way as to bring about what they perceive to be their personal good.

As described below, the perceived benefit model of language shift maintains that there is a limited inventory of language use motivations (LMs) which influence people to make language choice decisions. As individuals' language choices are the basic elements of communal language shift, a study of a community's LMs is essential to the understanding of present and future language shift.

LMs are not uniform within a community. A study of the variation in language use motivational patterns used by different subsections of the community is crucial to understanding present and future language shift.

Obviously, if there is variation across age in LMs, certain conclusions can be drawn concerning future language use patterns. If the younger generation has motivations to use language B and the older generation to use language A, a future communal shift from language A to language B is most likely indicated. Less obvious, but nevertheless true, there may be other variations in LMs, such as across gender lines, or based on educational factors. Furthermore, the same subgroups that are in the forefront of linguistic change (such as the introduction of new lexical items) in a community are often, if not always, in the forefront of language shift.

There appears to be something special happening to cause differences in language use motivation across age. The variation that is present appears to be influenced by a phenomenon whereby the LMs of younger generations are often a subset of their parents' motivations. This is labeled *cross-generation motivation simplification* and is discussed later. This phenomenon has important implications in predicting future language use patterns and in making a prognosis of a language's vitality.

General approach to language shift

Traditionally, language shift has been seen either as community-based phenomenon, or as an individual-based phenomenon. Seeking to understand the dynamics of language shift, scholars investigate either community factors, such as urbanization and population, or individual motivations and social factors relating more to individuals than to communities.

Fasold (1984) provides examples of language shift study taken from the community perspective. He maintains that certain factors are very pertinent in explaining and predicting language shift. These factors include: industrialization, urbanization, migration, proletarianization, and government policies prescribing and proscribing language use in education and other government institutions. Nevertheless, he holds that there has been "very little success in using any combination of [these factors] to predict when language shift will occur. In fact, there is considerable consensus that we do not know how to predict shift" (Fasold 1984:217).

Fishman's (1964, 1965) introduction and use of the concept of *domains of use* is also based on the community perspective. These domains, which would be seen as the conglomerate of factors which define typical communication situations—factors such as participants, location, topics of conversation, and formality level—are basically subdivisions of the speech community.

This domains approach is extremely useful in studying the language choice patterns in a community. It is also very useful in demonstrating language shift over time, summarizing the results of language shift from the community perspective. However, because it is an approach based on the community rather than on individuals, it is somewhat less adequate in dealing with the actual dynamics of shift.

John Edwards's approach is a good example of an individual-based viewpoint on language shift. Instead of dealing with factors such as industrialization and urbanization, he deals with factors that are directly related to individuals' motivations and goals. Noting that "history shows that language shift is the rule, not the exception" (1985:96), Edwards attributes code choice, and ultimately language shift, to "a pragmatic decision in which another variety is seen as more important for the future" (1985:71). He holds that different *pragmatic considerations* such as power, social access, and material advancement are of supreme importance in the study of language use and shift patterns. He also holds that in any language planning activity, these pragmatic considerations are the major determinants of success (1985:94). Because of the importance he attributes to them, Edwards concludes that the only way to influence language shift is to alter the entire social fabric of the language community (1985:98).

Other contributors to the field of language shift who base it more on the individual motivation perspective are Dorian, Gal, Kulick, Trudgill, Paulston, Bentahila and Davies, Wardhaugh, Haugen, Bourdieu, Grosjean, and Hymes.

Gal concluded that stating that social changes cause shift leaves out the "crucial step of understanding how that change has come to be interpreted by the people it is supposed to be influencing" (Gal 1979:9).

Kulick, agreeing with Gal's statement, declares:

> To evoke macrosociological changes as a "cause" of shift is to leave out the step of explaining how such change has come to be interpreted in a way that dramatically affects everyday language use in a community. If the investigation of language shift is modified to include such steps, the question that then

must be answered is: Why and how do people come to interpret their lives in such a way that they abandon one of their languages? Viewed in this way, the study of language shift becomes the study of a people's conceptions of themselves in relation to one another and to their changing social world, and of how those conceptions are encoded by and mediated through language. (Kulick 1992:9)

Thus, for Kulick, the key to understanding language shift is understanding how people view and manipulate their conceptions of themselves and of the world around them. Looking at language shift from the macrosociological perspective leaves out the important step of how societal values are interpreted, manifested, and even formed.

The perceived benefit model of language shift is an individual-based model, and deals with individuals' motivations which influence language choice.

The perceived benefit model

The perceived benefit model of language shift was introduced in Karan (1996). It is based on the observation that languages spread and shift occurs because individuals, consciously or subconsciously, make decisions to use certain languages in certain situations. These individual decisions are motivated by what people consider to be their personal good. Individuals exploit, modify, and expand their linguistic repertoires in order to gain personal perceived benefit (1996:42, 129–30).

A key component of this model is that the inventory of language choice motivations is limited. Motivations in this context are either communicative, economic, social, or religious (Karan 1996:125–30).

Following *communicative motivations*, people make language code choices that benefit communication. One of many possible examples of this is the spread of Swahili in East Africa. In that region there are many ethnic languages, and Swahili has become the language of choice for interethnic group communication. There is a strong and very realistic felt need to acquire and use Swahili (Wardhaugh 1987:193, Paulston 1992:60–61).

Guided by *economic motivations*, people will make the decision to acquire and use the code that they perceive will bring them the most fiscal gain. In diglossic situations, where in a community there is a functional difference between two languages, a high and a low language (Fishman 1967), knowledge of the high language is almost always a prerequisite to obtaining the higher-paying jobs and entry into the subsector of the community where wealth and potential wealth can be found.

Paulston writes:

> The basic incentive for learning Catalan for the immigrants is economic, just as it was for learning French for the Occitan speakers. In Brudner's (1972) terms: Jobs select language learning strategies. (1992:59)

There are two basic types of *social motivation* for language choice: (1) the social motivation that would give the incentive to use the prestige language in a quest after power, prestige, and influence; and (2) the social motivation that would call for the use of an in-group language, helping to bring about solidarity, unity, and acceptance. This power-solidarity distinction was first made by Brown and Gilman (1960), when discussing the use of *tu* and *vous* type pronouns.

Although these two types of social motivations of language choice seem very different at first sight, there are close parallels between the two. In both types, the goal is association with positive qualities attributed to the languages in question.

With the power/prestige type of social motivation, the positive qualities could include intelligence, technical superiority, and sophistication.

With the solidarity type of social motivation, the positive qualities could be friendliness, honesty, belonging to the neighborhood, acceptance, nonjudgmental attitude, straightforwardness, lack of pretension, good work ethics, and egalitarianism.

In diglossic situations where there is the potential for individual bilingualism, there are often strong social motivations to learn and use both the high and the low languages. The motivations to learn and use the high language are largely based on social-power/prestige motivations. As an example, Taber describes a particular situation in the Central African Republic in the early 1960s where "advancement and prestige are so completely tied to knowledge of French" (1979:197). The motivations to learn and use the low language in a diglossic situation are often based on social-solidarity motivations, as well as communicative motivations. In a situation where there are strong motivations to use more than one language, for instance in the Puerto Rican community of New York City, whose population is motivated to use Spanish for social-solidarity reasons and to use English for social-power/prestige reasons, it is easy to see how code-switching can be the natural result (Poplack 1978).

Concerning *religious motivations*, Romaine (1989:375) notes the importance of religion as a domain "either in language maintenance or in fostering linguistic differences." Often there are languages that are associated with God or a god or a religion, and adherents would have a perceived religious benefit of using or learning that particular language. In some Central African areas, for example, Sango is, in the minds of some people, connected to Christianity and God, while the ethnic mother-tongue languages are associated with the traditional religions.

Another example is given by Kulick (1992:20) who wrote of an association between the Tok Pisin language and the good half of the Gapun people's metaphysical world, and a complementary association between the Gapun language and the bad half of their metaphysical world. In general, even though the parents still use Gapun, the society holds that Tok Pisin is associated with the half of human nature associated with good, collectivism, masculinity, adulthood, Christianity, modernity, and education. Gapun is associated with the half of human nature associated with evil, individualism, femininity, immaturity, paganism, backwardness, and lack of education (1992:20). Kulick tells how children were motivated to speak only Tok Pisin because of these associations.

So, in this perceived benefit model, people seek their own perceived benefit in language choice decisions. These decisions are the basic elements of language shift. Thus, the way to understand and make projections concerning language shift is to understanding language-choice-related motivations in the community. As a corollary, the way to influence language shift (impede or encourage) is to modify those language choice motivations. Thus, in principle, I agree with Edwards when he concludes that the only way to influence language shift is to alter the entire social fabric of the language community (1985:98). I hold that the only way to influence language shift is to alter the motivational fabric of the language community (Karan 1996:133–48).

Vitality assessment via motivational studies

Giles, Bourhis, and Taylor (1977) discuss language shift from the perspective of language maintenance. They present the following three factors as greatly influencing language maintenance: status, demographics, and institutional support. They combine these three factors into the language characteristic *ethnolinguistic vitality*.

In the present discussion, *vitality*, as in *vitality assessments*, is not to be interpreted by the above definition, but rather to mean simply the amount of life in a particular language, including the prospects of it not dying out soon. Instead of seeing vitality as the combination of status, demographics, and institutional support, I see vitality as having more to do with motivations and opportunity—language use motivations and opportunity to learn and use the language.

The perceived benefit model provides a new avenue into the study of language vitality assessment. Present and future language use patterns in any community can be interpreted as the aggregate of the motivations plus the opportunities. This being the case, the data that are needed for assessments of future language vitality are (1) the present and projected motivations and (2) the present and projected opportunities to learn and use the language. I will first discuss assessments of present and projected future motivational structures.

Motivational structures data. New methods are needed to make assessments of language-related motivational structures in order to determine which language-related motivations are active in the differing subsections of a speech community. We need further development of survey methodology, designed to reveal present language related motivational patterns. These tools must be designed to enable discovery of all the different types of LMs and also to distinguish the magnitude or strength of an individual motivation, perhaps with a type of high, medium, or low motivation ranking.

It is necessary that these developments in survey methodology take into consideration all areas and types of motivations, and that they assess the motivations of a broad spectrum of the society. Motivational data are needed from a representative sampling of the community, with care taken to record relevant social factors of the individual subjects in the sampling.

We need to record these factors of the individual subjects so that studies of the variation in the motivational structures of the community can be made, such as variations across gender lines, based on educational factors, or correlated with the innovators of linguistic change.

Bourdieu and Boltanski (1975) present a model of language use and language shift which is based on what they call the *marché linguistique*. In this model, people "buy" by investing time to know a language well, or to know the prestige dialect as it should be spoken (legitimized language), and "sell" by using language, which has become a commodity. The proper use of language brings about profit in showing distinctiveness, authority, and symbolic power. As an example of the linguistic market, Bourdieu mentions how women are *plus promptes à adopter la langue légitime (ou la prononciation légitime)* (1982:35), stating that the motivation for this is that the major, or even exclusive, path of social advancement for women is through marriage, and thus, the women would sooner and more substantially buy into the symbolic gains of language to use those resources in finding a spouse who would bring about the desired social advancement.

Interestingly, when discussing the motivations that would bring about either a specific variant or a choice of code, Bourdieu often almost ignores the distinction between internal language variation/change and the choice of languages in a multilingual situation. He treats the two phenomena as one: a linguistic market transaction designed to benefit the speaker. In the above quote, he treats as the same phenomenon the choice of a code and the choice of a specific pronunciation. And indeed, the similarities between the social-factor-defined variation between languages and within a language warrant this treatment (Karan 1996:151).

In the light of this, it can be seen that not only is it the typical pattern that younger generations, women, and urban-centered people, for example, are in the forefront of linguistic change (such as the introduction of new lexical items, or a shift in vowel quality), it is also the typical pattern that these same groups of people are in the forefront of language shift (making language use choices that lead to the gain of vitality for one language and the loss of vitality for another). Thus, a study of LMs across different subsections of a population can provide very useful information as to the direction of language shift, not only present but also future.

In any given community, the subsections of the population who are in the forefront of language internal change should be identified, perhaps through areawide patterns of typical innovators of change or perhaps through studies of language internal change. Then the language use motivational patterns of those same subsections of the population can be seen to be more reflective of future communitywide language use motivational patterns.

When we have access to the LMs present in different subsections of a speech community, we are able to make projections of future LMs, based on the patterns of innovation of change in that particular society. New survey methodology providing LM data correlated with social factors will give access to the current and future LM patterns. This data, combined with present and future projections of the opportunities to learn and use the language, will help project the future vitality of a language.

Use and acquisition opportunities data. Tools are generally available to gather and treat data relating to present opportunities to learn and use languages in a society. Assessments of language use patterns would provide most of these data. A very useful tool in recording these data would be a domains-of-use analysis of language use in a community (Fishman 1964, 1965, 1972).

Another factor which must be considered in an analysis of opportunities to learn and use a language would be how well those using a language actually control it. For example, a community which has the competence to use a language of wider communication (LWC) for buying and selling, and for little else, would provide much less of an opportunity to learn and use that language than a community which has the competence to use that LWC for all aspects of life. A community where twenty percent of the population regularly use an LWC, but do not control it well, would provide less of an opportunity to learn and use that language than a community where twenty percent of the population regularly use and it and control it well.

Again, the tools are available to assess peoples' proficiency in various languages. Sentence repetition testing is one very good tool for accurately assessing a community's competence in a language (Radloff 1991).

Through the use of these available tools, current assessments of the opportunities to learn and use a language in a community are attainable.

Future projections can be extrapolated from the present opportunities and the current pattern of LMs in a community.

In a list form, the data needed for assessments of future language vitality are

1. present language use motivations,
2. projected future language use motivations,
3. present opportunities to learn and use the language, and
4. projected future opportunities to learn and use the language.

There is a need to develop survey tools to collect data for Number 1. Data for Number 2 can be arrived at by examining variation based on social factors in the data from Number 1. Motivational patterns exhibited by those in the forefront of change in the community can be estimated to reflect future LMs. Data for Number 3 can be gathered using typical language use assessments and bilingualism testing methods. Extrapolations for Number 4 can be made based on Numbers 1 and 3.

The actual projections of future language vitality can then be made by combining projections for Numbers 2 and 4. Projected future LMs, taken in the light of projected future opportunities to learn and use the language, can give valid estimates of future language vitality.

Cross-generation motivation simplification

There appears to be something special happening to cause differences in LMs across age. Often, the LMs of the younger members of a society are a subset of the motivations of the older generation. This phenomenon is labeled *cross-generation motivation simplification*.

One example of this is the Gapun situation studied by Kulick (1992), which was mentioned above. In that Gapun community, the adults were motivated to use both the Gapun language and also Tok Pisin. It can be surmised that the motivations they had to use Gapun were communicative and social-solidarity. The motivations to use Tok Pisin were most probably communicative, social-power/prestige, economic, and religious. The motivations of the younger generation in that same society seem to start from the above set of motivations, and be simplified to leave only the motivations relating to the Tok Pisin language. In a situation where the opportunity clearly existed to learn and use Gapun, the younger generation did not use Gapun. The difference between them and their parents was not the opportunity but rather their motivations.

Another example of this process is the difference in the LMs and the language use patterns between adult and children immigrant populations. Yet another example is the growing monolingualism in many large African cities, where the younger generations are using only the LWC, and are not using, nor are motivated to use, the ethnic languages found in the country.

Questions are raised as to why this phenomenon is so often seen. Is there validity to this concept of cross-generation motivation simplification? Is there some kind of natural language economy which encourages it? Is it possible that there is a re-prioritization of motivations by the younger generation in the light of the changed environment? Are there some kinds of natural limitations on motivational complexity? When survey methods become available to determine LMs in different subsections of a community, these questions should be addressed.

An implication to be drawn from this apparent pattern of cross-generation motivation simplification is that the phenomenon bolsters language shift patterns. Very often, the motivations that are not found in the younger generations' inventory of motivations are those related to the use or the learning of a language which previously was very important in the community, but from which the community is presently shifting away.

Conclusion

Viewing language shift from the individual motivation perspective is crucial to the understanding of language shift and also to forming prognoses of language vitality. The perceived benefit model of language shift is well suited to making these assessments of future vitality. Projections of future language use motivations, and projections of future language learning and use opportunities can be derived from the present motivations and opportunities in a community. Together, these projections of future motivations and language opportunities can be studied to give more accurate projections of future vitality.

At present, we need survey tools to gather data on the present language use motivational structures in a community, tools which allow the data to show the motivational variation within the community.

References

Bentahila, Abdelâi, and Eirlys E. Davies. 1992. Convergence and divergence: Two cases of language shift in Morocco. In Willem Fase, Koen Jaspaert, and Sjaak Kroon (eds.), Maintenance and loss of minority languages, 197–210. Amsterdam: John Benjamins.

Bourdieu, Pierre. 1982. Ce que parler veut dire: L'économie des échanges linguistiques. Paris: Fayard.

Bourdieu, Pierre, and Luc Boltanski. 1975. Le fétichisme de la langue. Actes de la Recherche en Sciences Sociales 4:2–32.

Brown, Roger, and Albert Gilman. 1960. The pronouns of power and solidarity. In Thomas A. Sebeok (ed.), Style in language, 253–76. Cambridge, Mass.: Technology Press of MIT. Also in American Anthropologist 4(6):24–29. Also in Pier Paolo Giglioli (ed.), 1972, Language and social context, 252–82. Harmondsworth: Penguin.

Brudner, Lilyan. 1972. The maintenance of bilingualism in Southern Austria. Ethnology (1):39–54.

Dorian, Nancy C. 1981. Language death: The life cycle of a Scottish Gaelic dialect. Philadelphia: University of Pennsylvania Press.

Edwards, John. 1985. Language, society, and identity. Oxford: Basil Blackwell.

Fasold, Ralph. 1984. The sociolinguistics of society. Oxford: Basil Blackwell.

Fishman, Joshua A. 1964. Language maintenance and language shift as fields of inquiry. Linguistics 9:32–70.

———.1965. Who speaks what language to whom and when? Linguistics 2:67–88.

———. 1967. Bilingualism with and without diglossia; Diglossia with and without bilingualism. Journal of Social Issues 23(2):29–38.

———. 1972. Domains and the relationship between micro- and macrosociolinguistics. In John J. Gumperz and Dell Hymes (eds.), Directions in sociolinguistics: The ethnography of communication, 435–53. New York: Holt, Rinehart, and Winston.

Gal, Susan. 1979. Language shift: Social determinants of linguistic change in bilingual Austria. New York: Academic Press.

Giles, Howard, Richard Bourhis, and Donald Taylor. 1977. Toward a theory of language in ethnic group relations. In Howard Giles (ed.), Language, ethnicity, and intergroup relations, 307–49. New York: Academic Press.

Grosjean, François. 1982. Life with two languages: An introduction to bilingualism. Cambridge, Mass.: Harvard University Press.

Haugen, Einar. 1981. Language fragmentation in Scandinavia: Revolt of the minorities. In Einar Haugen, J. Derrick McClure, and Derick Thomson (eds.), Minority languages today, 100–119. Edinburgh: Edinburgh University Press.

Hymes, Dell 1974. Foundations in sociolinguistics: An ethnographic approach. Philadelphia: University of Pennsylvania Press.

Karan, Mark E. 1996. The dynamics of language spread: A study of the motivations and the social determinants of the spread of Sango in the Republic of Central Africa. Ph.D. dissertation. University of Pennsylvania.

Kulik, Don. 1992. Language shift and cultural reproduction: Socialization, self, and syncretism in a Papua New Guinean village. Cambridge: Cambridge University Press.

Paulston, Christina Bratt. 1992. Linguistic minorities and language policies: Four case studies. In Willem Fase, Koen Jaspaert, and Sjaak Kroon (eds.), Maintenance and loss of minority languages, 55–79. Amsterdam: John Benjamins.

Poplack, Shana 1978. Syntactic structures and social function of code-switching. In Richard Duran, (ed.). Latino discourse and communication behavior, 169–84. Norwood, N.J.: Ablex.

Radloff, Carla F. 1991. Sentence repetition testing for studies of community bilingualism. Summer Institute of Linguistics and the University of Texas at Arlington Publications in Linguistics 104. Dallas.

Romaine, Suzanne. 1989. Pidgins, creoles, immigrant, and dying languages. In Nancy C. Dorian (ed.), Investigating obsolescence: Studies in language contraction and death, 369–83. Cambridge: Cambridge University Press.

Taber, Charles R. 1979. French loan words in Sango: The motivation of lexical borrowing. In Ian F. Hancock, Edgar Polomé, Maurice Goodman, and Bern Heine (eds.), Readings on creole studies, 189–97. Ghent: Story Scientia.

Trudgill, Peter. 1974. Linguistic change and diffusion: Description and explanation in sociolinguistic dialect geography. Language in Society 3:215–46. Reprinted as chapter 3 of Peter Trudgill, 1984, On Dialect. Oxford: Basil Blackwell.

Wardhaugh, Ronald. 1987. Languages in competition: Dominance, diversity, and decline. Oxford: Basil Blackwell.

Power and Solidarity as Metrics in Language Survey Data Analysis

M. Paul Lewis

Introduction

When confronted with a language contact situation, the question that vexes us most is, What is going to happen? During this conference, several references have already been made to the question of prediction. I think no one would disagree that our ability to foretell the outcomes of the sociolinguistic situations in which we work is inadequate.

Giles, Bourhis, and Taylor (1977:308) define ethnolinguistic vitality as "that which makes a group likely to behave as a distinctive and active collective entity in intergroup situations." There are a number of aspects of this definition which are of interest to us and which represent facets of the problem of prediction. Among them are how to define "group" and what levels of "distinctiveness" and "activity" are enough to constitute a separate "collective entity". Another question is what constitutes an intergroup situation, since language contact is generally realized as interactions between individuals involved in dyadic interchanges. Generally, the data we have to examine in the study of intergroup interaction is a sample made up of representative individual interactions.

In this paper I want to propose that the observations we collect of the linguistic behavior of individuals in interaction that are tokens of group behavior and that the same forces influencing individual behavior, when taken as an aggregate, influence group behavior. In agreement with Mark Karan (this volume), I want to propose that the assessment of motivational forces may well provide us with an extremely useful means of improving our predictions regarding the direction of ethnolinguistic vitality for a particular group. At the present stage of my thinking, I can do no more here than present a rather speculative hypothesis.

The pressure of politeness in language behavior

In *The Pronouns of Power and Solidarity*, the classic study of the usage of the so-called formal and informal pronouns of address in French, German, Italian, and Spanish, Brown and Gilman (1960) proposed that the use of these pronouns was governed by two semantics: *power* and *solidarity*. They observed that there are important differences between the linguistic behavior of speakers who are related primarily by the power semantic and those related primarily by the semantic of solidarity.

Brown and Gilman's study was foundational for the study of the relationship between linguistic form and social relations of politeness. *Power* relations are nonreciprocal. One participant has greater power than the other and this nonreciprocal relationship is encoded linguistically by the use of different forms of address. In the European languages which Brown and Gilman studied, the more powerful participant would use the *T* form (*tu* in French and Spanish) but would be addressed with the *V* form (*vous* in French, *vos* [later *usted*] in Spanish) by the less powerful participant in the relationship. To observe these norms is polite. To violate these norms was often seen by speakers to represent a questioning of the authority of the powerful participant or a mockery of the weakness of the subordinate participant in the relationship.

The *solidarity* semantic, on the other hand, is marked by reciprocity. It is based on the concept of shared history, ethnicity, geographic origin, age, gender, religious affiliation, or some other perceived commonality. While persons in a relationship may lack solidarity with each other, they lack it equally. Fasold thus states, "Solidarity implied a sharing between people, a degree of closeness and intimacy. This relationship was inherently reciprocal; if you were close to someone else, in the most natural state of affairs, that person was close to you" (1990:4). This reciprocal relationship of solidarity is encoded linguistically through the use of the *same* form of address by each of the participants in the relationship; the presence or absence of the perception of solidarity is marked by using the T form for solidary relations and the V form for nonsolidary relations.

The combination of the two semantics provides a great deal of flexibility for speakers to indicate their power and solidarity relationships, and to signal changes in that relationship "on the fly" as conversation takes place. Thus a mother, who normally addresses her child with the T form indicating both solidarity and superiority, can subtly signal disapproval by addressing that child with the V form, thereby signaling the withdrawal of her feelings of solidarity and a loss of intimacy.

Brown and Gilman originally proposed that of the two, power is, well, more powerful. Between those who are not power-equals, the power differential overrides any other commonalities. Solidarity relations seemed to affect language use only when the power relationship is not significant. Between power-equals, the important semantic is that of solidarity. Do the two parties perceive each other as belonging to the same affiliation categories, and are they willing to acknowledge those shared affiliations? If they are, their social behavior (including their way of talking to each other) will reflect it. If they aren't, they will, in the same fashion, demonstrate their affinity stance in their verbal and nonverbal behaviors.

One of the interesting findings of Brown and Gilman's study was that the priority of power and solidarity semantics had changed over time. By surveying the use of the pronouns of power and solidarity in written source material, they determined that the situation described above had gradually changed until, by the middle of the twentieth century, the priority of the two semantics had become reversed. Thus, even though the patron of a business is essentially more powerful than the clerk who works behind the counter and thereby ought to be expected to address the clerk with the T form, in practice, the solidarity semantic dictates that because the two share no commonalities that are deemed salient to the situation, they will address each other with the nonsolidary V forms. Another observation made by Brown and Gilman (1960:261) is that use of mutual T (power-equal, solidary), as opposed to mutual V (power-equal, nonsolidary), is increasing. They observe, "The direction of change is increased in the number of relations defined as solidary enough to merit a mutual *T* and, in particular, to regard any sort of camaraderie resulting from a common task or a common fate as grounds for *T*."

Clearly, the perceptions of power and solidarity which condition the linguistic choices are socially conditioned themselves. Whom we perceive to be powerful and with whom we wish to associate ourselves in a solidary relationship are features of our cultural and social value systems. The trend over time to use more solidary speech forms reflects the social trends of Western societies in the mid-twentieth century with their heightened focus on equality, the leveling of social and class distinctions, rights, and equal access to social and economic reward systems. In tests of French students attending American universities, Brown and Gilman (1960:272-74) reported a high correlation between the use of T forms and political radicalism, indicating in yet another way how closely the semantics of power and solidarity are related to social and political value systems.

I have referenced Brown and Gilman's work primarily in order to misappropriate their terms and to make linkages—in a way that is perhaps unwarranted at first glance—to several other threads of investigation in the area of the semantics of language use.

One such thread is the work of Brown and Levinsohn (1987) on politeness as a universal phenomenon in language usage, in which they identify the twin forces of positive and negative face. In their words,

> Central to our model is a highly abstract notion of "face" which consists of two specific kinds of desires ("face-wants") attributed by interactants to one another: the desire to be unimpeded in one's actions (negative face), and the desire (in some respects) to be approved of (positive face). This is the bare bones of a notion of face which (we argue) is universal, but which in any particular society we would expect to be the subject of much cultural elaboration. (Brown and Levinsohn 1987:13)

While *power* and *negative face* and *solidarity* and *positive face* are not precisely conceptually equivalent, I would like to link them as dealing with facets of the same basic motivational forces.

Another conceptual thread that I see as related is Garvin and Mathiot's (1956) *unifying* and *separatist* functions of language. These are quite similar to what Fishman (1972) describes as *contrastive self-identification*. Unification and self-identification are closely related to solidarity and positive face, while separation and contrast are analogs in many ways of power and negative face.

More recently, Schiffman (1993:121), in an examination of language shift and its relationship to diglossia, reported a clear link between changes in societal values and linguistic behavior. "In Tamil, for example, the political speech was once restricted to the domain of the H-variety, but nowadays political speeches only begin and end in H; in between, L-variety predominates (*probably as a mark of solidarity*)" [emphasis added].

Going further, Schiffman also relates the observable differences in language behavior to the dynamics of power and solidarity, noting that it was Rubin (1968) who made a similar extension of the analogy of T and V pronouns to the Low (L) and High (H) varieties she observed in use in Paraguay. Schiffman's summary is important to bear in mind: "The dynamics of H and L exchange, like the exchange of T and V, are specific to particular linguistic cultures and cannot be predicted without recourse to a knowledge of other aspects of the linguistic culture" (1993:126).

These are not the only strands of research. The use of politeness forms by individual speakers has been subjected to other analyses by Ervin-Tripp (1972), Lambert and Tucker (1976), Bates and Benigni (1975), Brown and Levinsohn (1987), and Brown (1980). A somewhat related kind of individual linguistic behavior, under the rubric of accommodation theory, has been studied by social psychologists Bourhis, Giles, and Lambert (1975), Giles (1979), Giles, Robinson, and Smith (1980), and Gallois et al. (1988), to name just a few. These scholars have described the linguistic strategies of speakers as they adjust their way of speaking to converge with or diverge from that of their interlocutor based on their intent to express their solidarity or their independence. A similar kind of phenomenon has been described by Le Page and Tabouret-Keller (1985) among speakers of Creoles who adjust their speech as *acts of identity*, to align themselves either more closely with the solidarity of the in-group or with the power of the out-group.

One other strand I might mention is the phenomenon of *covert prestige* described by analysts of linguistic variation. Here, solidarity-promoting forms are maintained in spite of negative associations attached to them by those in positions of power (e.g., promoters of standards). I would suggest that in these situations *overt prestige* represents the power semantic while *covert prestige* is the expression of the value given to solidarity.

And finally, from the perspective of anthropology, we can look at power and solidarity as being particular representations of the notions of *grid* and *group* (Harris, this volume). *Grid* is defined as the unequal distribution of, or access to, resources (the inequality of the power semantic), and *group* refers to the definition of membership in a group and equal access to its shared resources.

As stated earlier, I stress here that the interplay of power and solidarity as forces in individual behavior can also be demonstrated in the aggregate behavior of social groupings. My premise is that individuals modify their linguistic behavior in response to their solidarity and power needs, and that over time the aggregation of these individual decisions can result in an observable trend towards an orientation in which the power needs or the solidarity needs of the group tend to be more dominant.

Societal postures of power and solidarity

Paulston's (1987) analysis of two different language contact situations provides an extremely useful taxonomy of social postures. These, in my view, represent how a changing mix of saliency of the solidarity and power semantics influences a group's social relations with those around it and its tendencies in terms of language maintenance and shift.

Briefly summarized, Paulston has looked at linguistic groups in terms of the nature of their social mobilization and has produced a typology which includes four categories: *ethnicity, ethnic movement, ethnic nationalism,* and *geographic nationalism*. She proposes that each of these categories "under certain specified social conditions result in differential linguistic outcomes or language maintenance or shift" (Paulston 1987:34).

Ethnicity is the most solidarity focused of the orientations and is characterized to a great extent by its lack of self-consciousness. Paulston's own description says it best:

> Ethnicity tends to stress roots and a shared biological past and the common ancestors (factual or fictional). The basis of personal identity is cultural (including religion), and ethnicity is a matter of self-ascription. The cultural values and beliefs, which are held in common, are unconsciously learned behavior, and ethnicity is just taken for granted. The members tend to feel comfortable with past and future, and there is no opposition and no violence involved. (1987:34–35)

Ethnicity becomes *ethnic movement* when the group becomes aware of its unique identity and feels the need to promote and foster that identity in the face of some kind of contrasting or opposing alternative. The unquestioned assumption of group cohesion and solidarity is less in focus, and the acquisition of resources, tokens of power, becomes more salient. Again, Paulston's description:

> The major difference between ethnicity and ethnic movement comes when ethnicity as an unconscious source of identity turns into a conscious strategy, usually in competition for scarce resources. An ethnic movement is ethnicity turned militant, consisting of ethnic discontents who perceive the world as against them, an adversity drawn along ethnic boundaries. (1987:38)

It should be noted, however, that even though an ethnic movement is characterized by an increased focus on power, the solidarity dynamic is not lost. Indeed, in many cases it is the banner of group solidarity that is waved by the promoters of the ethnic movement as a means of rallying support for the movement itself. One way of viewing this phenomenon is that formation of group solidarity is not the ultimate purpose of the organizing activities, but rather a tool that is used to achieve the real ends of the activity, an increased participation in the structures of power.

Ethnic nationalism is an even stronger, more centralized realization of the drive for access to power as the ethnic movement gains strength and works not only for recognition but for remediation through legislative and administrative changes that will grant it an even greater level of control of its own destiny.

The ultimate, and most power-oriented, type of social mobilization described by Paulston is *geographic nationalism* that seeks territorial independence, absolute self-determination, focused around the chosen symbols of ethnic (now national) identity.

In Lewis (1993) I examined how the advent of the Mayan revitalization movement in Guatemala demonstrates many of the characteristics of this transition from ethnicity to an increasingly vocal and more and more militant ethnic movement and ethnic nationalism. Paulston's framework proved to be exceedingly useful in understanding the dynamics of that shift. However, I realized that while Paulston's framework provided a useful taxonomy of the social configurations, I was looking for the forces which were motivating the changes in that configuration and which would enable me to predict the outcomes of those changes.

As a result of that research, I'm prepared to propose a hypothesis for testing: In regards to the nonpowerful language in any contact situation, a predominance of individuals with a strong solidarity orientation is more likely to reinforce ethnolinguistic vitality and language maintenance, while a predominance of individuals with a strong power orientation is likely to motivate language shift towards the language of power.

This view focuses on the single continuum of increasing militance along which the progression from ethnicity to nationalism seems to move. It makes explicit that, at each stage in that progression, there is a unique combination of commonly held solidarity and power evaluations being made by a sufficient number of individuals so that a societal effect can be recognized.

Implicit in this view is the recognition that power and solidarity are not opposites but coexisting sociopsychological needs, as stated by Brown and Levinsohn (1987) in their description of negative and positive face needs.

In the case of Mayan Guatemala, these effects have been most clearly seen in the onset of widespread language shift. Previously disfranchised but solidary Mayans now seek empowerment through their relatively recent acquired access to Spanish language acquisition, Spanish education, and fuller participation (thereby) in the Spanish-dominated economic system.

It is important to recognize, as Mark Karan (this volume) has pointed out, that there is a distinction between (1) the current valence of solidarity and power factors in a static analysis of a situation and (2) the orientation of a society in regards to the balance of power and solidarity in the future and as a goal to be achieved through programmatic action.

While ethnicity may be identified primarily by strong characteristics of solidarity, a group may, as in the case of the Mayans, have power aspirations which are untapped and unrealizable because of the socioeconomic and political contexts (what Paulston refers to as *access and incentives*). Heath and Laprade (1982) noted the importance of economic and social rewards in reinforcing and amplifying the momentum of language shift. A similar theme is mentioned by Mufwene (1995) and more recently has been elaborated in considerable detail by Palmer (1996) and in Feenstra's (1996) response to Palmer on the LG-SHIFT mailing list. I believe that it is worth stressing in this regard that the rewards may not be entirely economic. Fishman (this volume) has noted that there are many who are engaged in reversing language shift who have taken what he calls the *road of self-denial* and are maintaining the use of their languages in spite of the economic disadvantages associated with that choice. I believe that the understanding of solidarity, as well as power, as primary motivating forces to be considered can account for this kind of language choice. While economic rewards (a kind of power acquisition) may not be the result, there are social rewards of (perhaps covert) prestige (a kind of solidarity acquisition) which may be more salient. Thus, ultraorthodox Jews, the Old Order Amish, and other groups which have maintained themselves in, or been forced into, isolation, very often justify that circumstance on the grounds of a highly valued solidarity.

Ethnicity, faced with an oppressive situation and no access to the means (political or economic) of power, may simply "hunker down", build strong boundaries, and reinforce its solidarity. My analysis (Lewis 1993 and 1994) of just such a situation among the Mayans in Guatemala is that once the doors opened for access to the symbols of power (formal education, cash-based economic activity, and the Spanish language), Mayans abandoned their solidarity focus very quickly and began rushing through those doors in large numbers.

A group characterized by ethnicity will be marked by a high level of solidarity and a diminished focus on power. If the L1 of the in-group is associated with power and solidarity, heightened ethnolinguistic vitality and language maintenance seem much more likely to be the result. The community can meet both of its *face needs* (an inclusive identity and a contrastive independence) through its L1. In a group characterized by ethnicity where the L2 is associated with power, one could expect less stability, particularly if the saliency of solidarity is giving way to a heightened interest in meeting the group's power needs. Over time, as the socioeconomic and political context undergoes change, the community may reevaluate its needs; the chances of language and culture shift increase as it gravitates towards the means of achieving independence and self-determination, in a word, power.

Each of the other stages on Paulston's (1987) continuum represents a specific configuration of the relative value given to the power and solidarity wants of the community. I believe an ethnic movement represents a heightened interest in the acquisition of power while maintaining a relatively high evaluation of solidarity. It is an attempt to have both power and solidarity at the same time, but with the balance tipped slightly towards the power semantic. Power is achieved by playing on the strong solidarity of the group. This is in contrast with ethnicity, where the balance would lean more towards the solidarity needs/wants of the community. Similarly, ethnic nationalism represents an even greater influence of a power-oriented motivation, and geographic nationalism represents the extreme end of the scale, where independence (unimpeded action, that is, negative face) is dominant and national solidarity is the handiwork of political and social engineering processes.

As evidence of this, I offer the tendency of these more power-oriented configurations to redefine identity in more powerful, modern, and sophisticated terms. The acquisition of power becomes more important than the maintenance of the traditional markers of identity. Cultural symbols (including language) are re-created. Language planning and development activities become a priority. The elaboration of dictionaries, grammars, and manuals of style, and the creation of new words for technological, educational, governmental, and scientific domains of use are all seen as essential identity-preserving/creating activities. In some cases, the monolingual elders who follow the traditional lifeways are seen as obstacles to this program of making the language and culture adequate for the modern (read power-oriented) world.

While there is much evidence around us that social configurations are moving towards a heightened evaluation of power, making language and culture endangerment the topic of the hour, we should not forget that the same process can also cause the focus to turn again towards solidarity. The point is that as human beings we have *both* power needs and solidarity needs and that we move between the two, meeting one—such as, our need for independent action—but then as that alienates us from our companions, we swing back to meet our need for acceptance by engaging in solidarity-reinforcing behaviors. I think that this insight, learned from the studies of politeness cited above, can lead us to a much more moderated approach to prediction.

Because trends in Guatemala at the time that my colleagues and I collected our data (ten years ago, now) were moving in the direction of an increased focus on power, it seemed reasonable to predict language shift as the eventual and inevitable outcome of the processes which we were observing. Such a view, however, did not allow for the possibility that a future change of ideology, socioeconomic factors, sociopolitical context, and even overt language planning efforts could very well cause those seemingly inexorable trends to be arrested and even reversed, resulting in a return to a solidarity focus and a more stable language maintenance.

While the view from that point in time may have shown only bleak prospects for the continued ethnolinguistic vitality of K'iche', we should not have ruled out the possibility of a change in the trends we were observing. The power semantic may, after a time, lose its charm. This is not to say that a value shift towards power will have no lasting effects on the language and culture. Fishman (1991) has shown how carefully and painstakingly and at what cost the reversal of language shift is achieved. The return to stable diglossia for the Maya-K'iche' of Guatemala will most likely be to a diglossic situation in which fewer domains are assigned to K'iche' than previously and where the variety of K'iche' that is spoken will inevitably demonstrate more evidence of contact with Spanish. This refocusing on solidarity is one which has, as its object, an ethnic identity that is changed—transformed by the effects of the drift towards power—and which has redefined markers of identity as the symbols of group solidarity.

Adams (1995) makes reference to this in regard to the most recent Guatemalan census; he observes that the number of people who report themselves to be speakers of a Mayan language has decreased while the number of respondents who identify themselves as Mayans has not changed appreciably from the census taken more than ten years earlier. Adams proposes that the cultural markers of Mayan identity are changing while the structure of Guatemalan society (divided sharply along the racial fault line of Latins and Mayans) remains unchanged. It is now more likely than before that members of the Guatemalan population will consider themselves to be authentically Mayan while not speaking a Mayan language. This "new" society, refocused on solidarity, will likely demonstrate a diminished pace of language shift and perhaps even a reversal of language shift if language proficiency is strongly emphasized as a marker of Mayan identity; but even so the new identity will differ from the old in many significant ways.

This oscillation between power and solidarity seems similar to the phenomena of focus and diffusion described by Le Page and Tabouret-Keller (1985) in their descriptions of the spontaneous identity delineation made by individual speakers of Creole languages. While the parallel group processes move at a more ponderous pace, they seem to be characterized by many of the same features. The loss of a solidarity orientation is analogous to diffusion, and the regaining of that focus analogous to refocusing. We should expect that communities will swing first in one direction and then in the other as they attempt to meet alternately and simultaneously their positive and negative face needs. Over time, a discernible trend may become evident, but even that trend is subject to course corrections.

Ethnolinguistic identity theory

The factors affecting language contact outcomes can be categorized in a variety of ways. Different disciplines have taken different approaches in how they divide up the factors. For the purposes of this paper, I will use the perspective of *ethnolinguistic identity theory* (EIT) (also summarized in Hatfield and Lewis 1996), which makes a primary distinction between objective ethnolinguistic vitality and subjective ethnolinguistic vitality.

Objective ethnolinguistic vitality factors are those concerned with the measurement of structural variables in the society which could influence the vitality of an ethnolinguistic group. Giles et al. (1991) label these the *diffusion climate* and the *internal colonialism climate*. These have to do with environmental factors such as demography, social structure, and political-legal factors.[1] Also included in these objective factors are such intergroup dynamics as access to language acquisition, sociocultural status, cultural core values, and interactional norms. *Subjective ethnolinguistic vitality factors* are those concerned with the perceptions of the members of a group regarding their own group's relative strength and prestige in relation to another group with which they have contact. Giles et al. (1991) emphasize the importance of these perceptions in affecting the outcome of language and culture contact situations. Furthermore, they emphasize that not only the subjective perceptions of the ingroup but those of the outgroup are important as well. "...[T]he potency of socio-structural and political-legal factors are

---

[1]Giles et al. (1991), while recognizing the threads of research begun by Giles and Bourhis, also trace the development of ethnolinguistic identity theory from the work of de Vries (1984), where these terms are used to describe what are referred to by the others as objective vitality factors.

necessarily mediated by individuals' subjective evaluations of languages and statuses in an *intergroup* context" (Giles et al. 1991:116).

Objective ethnolinguistic vitality factors

Three general categories of objective vitality factors have been identified: demographic, institutional support, and status factors. Not surprisingly, these correspond rather well with Fishman's (1991) major language-shift-supporting areas of dislocation: physical/demographic, cultural, and social. These broad categorizations take into account sociostructural factors relating to group size and distribution, political and economic dominance, institutional support, boundary maintenance, and relative status and prestige.

Demographic factors. The demographic factors include the size and distribution of the contact groups. Eight subcomponents of demographics have been identified (Giles, Bourhis, and Taylor 1977) which are divided between two larger subcategories: group distribution and group numbers.

Group distribution. Group distribution entails three subcomponents: national territory, group concentration, and group proportion. The first of these, national territory, "is related to the notion of ancestral homeland" (Giles, Bourhis, and Taylor 1977:312). Group concentration deals with the relative population density of a group. "Widespread diffusion of minority group members as individuals may discourage group solidarity..." (Giles, Bourhis, and Taylor 1977:313). The third group distribution factor is group proportion which refers to the number of speakers "belonging to the ethnolinguistic ingroup compared with that belonging to the relevant outgroup..." (Giles, Bourhis, and Taylor 1977:313). A lower proportion is likely to lead to lower ethnolinguistic vitality than a higher one.

Group numbers. Group number factors include five subcomponents: absolute numbers, birth rate, mixed marriages, immigration, and emigration. The relationship of each of these to ethnolinguistic vitality is straightforward.

Absolute numbers are important; a group with one million speakers is likely to be stronger than a group with only three living speakers. Joe Grimes's (1986) work on the significance of absolute numbers in various parts of the world is an important contribution to the interpretation of the absolute numbers and ought to be part of the presuppositional base of all surveys.

The birthrate of the in-group in relation to the birthrate of the out-group can also be an important predictor of vitality. If investigated in depth, it might provide valuable information about group members' optimism or pessimism regarding the future of their group, the economic and social pressures which the group is feeling, and the strategies for both economic and cultural survival which the group is adopting.

Similarly, the number of exogamous marriages is a possible indicator of vitality, though the significance of such marriage patterns to language and ethnicity needs to be evaluated carefully. Exogamous marriages in some cases may be seen as power-oriented as in the well-known situation described by Susan Gal (1978). However, the exogamous marriage patterns of the Vaupés region of Colombia and Brazil have resulted in a complex multilingual situation. People speak several languages, as well as Tucano, the lingua franca, but the father-language is primary, serving as a badge or emblem of identity (Sorensen 1967, Jackson 1974, B. Grimes 1985).

Finally, immigration and emigration patterns need to be evaluated as well, and the significance of the patterns must be interpreted. "Migrants can either contribute to the strengthening of a linguistic subordinate group by assimilating into it, or they can contribute to its weakening by assimilating into the linguistic dominant group" (Giles, Bourhis, and Taylor 1977:315). The rate and strength of such assimilation is yet another indicator of the value given to power (assimilation to the more powerful group) or solidarity (assimilation to the in-group). Fishman observes, "L[anguage]S[hift] occurs because interacting languages-in-cultures are of unequal power and, therefore, the weaker ones become physically and demographically dislocated" (1991:59).

Fishman's (1986) sociological analysis of these kinds of situations takes particular note of the differences between the immigrant minority ethnolinguistic group and the conquering minority ethnolinguistic group. Though both are few in numbers relative to the out-group, the balance is changed by the distribution of economic and political advantage. This again reminds us that such trends are likely only to go so far and then to be reversed for a time. The outcome is assured in favor of the group with positive status, but the status of a group can very well change over time. To use an historical example that is very close to home, we would expect that French would have become the dominant language in Great Britain following the Norman invasion (just as Spanish became the language of power in Spanish America) had the positive evaluation of Norman power not given way over time to the resurrection of English solidarity.

As the preceding has indicated, while the size and distribution of a group are significant demographic factors, they are not the only factors that need to be considered. Small groups which densely populate a delimited geographic area, if no factors change, may be able to maintain their identity more than groups which are widely spread and find their individual group members isolated from other group members. Rural groups that can remain intact, if everything stays as it is, are more likely to be successful than urban groups which have numerous out-group contacts. In this regard, an ideological orientation towards separation (boundary hardness, i.e., solidarity) facilitates the isolation and the identity maintenance of the group. Examples given by Fishman (1986) are the Old Order Amish and the Hassidim (one a rural group, the other urban), who not only through geographical location but more through ideology have maintained their isolation from the larger society and its erosive effects on identity and language.

It is at this point that the work of Milroy (1980) and the discussion of social network theory presented by Graham (this volume) come to mind and emphasize the important role of social networks as norm enforcement mechanisms. Where populations are close-knit, involved in dense and multiplex solidarity-enforcing social ties, there is a greater likelihood that language norms will also be enforced, whether these norms promote maintenance or shift. Widespread population groups where social ties are not dense nor multiplex experience a relaxation in the stringency with which behavioral norms are enforced. When the system of sanctions and rewards is weakened, there is a greater likelihood that behaviors will change as group members respond to the values (and rewards) of the out-group behaviors. Fishman has also noted the tensions which urbanization, industrialization, universal education, and other network-weakening phenomena place on close-knit groups.

Institutional support factors. Turner and Giles (1981) identified as institutional support factors those which relate to the kind of recognition and use given to a language or variety in education, media, government, religion, and other societal institutions. Giles, Bourhis, and Taylor (1977:315–16) observe that institutional support can be either formal or informal. "Informal support refers to the extent to which a minority group has organized itself in terms of pressure groups." Formal support is that built into the institutional structure itself. The kinds of institutions listed are many and diverse. It would seem likely that some are more crucial indicators than others and that some institutions will be associated with the power semantic (e.g., government, education) while others will be more likely to lend support to solidarity (e.g., home, religion). Giles, Bourhis, and Taylor emphasize the key role of the use and support of a language in education at all levels not only as objective indicators of vitality but also as being influential in the shaping of subjective perceptions of ethnolinguistic vitality. "... [T]he number of minority language medium schools and the number of speakers they produce are often scrutinized by linguistic minority group members who often feel that *une langue qu'on n'enseigne pas est une langue qu'on tue...*" (Giles, Bourhis, and Taylor 1977:316). It is my observation that the change in attitude toward formal education in Guatemala correlates with the underlying value shift from one of solidarity to one of power acquisition.

The societal roles assigned to a language are affected by ideological pressures. Institutional support (or lack thereof) is both a reflection of and a reinforcer of the underlying value orientation.

Status factors. Status factors are those which deal with the relative prestige of the linguistic variety. This prestige may be acquired because of compartmentalization of roles where a particular variety is recognized as the H variety and assigned functions which are associated with more prestigious activities. This prestige is derived from the prestige ascribed to the *speakers* of the language, not from any particular linguistic features of the language itself (though many speakers attribute greater beauty, eloquence, simplicity, etc., to H varieties). Fishman (1991) makes reference to this as well, noting that while a domain of use in a wider sense is related to and defined by societal institutions, in a narrower sense it is characterized by the role relationships that exist between the interlocutors. The prestige of the speakers is related to their economic, social, and political positions and to the values orientation of the interlocutors in regards to power and solidarity. Giles, Bourhis, and Taylor (1977) identify four kinds of prestige: economic status, ascribed (social) status, sociohistorical status, and language status.

Economic status. Economic status refers to the degree of participation in and control of (power over) the economy that a group has achieved. This is especially true of the degree of control a group has over its own economic destiny.

Social status. Social status parallels economic status in many cases and is equally important. Giles, Bourhis, and Taylor (1977) define social status as group self-esteem and, early in the development of the theory, included the need for consideration of the subjective vitality factors. Social status can also be that ascribed to a group by members of the out-group and, therefore, also has an objective component.

Sociohistorical status. Sociohistorical status refers to the history of the group and the perception of the group's past as being more or less "glorious". I would classify sociohistorical status as a measure of the solidarity semantic. "Regardless of the outcome...historical instances can be used as mobilizing symbols...to inspire individuals to bind together as group members in the present" (Giles, Bourhis, and Taylor 1977:310–11). The presence or absence of historical rallying points or the existence of a history that is perceived as shameful or embarrassing are factors which affect the sociohistorical status of an ethnolinguistic group.

Language status. Finally, language status refers specifically to the perceived status of the languages in contact. A language which has been standardized may have greater status than one that has not been standardized and thus may contribute to the overall perceived vitality of the group which associates with the language. Similarly, the existence of literature in the language may contribute to its prestige. Language standardization efforts are often portrayed as solidarity enforcers, but are frequently part of a larger strategy aimed at achieving power through the legitimizing of the group identity as modern, educated, urban, and sophisticated. Literature production may be subject to such a double interpretation as well. Literature may well contribute to group solidarity and strengthen solidarity ties among speakers of the language. In other cases, however, literature may be produced as a symbol of the sophistication and potency of the language group. Such literature is less likely to be *read* than displayed. Thus, our observations of literature use need to be more than cursory.

Subjective ethnolinguistic vitality factors

A group's own self-perception of its vitality, quite apart from the objective indicators, can be considered as well and analyzed as subjective vitality factors. In several studies (Bourhis and Sachdev 1984; Giles, Rosenthal, and Young 1985; Young, Giles, and Pierson 1986), the importance of this subjective evaluation is demonstrated to be even greater than that of the objective measures. Groups which perceive themselves as successful tend to behave in ways which will reinforce that success. Groups which perceive themselves as failing may react by engaging in language and identity maintenance efforts (solidarity reinforcement) or by shifting to behaviors which conform more to out-group (i.e., power acquisition) norms.

Included as indicators of a group's subjective ethnolinguistic vitality are: their skills and motivations to learn a second language, their intergroup attitudes, and their attitudes towards code switching or the use of a given language (Bourhis, Giles, and Rosenthal 1981). Allard and Landry (1994) provide a thorough description of the features of subjective ethnolinguistic vitality and a history of its study. In addition, they have included features of social network theory as a component of the measurement of subjective ethnolinguistic vitality. What they call *individual networks of linguistic contacts* (INLC) are used as measures of ethnolinguistic vitality.

> The structure and composition of these networks are directly affected by the relative E[thnolinguistic] V[itality] of the ethnolinguistic groups with which an individual is in contact. In effect, these networks determine the quantity and quality of a person's ethnolinguistic experiences. (Allard and Landry 1994:121)

In part, the INLCs are part of the objective measures of ethnolinguistic vitality since they represent, in many cases, the institutions of the society, family, school, church, etc. At another level, however, they contribute greatly to the individual's subjective ethnolinguistic vitality through that individual's psychological participation in social interactions. Linguistic competencies of various kinds are developed in and through the INLCs. Allard and Landry propose that "it is the individual's experiences in the INLC that give rise to perceptions of the relative vitalities of the ethnolinguistic groups with which he/she is in contact" (1994:122). As an individual makes social comparisons and categorizations of the INLCs in which he or she participates, positive or negative perceptions are developed. Negative perceptions can lead to actions aimed at attaining a more positive social identity. "In an interethnic group context, the language behavior of individuals may reflect a strong sense of belonging to an ethnic group or an equally strong desire to integrate another ethnic group" (Allard and Landry 1994:123).

Of the seven Mayan communities which my colleagues and I studied ten years ago, the ones with the highest levels of subjective vitality were also the ones most open to innovations, farthest along in their "economic development", and most affected by language shift.

This indicates that it is simply not enough to know if a group feels good about itself. The values that underlie that positive self-evaluation must also be understood. If the power semantic is most salient, the positive subjective vitality will be derived from the perceived level of power attributed to the group as a whole. On the other hand, if the solidarity semantic is more salient, the positive subjective evaluation will be derived from the sense of group cohesion and belongingness that has been developed within the group.

Assessing ethnolinguistic vitality by assessing solidarity and power

This synthesis of politeness theory with ethnolinguistic vitality theory should lead us to better methods of assessing the ethnolinguistic vitality of a community. On the basis of what I've described above, it doesn't seem that we need to collect a great deal of community data which is new and different from what we have been gathering in our standard sociolinguistic studies; rather, we need to look at these data with an awareness of the dynamics of solidarity and power, positive and negative face, overt and covert prestige, unifying and separating functions, contrastive self-identification, focus and diffusion, and grid/group orientations. Further, we should attempt to gather these data in such a way as to maximize their usefulness for this kind of analysis. What factors will help us assess the power and solidarity values of an ethnolinguistic group and thus be able to make some suggestion as to its trajectory in terms of ethnolinguistic vitality and language maintenance?

The following insights should be kept in mind as we analyze data from both initial sociolinguistic surveys and the ongoing assessment by language development field-workers.

1. The assessment of the power and solidarity orientation of any social group must be done not only in terms of the current status but also in terms of people's aspirations for the future. Is the group characterized by an overall orientation towards ethnicity, ethnic movement, ethnic nationalsim or geographic nationalism? Furthermore, what are the aspirations and values of the group in terms of the acquisition of power or the reinforcement of group solidarity? Answers to these questions require care in the selection of the interview sample. It will be helpful to interview subjects from a broad range of age groups, from both sexes, and from both "traditional" and "progressive" segments of society. Interviews and questionnaires should be designed to inquire not only about the status quo but also about aspirations, the ideal situation, and what interviewees see as components of the current situation that need to be changed.
2. Language attitude data should be analyzed not only for what they can tell us about positive or negative attitudes towards L_1 and L_2 (or L_n) but also for what they indicate about the group's orientation towards power and solidarity. As useful as it is to know if people like their language and think it is beautiful, we need to keep in mind that languages, like any cultural symbol, are part of a larger semiotic system. We need to discover what associations L_1 has with other symbols of power and/or solidarity. This same kind of

analysis needs to be done for each of the linguistic varieties in the community's repertoire.
3. The traditional objective and subjective categorizations of ethnolinguistic vitality data, while useful, are insufficient by themselves. It is simply not enough—in addition to the demography, institutional support and status data—to know if a group feels good about itself. If the power semantic is most salient, the positive subjective vitality indicators may be derived from the perceptions of achieved power and may actually be indicators of impending or even incipient language shift. On the other hand, if the solidarity semantic is more salient, the positive subjective evaluation may be derived from a sense of group cohesion and belonging, with the accompanying tendency towards language maintenance. These situations are not at all similar and have very different potentials for the future. It is also very likely that in either case the community will, at some point in the future, perceive a need to invoke the complementary semantic with its restraining and compensating influence. I believe that this point alone will help us to temper our predictions. We should expect that there will be a compensatory course correction. While languages do die, I don't believe they very often do so in a straight line.
4. Much of this information can be obtained only through longer-term analysis of a sociolinguistic situation. The analysis of early survey information can provide a good basis on which to draw tentative conclusions, but an in-depth understanding of the power and solidarity orientation and aspirations of a community requires acquisition of the language of the community, identification with and acceptance by members of the community, and sensitive participant observation. It is important, then, that fieldworkers engaged in long-term language development keep these dynamics in mind and be in a continuous assessment mode. Language surveyors can only provide part of the picture.

Summary and conclusions

In summary, the parallel forces of power and solidarity can be seen to affect not only individual linguistic behavior, but also the behavior of entire groups. I have proposed that changes in the relative saliency of these dynamics can be seen to influence the social orientation of groups and account for the shifts in posture described by Paulston (1987) along a scale of increasing focus on power and decreasing focus on solidarity—from ethnicity, to ethnic movement, to ethnic nationalism, to geographic nationalism. I have proposed that power and solidarity are not opposite ends of a single continuum but rather two separate continua and can therefore vary and co-vary in an infinite set of combinations.

Based on my analysis of the situation in Mayan Guatemala, I believe that in language contact situations—particularly where there is diglossia and a considerable power differential between the languages in contact with each other—a greater emphasis on solidarity tends to produce a greater degree of L language and culture maintenance, while a greater emphasis on power tends to promote language and culture shift towards H.

Finally, the orientation of a group towards power or solidarity changes over time and these changes in orientation account for the halting of trends which to the outside observer seem unassailable. Thus, a language heading for extinction will experience a cultural resurgence, or one that seems well established and strong will experience a period when attrition seems to be gaining speed. Sometimes these resurgences or losses are merely bumps in the road. Other times they represent a complete reversal.

These changes are the result of changes in the external environment accompanied by changes in the ideological orientations of the speakers of the languages involved. Our language assessment efforts, whether in the most cursory of rapid appraisals or in the lengthiest of long-term language programs, will be greatly aided, I believe, if we can learn how to interpret the data we collect in terms of the interaction of power and solidarity.

It would be helpful for us to begin collecting such data and their analyses and examining how the various kinds of data can be appropriately subjected to this sort of categorization and tested against empirical language use data over a period of time. As we begin to accumulate baseline data through our traditional surveys, and then build on that with longitudinal data through our language program assessment activities, we should be able to identify if there is indeed a correlation between language maintenance and power and solidarity orientations as I am hypothesizing here.

Such a development will not only lead us to a better understanding of the dynamics of language maintenance and shift, the character of ethnolinguistic vitality, and the process of transition from ethnicity to nationalism, but will enable us to make more appropriate and accurate plans for the character and direction of language development programs.

References

Adams, Richard. 1995. Identidad local, identidad nacional. Paper presented at Seminario: De la Etnia a la Nación: La discusión sobre la identidad nacional, base necesaria en la construcción de la paz y la democracia en Guatemala. Guatemala City, Guatemala, 18–19 July, 1995.

Allard, Réal, and Rodrigue Landry. 1994. Subjective ethnolinguistic vitality: A comparison of two measures. In Rodrigue Landry and Réal Allard (eds.), Ethnolinguistic vitality, International Journal of the Sociology of Language 108:117–44.

Bates, Elizabeth, and Laura Benigni. 1975. Rules for address in Italy: A sociological survey. Language in Society 4(3):271–88.

Bourhis, Richard Yvon, Howard Giles, and Wallace E. Lambert. 1975. Social consequences of accommodation of one's style of speech: A cross-national investigation. In Robert L. Cooper (ed.), Language attitudes II, International Journal of the Sociology of Language 6:55–72.

Bourhis, Richard Yvon, Howard Giles, and Doreen Rosenthal. 1981. Notes on the construction of a "Subjective Vitality Questionnaire" for ethnolinguistic groups. Journal of Multilingual and Multicultural Development 2:145–50.

Bourhis, Richard Yvon, and Itesh Sachdev. 1984. Vitality perceptions and language attitudes: Some Canadian data. Journal of Language and Social Psychology 3:97–126.

Brown, Penelope. 1980. How and why are women more polite: Some evidence from a Mayan community. In Sally McConnel-Ginet, Ruth Borker, and Nelly Furman (eds.), Women and language in literature and society, 111–36. New York: Praeger.

——— and Stephen Levinson. 1987. Politeness: Some universals in language usage. Cambridge: Cambridge University Press.

Brown, Roger, and Albert Gilman. 1960. The pronouns of power and solidarity. In Thomas A. Sebeok (ed.), Style and language, 253–76. Cambridge, Mass.: Technology Press of MIT. Also in Pier Paolo Giglioli (ed.), 1972, Language and social context, 252–82. Harmondsworth: Penguin Books.

de Vries, John. 1984. Factors affecting the survival of linguistic minorities: A preliminary comparative analysis of data for Western Europe. Journal of Multilingual and Multicultural Development 5:207–16.

Ervin-Tripp, Susan. 1969. Sociolinguistics. In Leonard Berkowitz (ed.), Advances in experimental social psychology 4:93–107.

———. 1972. Sociolinguistics. In J. B. Pride and Janet Holmes (eds.), Sociolinguistics, 225–40. Harmondsworth: Penguin Books. Excerpt from Ervin-Tripp, 1969.

Fasold, Ralph. 1990. The Sociolinguistics language. Introduction to sociolinguistics, vol. 2. Oxford: Basil Blackwell.

Feenstra, Jaap. [Jaap_Feenstra@SIL.org] July 1996. Language shift—A value-driven complex in a changing environment. [www.SIL.org/fileserv/lg-shift/ JAAPFE97.RTF].

Fishman, Joshua A. (ed.). 1968. Readings in the sociology of language. The Hague: Mouton.

———. 1972. Language and nationalism: Two integrative essays. Rowley, Mass.: Newbury House.

———. 1986. Bilingualism and biculturism as individual and as societal phenomena. In Joshua A. Fishman, Michael H. Gertner, Esther G. Lowyand, and William G. Milan (eds.), The rise and fall of the ethnic revival: Perspectives on language and ethnicity, 39–56. The Hague: Mouton.

———. 1991. Reversing language shift: Theoretical and empirical foundations of assistance to threatened languages. Philadelphia: Multilingual Matters.

Gal, Susan. 1978. Peasant men can't get wives: Language change and sex roles in a bilingual community. Language in Society 7(1):1–16.

Gallois, Cynthia, A. Franklyn-Stokes, Howard Giles, and Nikolas Coupland. 1988. Communication accommodation in intercultural encounters. In Young Yun Kim and William B. Gudykunst (eds.), Theories in intercultural communication, 157–85. Beverly Hills, Calif.: Sage.

Garvin, Paul L., and Madeleine Mathiot. 1956. The urbanization of the Guaraní language. In A. F. C. Wallace (ed.), Men and cultures: Selected papers from the Fifth International Congress of Anthropological and Ethnological Sciences, 783–90. Philadelphia: University of Pennsylvania Press. Also in Fishman 1968: 365–74.

Giles, Howard. 1979. Ethnicity markers in speech. In Klaus Scherer and Howard Giles (eds.), Social markers in speech, 251–89. Cambridge: Cambridge University Press.

———, Richard Y. Bourhis, and Donald. M. Taylor. 1977. Towards a theory of language in ethnic group relations. In Howard Giles (ed.), Language, ethnicity, and intergroup relations, 307–49. London: Academic Press.

———, Nikolas Coupland, Angie Williams, and Laura Leets. 1991. Integrating theory in the study of minority languages. In Robert L. Cooper and Bernard Spolsky (eds.), The influence of language on culture and thought: Essays in honor of Joshua A. Fishman's sixty-fifth birthday, 112–36. Berlin: Mouton de Gruyter.

———, W. Peter Robinson, and Philip M. Smith (eds.). 1980. Language: Social psychological perspectives. Selected papers from the first International Conference on Social Psychology and Language Held at the University of Bristol, England, July 1979. Oxford: Pergamon Press.

———, Doreen Rosenthal, and Louis Young. 1985. Perceived ethnolinguistic vitality: The Anglo- and Greek-Australian setting. Journal of Multilingual and Multicultural Development 6:253–69.

Grimes, Barbara F. 1985. Language attitudes: Identity, distinctiveness, survival in the Vaupés. Journal of Multilingual and Multicultural Development 6(5):389–401.

Grimes, Joseph E. 1986. Area norms of language size. In Benjamin F. Elson (ed.), Language in global perspective: Papers in honor of the 50th anniversary of the Summer Institute of Linguistics 1935–1985, 5–20. Dallas, TX: Summer Institute of Linguistics.

Hatfield, Deborah, and M. Paul Lewis. 1996. Surveying ethnolinguistic vitality. Notes on Literature in Use and Language Programs 48:34–47.

Heath, Shirley Brice, and Richard Laprade. 1982. Castillian colonization and indigenous languages: The cases of Quechua and Aymara. In Robert L. Cooper (ed.), Language spread: Studies in diffusion and social change, 118–47. Bloomington: Indiana University Press.

Jackson, Jean. 1974. Language identity of the Colombian Vaupés Indians. In Richard Bauman and Joel Sherzer (eds.), Explorations in the ethnography of speaking, 50–64. Cambridge: Cambridge University Press.

Lambert, Wallace E., and G. Richard Tucker. 1976. Tu, vous, usted: A social psychological study of address patterns. Rowley, Mass.: Newbury House.

Le Page, R. B., and Andrée Tabouret-Keller. 1985. Acts of identity: Creole-based approaches to language and identity. Cambridge: Cambridge University Press.

Lewis, M. Paul. 1993. Real men don't speak Quiché: Quiché ethnicity, Ki-che ethnic movement, K'iche' nationalism. Language Problems and Language Planning 17(1):37–54.

———. 1994. Social change, identity shift and language shift in K'iche' of Guatemala. vols. 1 and 2. Ph.D. dissertation. Georgetown University.

Milroy, Lesley. 1980. Language and social networks. Oxford: Basil Blackwell.

Mufwene, Salikoko S. 1995. Language shift and language death: Perspectives from new world creoles. Paper presented at LSA Parasession: Language South of the Rio Bravo. Tulane University, New Orleans, Louisiana, January 1995.

Palmer, Scott. 1996. The language of work, and the decline of North American languages. Notes on Literature in Use and Language Programs 49:42–63. [http://www.SIL.org/fileserv/lg-shift/49PLMER.RTF]

Paulston, Christina B. 1987. Catalan and Occitan: Comparative test cases for a theory of language maintenance and shift. In Robert L. Cooper (ed.), Language in home, community, region, and nation, International Journal of the Sociology of Language 63:31–62.

Rubin, Joan. 1968. Bilingual usage in Paraguay. In Fishman 1968: 512–30.

Schiffman, Harold. 1993. The balance of power in multiglossic languages: Implications for language shift. In Carol M. Eastman, (ed.), Language in power, International Journal of the Sociology of Language 103:115–48.

Sorensen, Arthur P., Jr. 1967. Multilingualism in the northwest Amazon. American Anthropologist 69(6):670–82.

Turner, John C. and Howard Giles (eds.). 1981. Intergroup behavior. Chicago: University of Chicago Press.

Young, Louis, Howard Giles, and Herbert Pierson. 1986. Sociopolitical change and perceived vitality. International Journal of Intercultural Relations 10:459–69.

Towards Predicting and Planning for Ethnolinguistic Vitality: An Application of Grid/Group Analysis

Sue Harris Russell

Introduction

While doing a sociolinguistic survey among the Murutic language groups in Sabah, I became aware of differing patterns of language use and levels of bilingualism among various villages, even within the same geographic area. Fishman's (1989) discussions on domains of language use and the relationship between diglossia on a societal level and bilingualism on an individual level proved useful in understanding some of the language use patterns that I observed. In these cases, there were discernible variables, such as contact, religion, intermarriage, and education level, that contributed to patterns of language use and the resulting language maintenance or language shift (Harris 1990a). However, there were some cases in which the variables for different villages seemed similar, yet the patterns of language use that had developed in these communities were vastly different. I could not discern a single factor or even a combination of factors that explained the different responses of these communities to the same variables. Further, there did not seem to be any way of predicting which communities were likely to maintain their language and which would shift to the national language. This kind of information would be extremely helpful in the placement of personnel in language development programs.

Theories and models of ethnolinguistic vitality provide a useful framework for studying, describing, and integrating variables contributing to the vitality of a language community. There is a strong relationship between the ethnolinguistic vitality of a community and the resulting language behavior of the participants. The stronger the ethnolinguistic vitality of a community the more likely the community will use and maintain its language. Ethnolinguistic vitality studies have sought to establish a relationship between variables that affect language behavior at the structural or sociostructural level, the psychological level, and the sociopsychological level, in order to explain and predict language behavior.

Generally, structural factors are those variables that originate outside the collective group—the environment, ecology, or external setting in which the speech community is situated. These factors include: economy, education, sociohistory, demography, institutions, religion, urbanization, contact, geography, and government policy. Although all of these factors affect ethnolinguistic vitality, it is difficult to predict how a community will respond to changes in these variables (Fasold 1984:240).

Subjective psychological variables take into account the individual's cognitive perception about vitality as a predictor of language behavior. The subjective variables have been discussed as values, (Smolics 1992; Edwards 1994; Dorian 1994; Young, Louw-Potgieter, and Giles 1986), a belief system (Allard and Landry 1986, 1992; Harwood, Giles, and Bourhis 1994), norms (Frase, Jaspaert, and Kroon 1992), and identity (Sanchdev and Bourhis 1990, Fishman 1989, Gudykunst 1989).

A third level of analysis is the sociopsychological level, which encompasses social interaction networks. Variables at any one of these three levels of analysis cannot predict ethnolinguistic vitality nor explain language behavior. Language behavior is the result of the interaction of variables at all three levels.

For the purposes of this discussion I wish to focus my discussion on the *collective* itself rather than the individual as the unit of research. For the purposes of this paper a collective is defined as a social unit that is distinguished from the rest of society by some kind of boundary, that which divides in-group from out-group (Edwards 1994, Abrams and Hogg 1990, Cohen 1994a, Barth 1994, Verdery 1994). Collective identity includes common values, beliefs, and norms of the social unit. Often collective identity is tied to a particular symbol, such as religion, dress, language, common history or ancestors, geography, or a political leader. Although language is a powerful symbol of collective identity, it is not the only one, so collective identity may be maintained even if language is not (Gudykunst 1989; Paulston 1992, 1994).

The collective is a key component of the concept of ethnolinguistic vitality, that which makes a group likely to behave as a distinctive collective within an intergroup setting (Harwood, Giles, and Bourhis 1994; Landry and Allard 1994; Giles, Bourhis, and Taylor 1977). Although there has been much discussion recently on the interrelationship of objective and subjective factors, there has been little discussion on how the collective itself may influence individual language behavior.

Analysis of the collective is important to studies of ethnolinguistic vitality because collective behavior influences and is influenced by subjective variables at the psychological level. There is a common understood identity, values, and belief system of the collective that influences individual choice and behavior. Individual behavior also produces changes in the shared values of the collective (Archer 1988, Adams 1975). The social structure of the collective also enables and constrains individual behavior; at the same time individuals are able to influence and change the social structure of their collective (Giddens 1984).

The collective also responds and adapts to changes in objective or environmental variables (Milroy and Milroy 1992; Brenzinger and Dimmendaal 1992; Cohen 1994a, 1994b). Some collectives are able to easily assimilate changes in their environment while other collectives experience extreme dislocation, resulting in the breakdown of the collective itself. The problem of predicting ethnolinguistic vitality is that all collectives do not hold the same value for a collective identity, nor do they all respond equally to changes in their environment.

Douglas (1982a) and others who have focused on the collective as a unit of research have proposed that there are only a limited number of social models on which people form their social relations, and therefore a limited number of models on which collectives operate (Douglas 1982a; Lingenfelter 1992, 1996; Malina 1986; Fiske 1991; Thompson, Ellis, and Wildavsky 1990; Thompson 1982; Gross and Rayner 1985; Ostrander 1982). I propose (1) that for each type of collective there are predictable values and beliefs in relation to collective identity and symbols (including language) and predictable responses to environmental changes, and (2) certain types of collectives will maintain stronger ethnolinguistic vitality when exposed to environmental changes.

In this article I will introduce a typology that classifies collectives into four distinct types; then describe ethnicity, collective behavior, and probable responses to changes in their external setting; and finally use the typology to describe and explain changes in language behavior and social identity in three case studies.

Typologies of social relations

Previous discussions of ethnolinguistic vitality have employed one-dimensional dichotomies from sociology to provide a framework for the study of language behavior. The typology I propose to use for the study of ethnolinguistic vitality is a two-dimensional classificatory scheme first proposed by Douglas (1982a) and elaborated by Thompson, Ellis, and Wildavsky (1990). It is based on two dichotomies—group and grid, roughly—reflecting the general spheres in which social environment limits and enables an individual's interaction with others.

The first dichotomy reflects the degree of restriction the social environment places on *whom* a person relates to, or what Douglas refers to as *group*. Group describes the degree in which a social environment constrains the behavior of an individual. At one end of the continuum is *high group* which describes an environment that has a distinct criteria for membership, strong in-group/out-group boundaries. Individual actors are constrained by those boundaries and participate in collective goals and activities.

At the other end of the continuum is a *low group* social environment. In a low group, social environment relationships are instrumental in nature. People may form groups to complete activities, but they generally participate in activities because it meets their personal agenda rather than because they are part of a group. Individuals in a low group social environment are free to manipulate resources for their personal gain. Competition rather than cooperation best characterizes low group social environments.

The second dichotomy is the degree to which the social environment restricts an individual in *how* he relates to people, the component which Douglas refers to as *grid*. A *high grid* social environment has several layers of role distinctions. These roles constrain the actions of individuals and interaction between them. Roles may be ascribed or achieved and are usually arranged in the society in a hierarchical manner, with fewer at the top than at the bottom.

In contrast to this, a social environment that is *low grid* has very few role distinctions and very little specialization. The most basic role distinctions may be those of young/old, men/women. In this kind of social environment, people are known for who they are and their character, rather than by role distinctions. Relationships tend to be made on the basis of person rather than role.

The combining of grid/group into a matrix produces four distinct structures for sociocultural interaction: *Individualistic*, low grid/low group; *Collectivist*, low grid/high group; *Corporate*, high grid/high group; *Bureaucratic*, high grid/low group, as seen in figure 1.

Figure 1. Four structures of sociocultural interaction
(Source: Lingenfelter 1992)

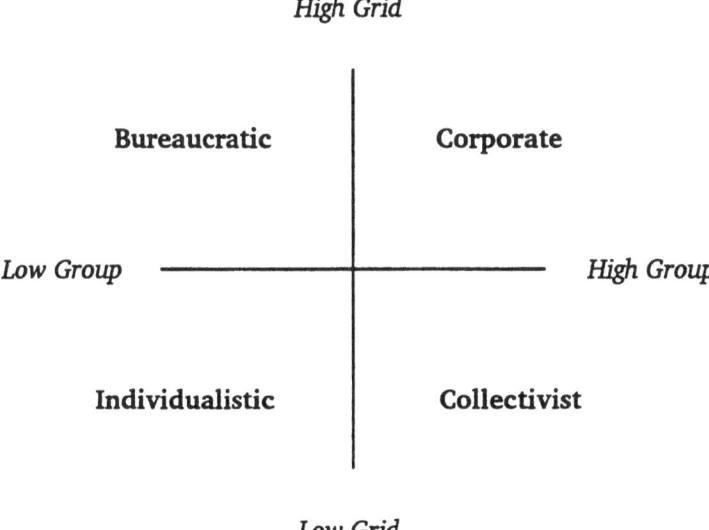

Four types of social environments

Each of the four types of social environments formed through the combination of grid and group has its own particular cosmology and way of life. These prototypes have been helpful in describing predictable differences in theological interpretations (Wildavsky 1984, Atkins 1991, Malina 1986), perceptions of risk and change (Douglas and Wildavsky 1982, Gross and Rayner 1985), perceptions of science and nature (Bloor and Bloor 1982), and perceptions towards resources, labor, and authority (Lingenfelter 1992, Harris 1996). I propose that each type of social environment also has its own perceptions, values, and attitudes toward language, ethnicity, and changes in its external setting. Through the study of the variables of grid and group, a researcher should be able to predict probable long-term ethnolinguistic vitality for a collective within a particular setting and the collective's probable response to changes in its external setting.

For the purpose of this discussion, I will limit my descriptions of the four prototype social environments to the factors that directly relate to the study of ethnolinguistic vitality. For each social environment I will seek to answer two basic questions:

1. How does a particular social environment respond to changes in its external setting?
   The answer to this question involves perceptions toward the external setting, risk taking, innovations, and the adaptability of the social environment to change.
2. How does the social environment affect people's values, beliefs, and perceptions toward the collective?
   To answer this question I will discuss how much individuals are restricted or enabled by the collective to pursue individual goals, and the importance of the collective in the formation of social identity. I will use Paulston's (1994) framework of social movements to describe ethnicity for each prototype and the implications for maintenance of ethnolinguistic vitality.

Low grid/low group: Individualistic

The individualistic social environment is characterized by maximum options for negotiation of contracts and choosing allies. It allows maximum individual mobility, both up and down the scale of prestige and influence. People may grant power to another for a particular task, or they may work together to accomplish a goal, but generally the goal is in the interest of the individuals participating rather than a group. Relationships are instrumental in nature and activities are directed to accomplish individual goals. Competition rather than cooperation tends to characterize this social environment.

A collective identity has very low value, unless it is useful for individual gain. No one cares especially about the history or ancestry of individuals. People have no roots and can move on easily if necessary. They freely manipulate group membership for their own advantage. If language is necessary for membership or to obtain resources, then individuals will learn it.

The individualist perceives risk as a part of life. Advancement does not come apart from risk, and a person must evaluate whether the risk is worth the potential gain from a venture. The individualist tends to be optimistic towards the future and towards risk. But it is the individual who both gains and loses rather than a group. Individuals will seek to take advantages of resources from which they will gain the most, including those from a dominant culture.

In individualistic social environments, ethnicity is found in terms of a shared biological and historical background, rather than a collective identity—what Paulston (1994) describes as ethnicity rather than social movement. Geographic boundaries may promote language maintenance, but when barriers are removed and resources are made available, individuals are free to obtain those resources. Language maintenance and acquisition will be based on instrumental rather than sentimental factors. If the dominant group makes resources available, people in this particular social environment will be assimilated into the dominant culture, and language shift will take place.

Low grid/high group: Collectivist

The most dominant feature of the collectivist social environment is the external boundary that identifies who is part of the group and who is not. The boundary may be defined by characteristics of commonality or by characteristics of contrast, that which sets it apart from the rest of society. Social identity of individuals is located in group membership. There is often an assumption of groupness; symbols of group identity are often unelaborated and assumed as part of the identity of the group.

Within the group there are no restrictions for relating to other members. Decision making is by consensus, with each having an equal voice. Leadership is charismatic and there is a lack of clear rules for succession. Groups may be enduring but larger groups tend to be unstable and break off into factions and smaller groups.

In the face of risk the collectivist social environment tends to strengthen its borders. There is a paranoia within the group; anything or anybody that threatens the group's existence, whether real or imagined, is viewed with suspicion. There is a strong good/evil dichotomy which generally corresponds to the in-group/out-group boundary. Although the collectivists see themselves as part of their external surroundings, these surroundings are viewed negatively and are threatening to the group. Changes in the surroundings are seen as dangerous, and when faced with domination, the collectivist social environment will strengthen its boundaries.

The collectivist is best described by Paulston's ethnic movement. Ethnic movements stress boundary maintenance; an *us* against *them* struggle (Paulston 1994). The rallying point for an ethnic movement may be language, or it may be some other symbol, such as religion. If the collectivist social environment is threatened by the dominant culture, people may strengthen their boundaries but in doing so reject resources available from that culture. However, collectivist groups tend to be small and fracture easily. They often do not have the institutions within the group itself which could provide educational, economic, and religious resources, and must look to the dominant culture if they wish to obtain them. If language is used as a symbol of boundary maintenance in the threat of environmental changes, language maintenance will continue until the collective is no longer threatened by the dominant culture. Then when conditions are more favorable, they may assimilate to the dominant culture through participating in its institutions in order to gain new resources.

High grid/high group: Corporate

The corporate social environment is characterized by enduring institutions. Security is found within these social institutions in which everyone knows their role and what is expected of them. Roles are assigned and ranked; opportunities for mobility are limited.

Authority within the community is allocated to leaders of high status within a hierarchy. Decision making is often through a "net like" social network—fathers, clan leaders, lineage leaders, king. Leaders remain in their positions of authority because people recognize and respect the office and the symbols of the office, which tend to be highly elaborated. Leaders control the resources of the community, including education, political power, and supernatural resources, but their followers expect them to use these for the benefit of all. If leaders fail to do so people may choose to withdraw their support.

The corporate social environment tends have large, stable organizations that persist and adapt to changes in the external environment. Social identity is found in the collective identity and one's role and status within the collective. Religious and political institutions reinforce the role and status of individuals, and symbols, including language, are important in the maintenance of these roles. Stability and security for the individual is often valued over innovation or individual gain which limits possibilities for competition or social mobility.

Risk is minimized through routine and symbolic actions. There are traditions and procedures to deal with possible risk, and people place their confidence in the enduring institutions. The corporate social environment is able to adapt to changes in its external setting. It incorporates and adapts the resources from the dominant culture so that they become a part of the collective itself.

In Paulston's framework, ethnic nationalism best describes the social movement of the corporate social environment. This social environment has the most persistent ethnolinguistic vitality, even in the midst of changes in its external setting. The corporate environment reflects the strongest attachment to symbols and places the greatest value on collective identity. However, unlike the collectivist social environment, the corporate environment generally has control of political, economic, and religious resources within the institutions of its environment and is able to incorporate resources from the dominant culture within these institutions. While they may not achieve statehood or territorial autonomy as Paulston describes for nationalism, their autonomy may result from their control of political, economic, and religious resources. Individuals' loyalties are to the institutions within the corporate social environment rather than those outside the collective.

High grid/low group: Bureaucratic

The bureaucratic social environment, like the corporate, has role specialization which is usually arranged in a hierarchy. However, unlike the corporate environment, there is little commitment to the collective whole. Resources and power are consolidated at the top of the hierarchy, but those at the top have independent power and make decisions that may or may not benefit others in the social environment. People at the bottom of the hierarchy feel powerless and restricted by the social environment.

Social identity within the bureaucratic social environment is found in the role or job within the hierarchy. Jobs are well defined and success is measured by how well people perform the job according to rules and procedures. Symbols are used to reflect status within the bureaucratic environment. Language in this environment may also be used to gain status and power.

In a bureaucratic social environment, people view risk and innovation differently depending on their place within the hierarchy. People at the top of the hierarchy view risk and innovation positively since they will not be affected by the outcome. People at the bottom of the hierarchy are less willing to take risk; it is viewed as a threat. They religiously follow rules and procedure in order to avoid risk and blame.

Bureaucratic social environments are often part of what Paulston (1994) describes as geographic nationalism or territorially-based nationalism. In these cases a political state is formed, and language planners seek to use a national language to form a collective identity. The national language becomes the means by which the state distributes its resources, and at the same time becomes a symbol for the new collective.

It is often within the context of geographic nationalism that many groups become part of the lower rungs of a large bureaucracy. Any group may be incorporated into the bureaucratic system when they are dominated by a larger group and lose control of and access to resources. Slavery is the extreme case; economic and political oppression are milder forms of the same phenomenon. In both cases people feel powerless against the greater economic, political, and religious forces thrust upon them. These groups become marginalized and lose their traditional culture and language; at the same time they do not share or benefit from the new resources. They may respond by choosing ethnic suicide or develop a fatalistic attitude toward life.

Implications of social environment on ethnolinguistic vitality

Table 1 provides a summary of the subjective variables of the four different social environments and table 2, the objective variables. Several conclusions may be drawn about collective behavior within a particular social environment and probable long-term ethnolinguistic vitality.

The individualistic social environment provides the maximal individual access to resources and the lowest value on a collective identity. People participating in this environment are unlikely to act as a collective unit in an intergroup setting.

The collectivist and corporate social environments both place a strong value on a collective identity. The expectation is that people in both of these environments would act as a collective in an intergroup setting. However the collectivist social environment tends to be small and unstable and will not withstand extreme outside pressure. Nor does it have the resources necessary for boundary maintenance. Of the four types of social environments, the collectivist social environment is most likely to maintain ethnolinguistic vitality when exposed to changes in its external setting.

Table 1. Summary of objective grid/group factors

Objective factor	Individualistic	Collectivist	Corporate	Bureaucratic
Perception of environment/ external setting	Individuals are separate from environment. Additional source of resources.	Group is part of environment but it is seen as a threat to the group.	Collective is part of environment so resources are available for use in the collective.	Seen as apart from environment but the environment can threaten status quo.
Perception of risk	Individuals take risk, seen as part of life. No risk, no gain.	Risk is not good, a threat to status quo.	Not threatened by risk, institutional procedures to minimize risk.	Risk is uneven, those at bottom of hierarchy lose more than those at top.
Perception of innovation/ change	New contacts, new potential resources to compete with neighbor.	Viewed with suspicion.	Incorporate what is useful to institutions, become a part of institution.	Uneven, those at top positive. Those at bottom see them as threat.
Adaptability toward change	Adaptable, go with flow.	Unstable, factions form.	Stable, security found in institution.	Unstable, paranoia that status quo will change.

Table 2. Summary of subjective grid/group factors

Subjective factors	Individualistic	Collectivist	Corporate	Bureaucratic
Collective restriction on individual choice	Individuals grant power to one another, Maximum individual freedom.	Strong in-group/out-group boundary. Resources held by group.	Individual role and status defined by collective. Authority and resources consolidated at top.	Resource controlled at top. Decisions top-down, those at bottom feel little individual choice.
Collective enablement to pursue individual goals	Maximum freedom to pursue individual goals.	Individuals contribute toward group goals, but have freedom on how they contribute.	Individuals contribute toward group goals in specialized roles.	Individuals restricted by role in hierarchy. Little individual freedom.
Value of collective identity in formation of social identity	Identity found in objects rather than people.	Strong collective identity. Social identity is part of groupness.	Strong collective identity, reinforced through elaborate symbols.	Social identity found in economic role or job in system.
Perception of ethnicity	Ethnicity: history, race, geography.	Ethnic movement: defines the group.	Ethnic nation.	Territorial nation.
Prediction of ethno-linguistic vitality	Language shift to language that provides resources.	In hostile environment: language maintenance. In benign environment and resources available: language shift.	Language maintenance: unless breakdown of religious, political, or economic institutions within community.	Language spread through superior resources and conquest.

Application of grid and group

In the previous section I described four different types of social environments and specific variables that affect ethnolinguistic vitality. In this section I will apply the concept of grid/group to analyze and describe language shift and maintenance in three different case studies. Each of these case studies will illustrate specific principles in the use of grid/group analysis.

Principle One: The grid/group typology is a comparative tool rather than an absolute measure. As in other typologies there are many variations in communities that reflect each of the social environments. The tool alone will not predict ethnolinguistic vitality, but it does provide a means for discovering how and why communities respond differently to similar changes in their external setting. It is particularly useful in explaining why communities with similar dense social networks respond differently to external change, particularly the introduction of economic resources. The Gapun case study demonstrates activity that seems to reflect a high group environment but is actually an arena for competition in an individualistic social environment.

Principle Two: Social environments are not static but change over time. Leach (1968) noted the shifting political arrangement of Kachin society in the Burma highlands between *gumsa* and *gumlao*, a shift from individualistic to corporate social environments. Wildavsky (1984) provides a description of the people of Israel as they moved through different social environments. They started in a Bureaucratic social environment under Egyptian slavery. They moved to anarchy or an Individualistic social environment as evidenced in rebellion and worship of the golden calf. Then they became a Collectivist social environment under the law, which provided a distinct in-group/out-group boundary, setting them apart from surrounding nations. And finally they moved to a Corporate environment under priestly rule, in which revelation from God came to the people only through the leaders. The study of the changes of social environments over time provides possible explanations for language shift and revitalization. In the Gweno case I will trace language shift and revitalization in relation to the changes in the social environment.

Principle Three: The study of grid and group provides a tool to study specific institutions within a society. Within a society or even within small communities all four of the different social environments may be found in the institutions in which the people of the community participate. The study of institutions rather than society as a whole enables the researcher to identify the institutions that are the most important in the formation of social identity. Changes in these institutions provide an explanation for the changes in social identity and the resulting language maintenance or shift. The Tagal case provides a unique illustration of the changes in social environment of three social institutions and the resulting shift in social identity.

The Gapun case

The first case I will analyze is the Gapun of Papua New Guinea (Kulick 1992). This particular case study is an example of a small-scale face-to-face society which, on the surface, seems to have a high group cohesion because of dense multiplex networks of communication. However, a grid/group analysis of the social environment reveals that it is not high group, but rather low group with interactions being instrumental to achieve individual goals.

The Gapun speakers number about 98; no children under 10 actively use the Gapun language. Kulick (1992:101-2) describes children being treated by caregivers as "aggressive individuals". Within the village there are public proclamations of conflict. People, especially women, sit outside their houses and publicly accuse one another in open confrontation. These factors are characteristic of low group social environments.

The men's house is the place of collective activity. There is a sense of social solidarity in male group activities, cooperative work activities, drawing men into consensus, and covering overt conflict. These seem to indicate a high group social environment. However, the men's house is also the arena of overt competition between men vying for the status of "big man". Men bring meat to share in communal meals, not to contribute to group goals but to achieve their own personal goals of raising their personal status. This shows how collective cooperation is necessary to achieve individual goals. It indicates low group rather than high group in which collective activities achieve group goals. The social environment of the Gapun is low group/low grid, where competition rather than cooperation is the norm.

Language is used as part of this competition. Tok Pisin, the language of wider communication in Papua New Guinea, became associated with modernization and Christianity. Men who worked outside the village used Tok Pisin in the village as a means of indicating their new status. Others learn and use Tok Pisin as a means of raising their status within the community.

In this case, language was maintained in a low group setting when there were no other options and no other opportunities were available. When Tok Pisin became a commodity to achieve individual goals, that of raising one's status in the community, people learned and spoke Tok Pisin at the expense of Gapun. So even though Gapun had the appearance of a high group social environment because it was a small face-to-face community, in actuality it was a low group social environment in which language shift is predictable when resources become available through another language.

The Gweno case

Winter (1992) presents a diachronic study of language shift among the Gweno, a member of the Kilimajaro Bantu language family of northeastern Tanzania. Gweno provides a complicated and interesting case of language shift over a long-term period. Although there is not enough ethnographic data available for a full description of changes in social environment, the description of the changes in political structure provide some insight into the mechanism of language shift.

In the beginning of his study of language shift, Winter (1992) describes a political system that was high grid/high group. The Gweno were a unified political unit with a paramount chief ruling by ritual power over ten subchiefdoms, as illustrated in figure 2. These centered on clans; people in these clans were further divided into age sets.

The paramount chief was able to acquire cattle which were used to acquire goods from other regions. He held a virtual monopoly on trade which increased his military dominance and power. He was able to use that power to impose levies on trade and labor, which in turn he used to reward his loyal followers. Economic, political, and religious power were consolidated in the office of the paramount chief.

Figure 2. Political structure of Gweno before language shift

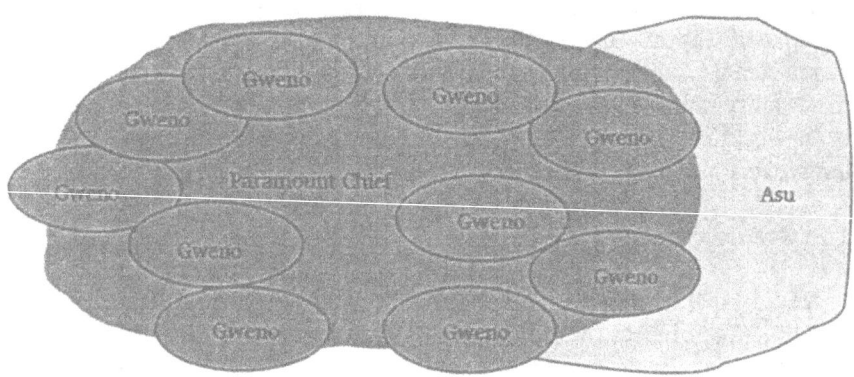

Winter notes that the process of language shift has its earliest roots in 1750, when the paramount chief invited an Asu ritual expert and his family to stay within Gweno territory. These immigrants developed into their own clan and subchiefdom, Sangi, which was given special privileges and rights. In the early 1800s the Sangi attempted to obtain independence from the Gweno paramount chief but failed to do so. However, the Sangi placed Asu troops between them and the paramount chief as a buffer. The Sangi subchiefdom continued to grow in power through access to trade with coastal caravans.

Over the succeeding years several factors contributed to the erosion of the power of the Gweno paramount chief. First, the Sangi subchiefdom grew economically powerful enough to gain independence from the Gweno paramount chief. This further diminished both the economic and political power of the paramount chief. The social environment was still high grid; however, it was weaker grid and weaker group as well. Then, several Gweno subchiefdoms were cut off from the paramount chief because of the independent Sangi subchiefdom between them (figure 3).

Figure 3. Political structure after Sangi independence

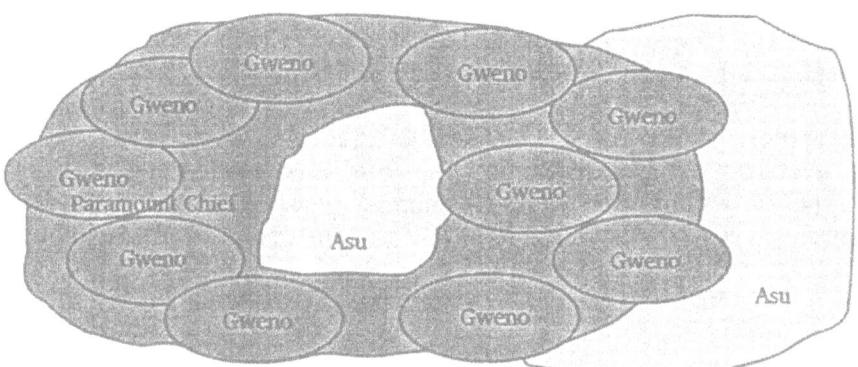

The separated Gweno thrived because of access to trade with the Asu. Eventually, they also gained independence from the Gweno paramount chief and became more oriented towards an Asu identity (figure 4). Language shift toward Asu began.

Figure 4. Beginning of language shift

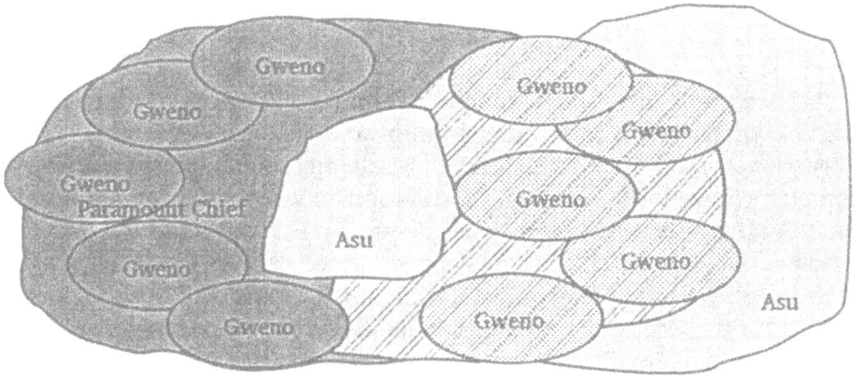

The remaining subchiefdoms still under the rule of the paramount chief were cut off from trade and at the same time became the object of cattle raids. The paramount chief no longer had economic resources to maintain political control. These Gweno subchiefdoms became impoverished and the area depopulated. The political structure completely collapsed, resulting in a low grid/low group environment where each family was free to negotiate economically with their Asu neighbors to obtain resources (figure 5).

These events slowly eroded the religious, economic, and political power that was once consolidated in the office of paramount chief. This weakened the high grid social structure of Gweno. The changes also resulted in former Gweno subchiefdoms participating in economic institutions outside of the Gweno chiefdom, using the Asu language as a means of acquiring economic resources. The shift in economic networks from Gweno to Asu resulted in the beginning of the independent Gweno subchiefdoms' language shift to Asu.

Figure 5. After political collapse of paramount chief

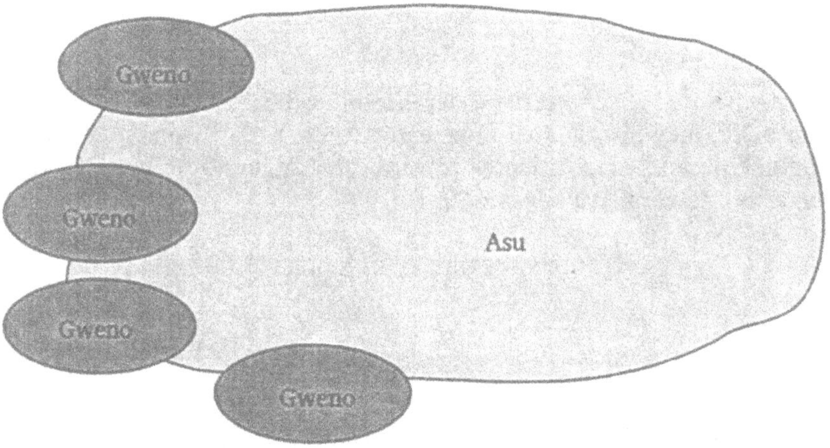

In 1926 the office of the Gweno paramount chief was revived, recreating a high grid/high group social environment. During this period the Gweno recovered their ethnic pride and identity, and language shift was for a time slowed, representing a correlation between the corporate social environment and ethnolinguistic environment. However, in 1963 the position of paramount chief was again abolished, and by 1989 language shift to Asu was complete; only older people understood Gweno.

This particular case shows the movement of one group through various types of social environment and resulting language maintenance and shift. Language maintenance prevailed when there was a high grid political structure with economic, political, and religious resources consolidated in the office of the paramount chief. Language shift occurred in the absence of a social structure supporting the corporate social environment.

The Tagal case

The Tagal Murut language group in Southeast Asia consists of about 30–40,000 speakers. The Tagal case illustrates that shifts in social institutions within a community over a period of time explain resulting shifts in social identity.

In precolonial times the Tagal practiced headhunting and lived in communal longhouses of about thirty doors. Heads were taken from known enemies, which included any other house, even those on the same river (Rutter 1929). Headhunting was a corporate activity of the house and reflected the house's ability to protect its resources and territory. Houses kept score of heads taken from other houses and made revenge raids to maintain a balance of heads with their enemies. Enemies were whole houses rather than individuals; everyone in an enemy house was at risk until the balance of heads was restored. The success of a headhunter was celebrated corporately as a success of the whole house. Community activity was high group, with the house itself being the in-group/out-group boundary (Harris 1995).

The house was also low grid. Any male in the house could become a leader on a raid, not necessarily the head of the house. Although the head of the house was the man who related to outsiders, he did not necessarily make decisions about raids, nor did he lead them. There were no rules to succession for leadership and few role specializations in the house (figure 6).

Two other social institutions were also important in precolonial Tagal, marriage and religion. In contrast to headhunting which was a collective activity, marriage and religion were a low group activity. Marriage was, in reality, a contract between two fathers who exchanged gifts throughout the lifetime of their children. Religion was also a low group activity. Individuals were free to seek out their own supernatural resources. Actions of individuals did not necessarily place the whole house at risk of supernatural sanction but generally only the family. As shown in figure 6, both marriage and religion were low grid/low group in precolonial Tagal society.

From 1900 to early 1950 the Tagal experienced a series of external changes. First, British colonial powers sought to abolish headhunting, impose taxes, and open the area for economic trade. Then, during World War II, the Japanese occupied Tagal territory and controlled labor and economic resources. Finally, in the early 1950s, Christianity was introduced in the Tagal area and became established in three of the five Tagal river watersheds. By the 1980s, two distinct Tagal societies developed simultaneously, one a Christian Tagal society and the other traditional.

Figure 6. Grid/group of three social institutions in Tagal precolonial society

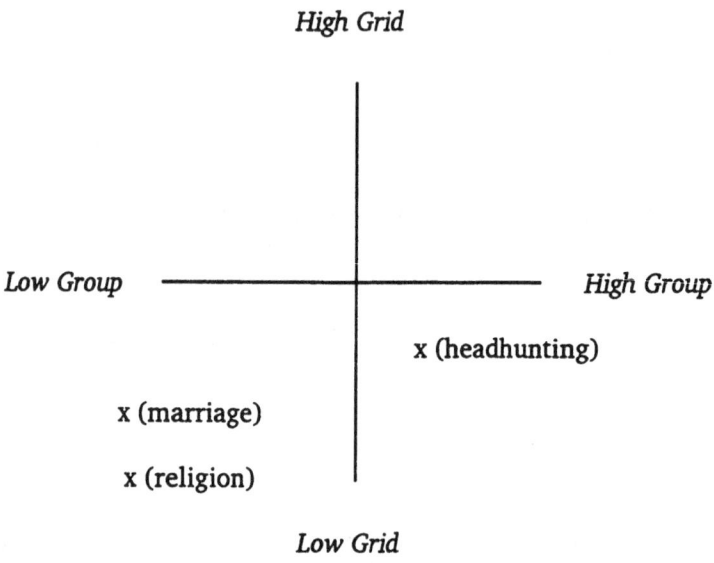

In both traditional and Christian communities, marriage and religion remain two important social institutions. However, in traditional society *marriage* is a collective activity, and in Christian communities *religion* has become a collective activity. This has resulted in these communities forming two different social identities.

In traditional society, the bridewealth required for a wife has inflated to the point where one family cannot obtain the resources necessary for marriage and the obligations of its feasts. Bridewealth exchanges often require 200–300 people to participate in the exchanges and food preparation. Also, traditional Tagal are obligated throughout their lifetime to participate in the exchanges with relatives and in-laws who call upon their resources. The nature of bridewealth practices has changed from a low group activity to a high group activity, involving both affinal and consanguineal kin. Bridewealth obligations require sons to live with their father, who controls their labor and resources. These obligations also require a man's in-laws to help with food production activities (Harris 1990b).

Supernatural resources are still important in Tagal traditional culture. However, there is no ritual specialist; individuals obtain and use supernatural resources to meet their needs. The social exchange for supernatural resource in traditional society is still low group (figure 7).

Figure 7. Grid/group of traditional Tagal social institutions

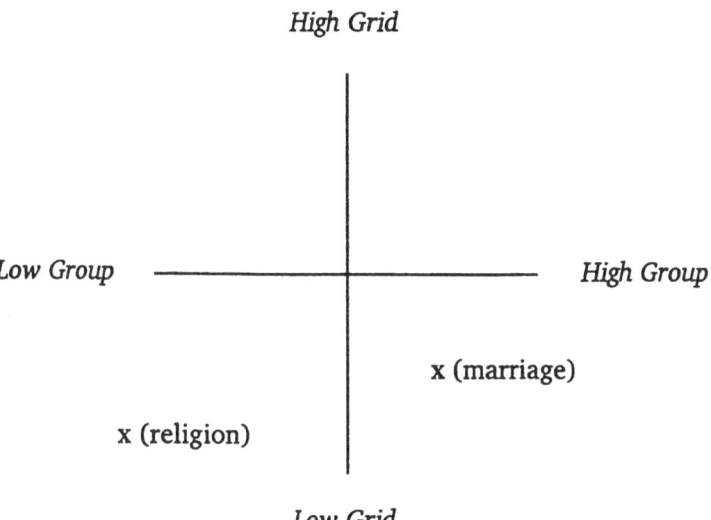

The distinct bridewealth practices serve as an in-group/out-group boundary. Rarely do Tagal intermarry with other ethnic groups, and marriages usually take place along the same river watershed. These bridewealth exchanges and their obligations create closed exchange networks along a river watershed, resulting in a social identity based on river rather than house. When asked where they are from or what race they are, traditional Tagal will provide the answer based on the river on which he resides, *ulun nu Tahol* 'person of the Tagal'. Tagal living along a specific river also claim their dialect is distinct from dialects spoken along other rivers.

In Tagal Christian society religion has become the collective activity. The church controls supernatural resources. People who wish to obtain supernatural resources do so through the church. Anyone who belongs to the church is able to obtain the resources other individual members have; they are considered group resources rather than individual resources. The exchange for supernatural resources has shifted from low group to high group in Tagal Christian society (figure 8).

Figure 8. Grid/group of Christian Tagal social institutions

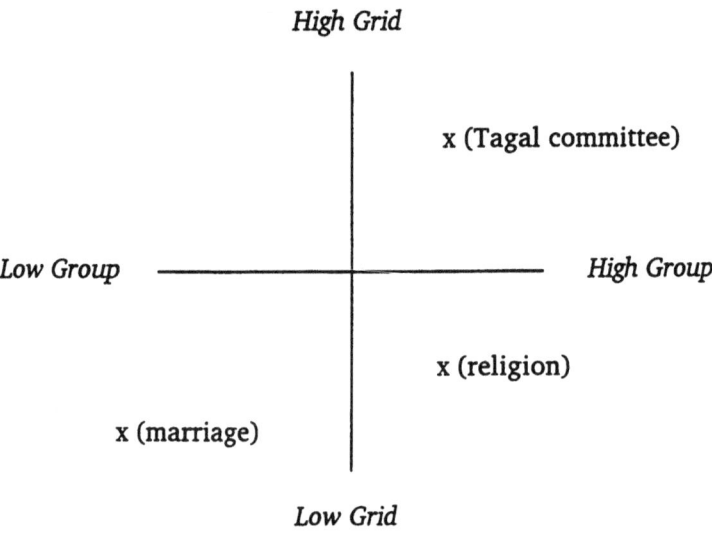

Although official church structure is high grid with specific role distinctions, the Tagal church does not make the same role distinctions. Most heads of households occupy the role of deacon and participate in consensus decision making. Although there is a pastor, anyone who has the ability can fill any of the functions within the church—such as preaching, praying for the sick, teaching, or leading worship—characteristic of a low grid environment.

Marriage in Christian Tagal society is low group. Christians have decreased the amount of bridewealth they require, and now nuclear families are able to pay it without involving extended consanguineal kin. Many Christians no longer have the traditional bridewealth exchange feasts, further eliminating participation of consanguineal and affinal kin in marriage negotiations.

In addition to the reduction in bridewealth, many of the social obligations and privileges that were once obligations of bridewealth have been incorporated into church functions. People can negotiate with the church for help with fields, church members are responsible for hospitality, and church members also participate in most of the life cycle events of their members.

Identity for Christians is based on the church. The church sponsors collective feasts, hosts guests from other villages, and provides a distinct in-group/out-group boundary. When asked where they are from, Christian Tagal will often answer according to the church rather than village—*Sidang Maligan* 'Maligan church'.

This case shows that different institutions within a society may have a different type of social environment. Identity is based around the institution with a high group social environment: house in pre-colonial Tagal society, marriage in traditional Tagal society, and church in Christian Tagal society.

At present the Tagal language is used in the activities and exchanges of both the institutions of marriage and church. However, in high group/low grid social environments identity is often assumed and symbols unelaborated. Language use is unconscious, identity is not based on the language used for the activities but the collective activities themselves. I predict that if people begin using a different language for the activities of these institutions on which their identity is based, language shift will occur.

In the 1990s a committee comprised of members of Tagal churches throughout the area was formed specifically to develop Tagal Christian literature. Over a period of time the committee began to develop specialized roles that provided an infrastructure to coordinate the activities of the churches, resulting in a high grid social environment. The committee also acquired property and sponsored activities to accomplish group goals. The social environment of the committee was high grid/high group.

One result of the committee's activities was the spread of a Tagal identity based on language. There were probably two reasons for this. First, the committee developed an infrastructure that was high grid/high group allowing them to transcend river and church boundaries to acquire and utilize resources for the good of the whole Tagal community. They were able to achieve goals that individual churches had neither the resources nor personnel to accomplish. The second reason is that language became an elaborated symbol: the focus of activity and the in-group boundary for membership in the committee.

Conclusion

Grid/group analysis provides a tool to identify the structure of social relations and the underlying values and beliefs that reinforce these structures. This analysis allows a comparative study of cultural processes found in the world through using a framework that focuses on the underlying patterns of social change rather than specific factors that are often difficult to identify.

For instance, in the Tagal case, some leaders wish to discontinue traditional bridewealth practices because they believe them to be a barrier to economic and educational advancement. However, the bridewealth system provides Tagal with a strong group boundary and is the institution in which collective activity takes place. If bridewealth practices were discontinued with no other collective activity initiated to replace it, Tagal traditional society would become a low grid/low group environment. If resources become available in the dominant language, language shift would occur.

The study of grid/group provides insight into how and why communities respond differently to the same environmental changes and has been especially helpful in explaining, at least in part, some of the dynamics of language shift.

References

Abrams, Dominic, and Michael A. Hogg. 1990. An introduction to the social identity approach. In Abrams and Hogg 1990:1–9.
——— (eds.). 1990. Social identity theory. New York: Harvester Wheatsheaf.
Adams, Richard Newboldt. 1975. Energy and structure: A theory of social power. Austin: University of Texas.
Allard, Réal, and Rodrigue Landry. 1986. Subjective ethnolinguistic vitality viewed as a belief system. Journal of Multilingual and Multicultural Development 7(1):1–12.
———. 1992. Ethnolinguistic vitality beliefs and language maintenance and loss. In Frase, Jaspaert, and Kroon 1992:171–96.
Archer, Margaret. 1988. Culture and agency: The place of culture in social theory. Cambridge: Cambridge University Press.
Atkins, Robert A. 1991. Egalitarian community: Ethnography and exegesis. Tuscaloosa: The University of Alabama Press.
Barth, Fredick. 1994. Enduring and emerging issues in the analysis of ethnicity. In Vermeulen and Govers 1994:11–32.
Bloor, Celia, and David Bloor. 1982. Twenty industrial scientists: A preliminary exercise. In Douglas 1982b:8–102.
Brenzinger, Matthias (ed.). 1992. Language death. Berlin: Mouton de Gruyter.
Brenzinger, Matthias, and Gerrit J. Dimmendaal. 1992. Social contexts of language death. In Brenzinger 1992:3–5.
Cohen, Anthony. 1994a. Boundaries of consciousness, consciousness of boundaries. In Vermeulen and Govers 1994:59–80.
———. 1994b. Self consciousness: An alternate anthropology of identity. London: Routledge.

Dorian, Nancy C. 1994. Choices and values in language shift and its study. In Joshua A. Fishman (ed.), Ethnolinguistic pluralism and its discontents: A Canadian study, and some general observations, International Journal of the Sociology of Language 110:113–24.
Douglas, Mary. 1982a. Cultural bias. In Mary Douglas (ed.), The active voice, 183–254. London: Routledge and Kegan Paul.
———, ed. 1982b. Essays in the sociology of perception. London: Routledge and Kegan Paul.
———, and Aaron Wildavsky. 1982. Risk and culture: An essay on the selection of technical and environmental dangers. Berkeley: University of California Press.
Edwards, John. 1994. Multilingualism. London: Routledge
Fasold, Ralph. 1984. The sociolinguistics of society. Oxford: Basil Blackwell.
Fishman, Joshua A. 1989. Language and ethnicity in minority sociolinguistic perspective. Clevedon: Multilingual Matters Ltd.
Fiske, Alan Page. 1991. Structures of social life. New York: The Free Press.
Frase, Willem, Koen Jaspaert, and Sjaak Kroon, eds. 1992. Maintenance and loss of minority languages. Amsterdam: John Benjamins.
———. 1992. Maintenance and loss of minority languages: Introductory remarks. In Frase, Jaspaert, and Kroon 1992:3–14.
Giddens, Anthony. 1984. The constitution of society. Los Angeles: University of California Press.
Giles, Howard, Richard Y. Bourhis, and Donald M. Taylor. 1977. Towards a theory of language in ethnic group relations. In Howard Giles (ed.), Language ethnicity and intergroup relations, 307–49. London: Academic Press.
———, Doreen Rosenthal, and Louis Young. 1985. Perceived ethnolinguistic vitality: The Anglo- and Greek-Australian setting. Journal of Multilingual and Multicultural Development 6(3–4):253–69.
Gross, Jonathan L., and Steve Rayner. 1985. Measuring culture: A paradigm for the analysis of social organization. New York: Columbia University Press.
Gudykunst, William B. 1989. Cultural variability in ethnolinguistic identity. In Stella Ting Toomey and Felipe Kozenny (eds.), Language communication and culture, 222–43. Newbury Park, Calif.: Sage.
Harris, Annette Suzanne. 1995. The impact of Christianity on power relationships and social exchanges: A case study among the Tagal Murut, Sabah, Malaysia. D. Miss. dissertation. Los Angeles, Calif.: Biola University.

Harris, Sue. 1990a. Implications of language use in language planning for Murutic languages of Sabah. Paper presented at the Eighth Annual Conference of the Asian Association on National Language, University of Malaya, Kuala Lumpur, Malaysia, 28–31 May 1990.
———. 1990b. The Tagal Murut. In Sherwood G. Lingenfelter (ed.), Social organization of Sabah societies, 39–61. Kota Kinabalu, Sabah: Sabah Museum.
———. 1996. An introduction to grid/group analysis. Notes on Literature in Use and Language Programs 50:3–16.
Harwood, Jake, Howard Giles, and Richard Y. Bourhis. 1994. The genesis of vitality theory: Historical patterns and the discoursal dimensions. In Rodrigue Landry and Réal Allard (eds.), Ethnolinguistic vitality, International Journal of the Sociology of Language 108:167–206.
Kulick, Don. 1992. Language shift and cultural reproduction: Socialization, self, and syncretism in a Papua New Guinean village. Cambridge: Cambridge University Press.
Landry, Rodrigue, and Réal Allard. 1992. Ethnolinguistic vitality and the bilingual development of minority and majority group students. In Frase, Jaspaert, and Kroon 1992:223–52.
———. 1994. Diglossia, ethnolinguistic vitality and language behavior. In Rodrigue Landry and Réal Allard (eds.), Ethnolinguistic vitality, International Journal of the Sociology of Language 108:15–42.
Leach, Edmond. 1968. Political structures of Highland Burma. Boston: Beacon Press.
Lingenfelter, Sherwood. 1992. Transforming culture. Grand Rapids, Mich.: Baker Book House.
———. 1996. Agents of transformation. Grand Rapids, Mich.: Baker Book House.
Malina, Bruce J. 1986. Christian origins and cultural anthropology. Atlanta, Ga.: John Knox Press.
Milroy, Lesley, and James Milroy. 1992. Social network and social class: Towards an integrated sociolinguistic model. Language in Society 21(1):1–26.
Ostrander, David. 1982. One and two dimensional models of distribution of beliefs. In Douglas 1982b:14–29.
Paulston, Christina Bratt. 1992. Linguistic minorities and language policies: Four case studies. In Frase, Jaspaert, and Kroon 1992:55–80.
———. 1994. Linguistic minorities in multilingual settings. Amsterdam: John Benjamins.
Rutter, Owen. 1929. The pagans of North Borneo. London: Hutchinson and Co.

Sachdev, Itesh, and Richard Y. Bourhis. 1990. Language and social identification. In Abrams and Hogg 1990:211–29.
Smolics, Jerzy J. 1992. Minority languages as core values of ethnic cultures: A study of maintenance and erosion of Polish, Welsh, and Chinese languages in Australia. In Frase, Jaspaert, and Kroon 1992:277–306.
Thompson, Michael. 1982. The problem of the center: An autonomous cosmology. In Douglas 1982b:302–27.
———, Richard Ellis, and Aaron Wildavsky. 1990. Cultural theory. Boulder, Colo.: Westview.
Verdery, Katherine. 1994. Ethnicity, nationalism and state-making. In Vermeulen and Govers 1994:33–58.
Vermeulen, Hans, and Cora Govers, eds. 1994. The anthropology of ethnicity: Beyond ethnic groups and boundaries. Amsterdam: Het Spinhuis.
Wildavsky, Aaron. 1984. The nursing father: Moses as a political leader. Tuscaloosa: University of Alabama Press.
Winter, Christopher. 1992. 175 years of language shift in Gweno. In Brenzinger 1992:285–99.
Young, Louis, Joha Louw-Potgieter, and Howard Giles. 1986. Values as a function of ethnicity and socio-economic status: A cross-national study. Journal of Multilingual and Multicultural Development 7(4):253–67.

Social Network Analysis: More Toward an Application to Sociolinguistic Research and Language Development Assessment

Steve Graham

Introduction to social network analysis

A social network is seen as a web of cultivated and maintained relationship ties that spread through society, serving to link individuals to one another, forming a meaningful, purposeful community for these linked individuals. The historical development of social network analysis is difficult to trace, as its roots weave in and out of numerous disciplines and special interests. Hence, this introduction is merely a summary review to furnish some background for using social network analysis in sociolinguistic research.

A systematic approach to social network analysis began to develop in the 1930s. In 1934 the psychologist Jacob Moreno introduced the sociogram as a tool for psychological geography, or sociometry. In 1936 Kurt Lewin introduced the study of social spaces and forces using discrete mathematics such as set theory and topology. At the end of World War II, Alex Bavelas (1948) founded the Group Network Laboratory at M.I.T., and in 1953 Frank Harary provided a systematic graph theory for the visual representation of networks.

Social network analysis spread and developed within the field of social anthropology in the 1960s and 1970s, largely through the work of Clyde Mitchell (1969). The concept was advanced in response to dissatisfaction with a structural functional view of society, generally credited to Emile Durkheim (1964). Structural functionalism tended to view society as a system with a structure for distinct segments that sustain distinct functions. Anthropologists perceived the need for a broader framework for the identification of social distinctions. Sociologists were also troubled by the inadequacy of a determinist perspective with respect to the structure of society. Sociolinguists were also struggling with structural functional multi-index scales, used to give a functional structure to social/linguistic variables.

Class-based, multi-index scales had developed primarily in the study of circumscribed rural cultures, but a general weakness became apparent in their application to complex, changing urban societies. The boundaries of large, changing, complex societies are somewhat obscure, making the structure of the whole difficult to fathom. Hence, the functions of the classes, in this obscure structure, are also difficult to determine. Macaulay (1976) points out that multi-index scales may not be accurate, as they may not adequately address economic and power issues. Kerbo (1983) also points out that social class, gender, and ethnicity are interrelated, and thus the nature and significance of social stratification may vary from one community to the next. Hence, multi-index scales may prove problematic, as they may not represent the actual stratification of a community.

Social network analysts did not accept the option of assuming chaos in response to the evident failings of structural functionalism to account for the data. Social networks were thus seen to transcend social class barriers. Social network analysts suggested that individual lives depend on how individuals are tied into a larger web of social connections. They proposed the notion of innate, self-organizing network principles apparent in the structure of society, and they advocated the study of these principles in order to ascertain this structure. Therefore, the introduction of the social network concept resulted in the notion that individuals create communities, and Mitchell (1986) suggests that they do so to create a meaningful framework for solving the problems of their everyday existence. This is quite a change from the structural functional view in which the individual was viewed simply as a constituent of a class that sustained a coglike function in the structure of a society.

Social network analysis thus suggests a basic self-structuring human tendency to stratify into social networks. Some have suggested a human tendency to stratify into smaller and smaller social networks with greater and greater power, and that larger social networks are cultivated primarily in response to the need for greater collective power to resist smaller social networks with extensive power. Some of the research also suggests that visual homophyly (skin color, facial features, body size, etc.) may be a very significant attribute in the initial development of social networks.

In recent years the gains in social network analysis have been linked to the developments in computer technology, as social network analysis involved intensive mathematical processing of the data. Also, Frank Harary's (1953) graph theory set the stage for computer graphic modeling for the visual interpretation of social networks. Today, social network analysis has developed into an interdisciplinary field of research including anthropology, sociology, history, social psychology, political science, human geography, biology, economics, communications science, pedagogy, and many other disciplines that share an interest in the study of the structure of human relations and associations that may be expressed most appropriately in network form. It has become an international endeavor with specialized professional organizations focusing on such issues as contagious diseases, social organizations, social support, organizational behavior, intraorganizational and interorganizational relations, and the diffusion of information. Each of these has its own literature, establishments, training, Web pages, and computer programs designed to facilitate the analysis of social networks related to these areas of concern. In 1997 I attended the seventeenth annual conference of the International Network for Social Network Analysis, with approximately 300 international participants attending to listen to the presentation of 176 papers, written by social network analysts representing most of the distinct areas currently covered by this field of research.

Some basics of social network analysis

Social network analysis is a healthy field of research that continues to develop in terms of refined intricacies. This section is a very basic introduction, provided to furnish some background for the consideration of social network analysis in *language development assessment* (term used in this paper referring to sociolinguistic research that focuses exclusively on issues related to language development). For a detailed presentation of social network analysis see Wasserman and Faust (1994).

Social network analysis contends that social structure is derived from relationships between individuals. Hence, it focuses on the *quantity* and *attributes* of relationship links between individuals in social networks. The social network is thus seen as a construct of ties that link a group of people to one another. The success or failure of individuals, groups, and organizations is dependent on the patterning of their internal relationship constructs. Therefore, social network analysis is the dyadic study of relationships between sets of individuals. It is thus distinguished from mainstream sociology, which tends to study the individuals.

In art, some advocate focusing on the spaces between objects in a scene, rather than the objects themselves. They suggest that in drawing or painting the spaces between the objects, the objects will be revealed. In physics, *field theories* suggest that an understanding of matter will come through the study of the matrix of forces between particles. Correspondingly, social network analysis suggests that the study of the relationships between the individuals will reveal the individuals.

The topic of research. The topic of social network analysis is not the attributes of individuals, but rather the attributes of relational links between individuals. These relational links are quantified on the basis of distinctions in relational attributes. For example, *is amused by, gives advice to, lends money to,* and *hears news from,* would be viewed as four distinct relational links. These shared links, or ties, are termed edges in social network analysis. Each edge is diagramed as a labeled line. In figure 1, a could represent an *is amused by* edge, b could represent a *gives advice to* edge, c could represent a *lends money to* edge, and d could represent a *hears news from* edge.

Figure 1. Edges a through d

Edges
a
b
c
d

Borgatti (1994) suggests that the attributes of these ties can be categorized as relating to the individual level of relationships, such as

1. role-based relationships such as *friend of, enemy of, brother of, father of, reports to;*
2. perception-based relationships such as *likes, respects, is amused by, knows;*
3. action-based relationships such as *lends money to, gives advice to, hears news from, sells to, infects, talks to, dates, marries, corresponds with, calls on the phone, sends e-mail to, argues with, fights with, attacks;*
4. influence-based relationships such as *convinces, persuades, coerces;* or
5. distance-based relationships such as *proximity, homophyly.*

He also suggests that they can be categorized as relating to the organizational level of relationships such as *sells to, buys from, sends personnel to, owns, has joint venture with, licenses, competes with;* and finally, the level of relationships between nations such as *has diplomatic ties with, is at war with, is an ally of, negotiates with, trades with, sells manufactured goods to, sells raw materials to, is near.*

The basic unit. The basic unit of research in social network analysis is the dyad, consisting of two nodes (also known as individuals, actors, or vertices), linked by one or more relational edges. The analysis does not provide for the study of a single node, as a single node does not provide the requisite edges to another node. Figure 2 illustrates the diagramming of two nodes being linked into a dyad by multiple edges.

Figure 2. The dyad

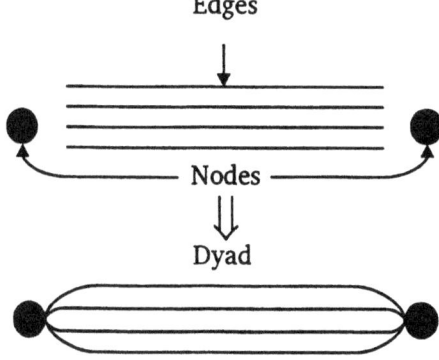

When nodes are linked into a dyad, with one or more edges, they are said to be adjacent. Each node is also given a label. In figure 3, nodes 1 and 2 are adjacent, sharing edge a, *being amused by the other*.

Figure 3. Labeled dyad

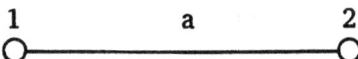

The building block. The triad is the building block of social networks. The edges of a dyad provide for the development of social networks. For example, if one individual node in a particular dyad also holds a dyadic adjacency relationship with a third individual, with many similar edges in the two dyads, the unlinked individual nodes in the two dyads are likely to form a dyadic adjacency relationship if they meet. Figure 4 illustrates the development of a triad, from two dyads, which then serves as the building framework for ongoing development as the social network is bound together by the overlapping triad edges.

Figure 4. The triad building block

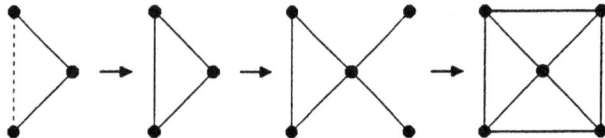

The triad is thus viewed as a stabilizing building unit, as any two nodes can exert a great deal of influence and pressure on the other node in a triad, motivating the third to settle, resulting in the growth of the social network. Also, one node can leave without total destruction of the edges, because the edges are maintained by a remaining dyad, the basic unit in social network analysis.

Methodology. Participant observation can be used to collect data on social networks. For example, some researchers have joined the homeless to chart the social support networks of the homeless or to study how drug dealers use social networks to develop their drug business. There may also be existing sources that provide helpful data on social networks. For example, some researchers have been charting the way the Supreme Court Justices vote in relation to their position papers to see if social networks

Social Network Analysis 137

in the Supreme Court have an impact on the decisions of the court. The most common method for gathering edge data is the *nomination method*:

1. Who do you go to for information about x, y, z?
2. Who do you go to for help with x, y, z?
3. Who do you go to when you need to borrow x, y, z?
4. Who do you go to for advice about x, y, z?

Symmetric and nonsymmetric edges. The nomination method may or may not produce reciprocal nominations. For example, in figure 5, node *3* nominated node *1*, but node *1* did not nominate node *3*. These nonreciprocal nominations provide information about the structure of a social network that is of interest to the social network analyst, as they may represent edge stigmatization or aspiration on the part of some nodes. Also, there are some edges in social networks that are never symmetric. For example, it is not possible for the edge *the father of* to be symmetric. These *directed* edges are noted on the graph using an edge with a directional notation somewhere on the edge. In the *directed graph*, figure 5, nodes *1* and *2* share the reciprocal edge *a* of *amusing each other*, and nodes *2* and *3* share the reciprocal edge *c* of *loaning money to each other*. However, edge *b* is a directed edge between nodes *1* and *3*, where node *1* *gives advice to* node *3*, but node *3* does not *give advice to* node *1*.

Figure 5. Directed graph

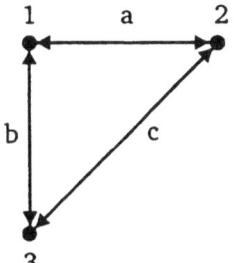

First-order and second-order network ties. Within the system of network ties, there are *first-order network ties*, which are the strong uninterrupted edges between nodes, or adjacent nodes. This system of ties is mapped using a sociogram. In figure 6, the uninterrupted edges between nodes are represented by solid lines of contact between Ego and the other nodes in the sociogram.

Figure 6. First-order network ties to *Ego*

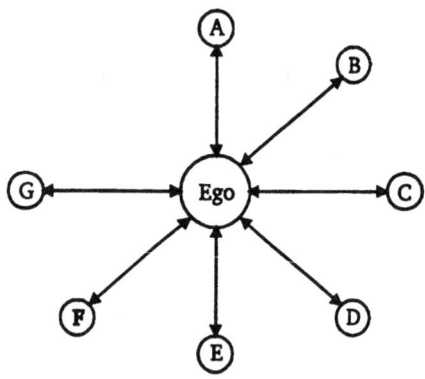

Within the system of ties there are also *second-order network ties*, which are the weaker ties between individuals. They are indirect links between individuals, through other intermediary individuals. Mitchell (1969) defines these second-order network ties as relations in which there are no lines which link a point back to itself directly without passing through some other point. In figure 7, the tie between *Ego* and *H* is a second-order network tie. *Ego* and *H* have a second-order network relationship through *B*. Hence, *B* serves as a *bridge* or *gatekeeper* between individuals with no direct contact, *Ego* and *H*.

Figure 7. Second-order network tie between *Ego* and *H*

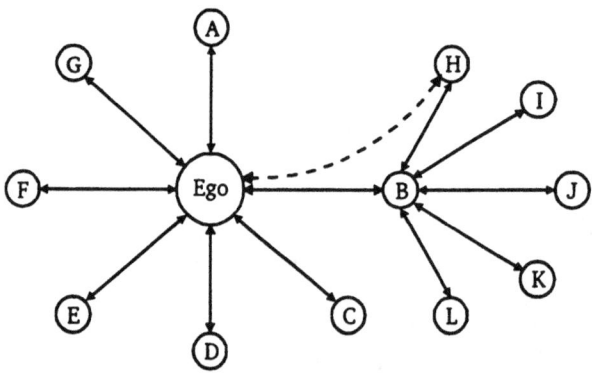

Density. The concept of *density* refers to the number of first-order network edges between all the nodes in a network. In the *low-density* social networks of figure 8, first-order network ties have not developed between *Ego's* first-order network ties. Hence, all of *Ego's* contacts have contacts with each other through *Ego* only. In the *high-density* social networks of figure 8, first-order network ties have developed between *Ego's* first-order network ties, to the point that almost everyone in the social network maintains a first-order network tie with almost everyone else in the social network.

Figure 8. Contrastive sociogram of a low-density network and a high-density network

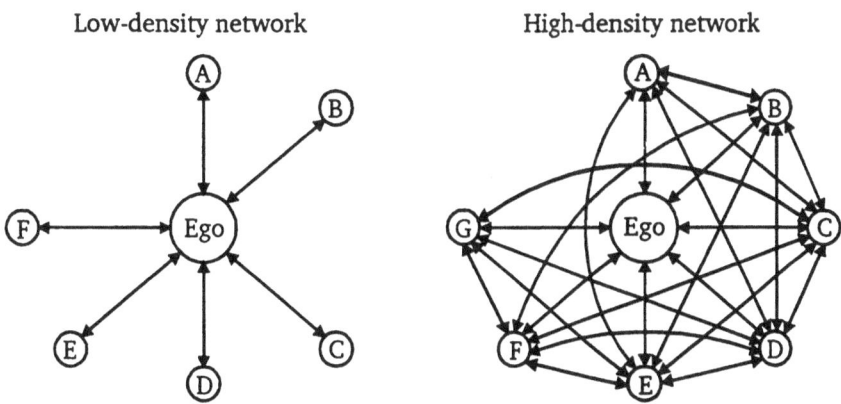

Multiplex attribute edges. In the study of social networks, a variety of attributes are examined in the dyad edges. The hypothesis is that the more frequently individuals interact with one another, the more similar they are likely to be with respect to the number of distinct attribute edges that they share in the dyad. Kapferer (1969) proposes that the *multiplexity* (the quantity of distinct attribute edges shared in the dyad) dictates the strength of the dyad-the greater the multiplexity of attribute edges in a dyad, the greater the strength of the dyadic link. Hence, interaction is directly related to the quantity of shared attribute edges. In figure 9, the multiplexity of shared dyadic edges are represented on a sociogram using multiple lines representing distinct attribute edges. Hence, the dyadic link between *Ego* and *C* is stronger than the dyadic link between *Ego* and *B*.

Figure 9. Sociogram with multiplexity of attribute edges between *Ego* and *C*

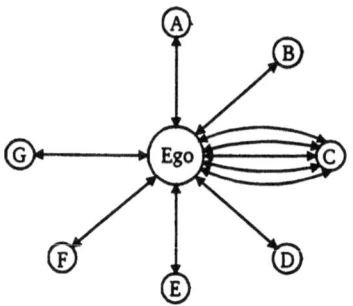

These multiplex edges are seen to provide for further development of the social network. For example, in figure 10, if *Ego* and *B* have numerous attribute edges, and *B* and *H* have numerous attribute edges, *Ego* and *H* are likely to be similar, and are likely to form strong first-order network ties if they meet.

Figure 10. Sociogram with a second-order network tie, *Ego* to *H*, changing to a first-order network tie

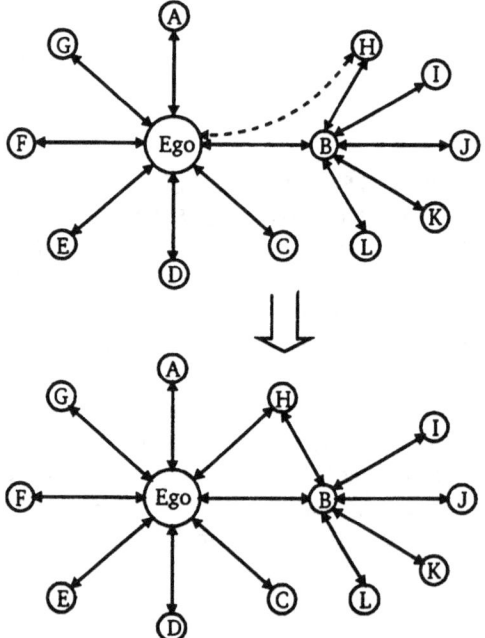

Path. The notion of passing through one node to another node is called *path*. Social network analysis tends to indicate that one node is not likely to have the *reachability* to pass through more than two nodes. For example, an employee's supervisor's supervisor's supervisor, is likely to have little knowledge of the employee's work. When ties pass through two nodes, the need for comparable ties is less crucial. In figure 11, nonpositive ties between *Ego* and *H* would put a psychological strain on the relationship between *Ego* and *B*, and the relationship between *B* and *H*, as *B* wants *Ego* to have comparable ties with *H*. However, the absence of comparable ties between *A* and *H* does not place a psychological strain on the first-order network relationships between *Ego* and *B*.

Figure 11. Sociogram with nonpositive network ties between *A* and *H*

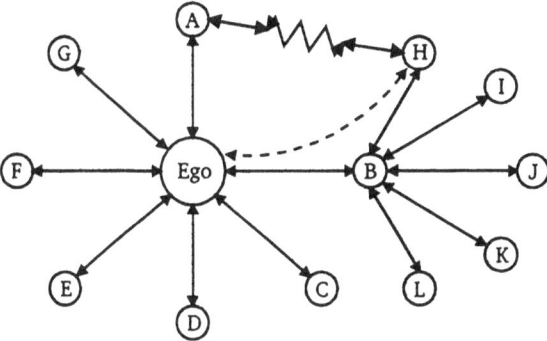

Nevertheless, *fourth-order* network ties are sometimes accessed to find employment, and some research has also been done on the theory that it is possible to connect any individual to any other individual in a path with six steps. John Gurae (1990) developed his book *The Six Degrees of Separation* on this notion. Fass, Ginelli, and Turtle (1996) have also studied links to Kevin Bacon in relation to this theory. There are also a number of games on the Internet that explore the six degrees theory.

Sampling and analysis. Social network analysis has tended to favor bounded social networks such as organizations, schools, social clubs, monasteries, and prisons. The social network data is processed using a separate *adjacency matrix* for each of the attribute edges. Each adjacency matrix provides *from rows* and *to columns,* relating to the nodes concerned. A *1* or a *0* is placed in the column and row representing the *in-degree* and *out-degree*, respectively, for the attribute edge of every possible dyadic relationship addressed by each matrix. A weighted *n-degree* can also be placed in the columns and rows to represent a weighted attribute edge for the dyadic relationships addressed by the matrix.

The adjacency matrix in figure 12 represents the data for priests that discuss a particular controversial issue within the confines of a monastery (Sampson 1969). The highlighted rows and columns on this adjacency matrix indicate that priest no.1, Acciaiuol, discusses this controversial issue only with priest no. 9, Medici. The adjacency matrix also indicates that Medici reciprocates in the discussion of this controversial issue with Acciaiuol; but Medici also discusses this issue with priest no. 2, Albizzi, priest no. 3, Barbadori, priest no. 13, Ridolfi, priest no. 14, Salviati, and priest no. 16, Tornabuon.

Figure 12. Example of an adjacency matrix for a monastery

From \ To	1. Acciaiuol	2. Albizzi	3. Barbadori	4. Bischeri	5. Castellan	6. Ginoti	7. Guadagni	8. Lambertes	9. Medici	10. Pazzi	11. Peruzzi	12. Pucci	13. Ridolfi	14. Salviati	15. Strozzi	16. Tornabuon
1. Acciaiuol	0	0	0	0	0	0	0	0	1	0	0	0	0	0	0	0
2. Albizzi	0	0	0	0	0	1	1	0	1	0	0	0	0	0	0	0
3. Barbadori	0	0	0	0	1	0	0	0	1	0	0	0	0	0	0	0
4. Bischeri	0	0	0	0	0	0	1	0	0	0	1	0	0	0	1	0
5. Castellan	0	0	1	0	0	0	0	0	0	0	1	0	0	0	1	0
6. Ginoti	0	1	0	0	0	0	0	0	0	0	0	0	0	0	0	0
7. Guadagni	0	1	0	1	0	0	0	1	0	0	0	0	0	0	0	1
8. Lambertes	0	0	0	0	0	1	0	0	0	0	0	0	0	0	0	0
9. Medici	1	1	1	0	0	0	0	0	0	0	0	0	1	1	0	1
10. Pazzi	0	0	0	0	0	0	0	0	0	0	0	0	1	0	0	0
11. Peruzzi	0	0	0	1	1	0	0	0	0	0	0	0	0	0	1	0
12. Pucci	0	0	0	0	0	0	0	0	0	0	0	0	0	0	0	0
13. Ridolfi	0	0	0	0	0	0	0	0	1	0	0	0	0	0	0	0
14. Salviati	0	0	0	0	0	0	0	0	1	1	0	0	0	0	0	0
15. Strozzi	0	0	0	1	1	0	0	0	0	1	0	1	0	0	0	0
16. Tornabuon	0	0	0	0	0	0	1	0	1	0	0	0	1	0	0	0

Symmetric edges can be represented with a *1*, representing an in-degree link, in the *from row* and *to column* for both nodes in a dyadic relationship on the adjacency matrix. Nonsymmetric edges are represented with a *1*, representing an in-degree link, in the *from row* and *to column* for one node, and a *0*, representing an out-degree link, in the *from row* and *to column* for the other node in a dyadic relationship concerned.

Multiplex data can be represented by preparing an adjacency matrix for each edge in a multiplexity of edges in a dyad. These adjacency matrices can be combined and represented on a *hierarchical equivalency clustering matrix*. For example, figure 13 represents the hierarchical equivalency clustering of friendship nominations between inmates in a prison (MacRae 1960), processed through the *UCINET IV* software (Borgatti, Everett, and Freeman 1996). The lower levels of the hierarchical equivalency clustering matrix represent fewer equivalent friendship nominations. Hence, the lower levels tend to break into larger clusters. The higher levels represent a greater degree of equivalency in friendship nominations, and thus tend to break into smaller clusters or *cliques*, building hierarchically from equivalencies in the larger clustering of fewer shared equivalent nominations at the lower levels.

Figure 13. Example of a hierarchical equivalency clustering matrix for friendship nominations in a prison

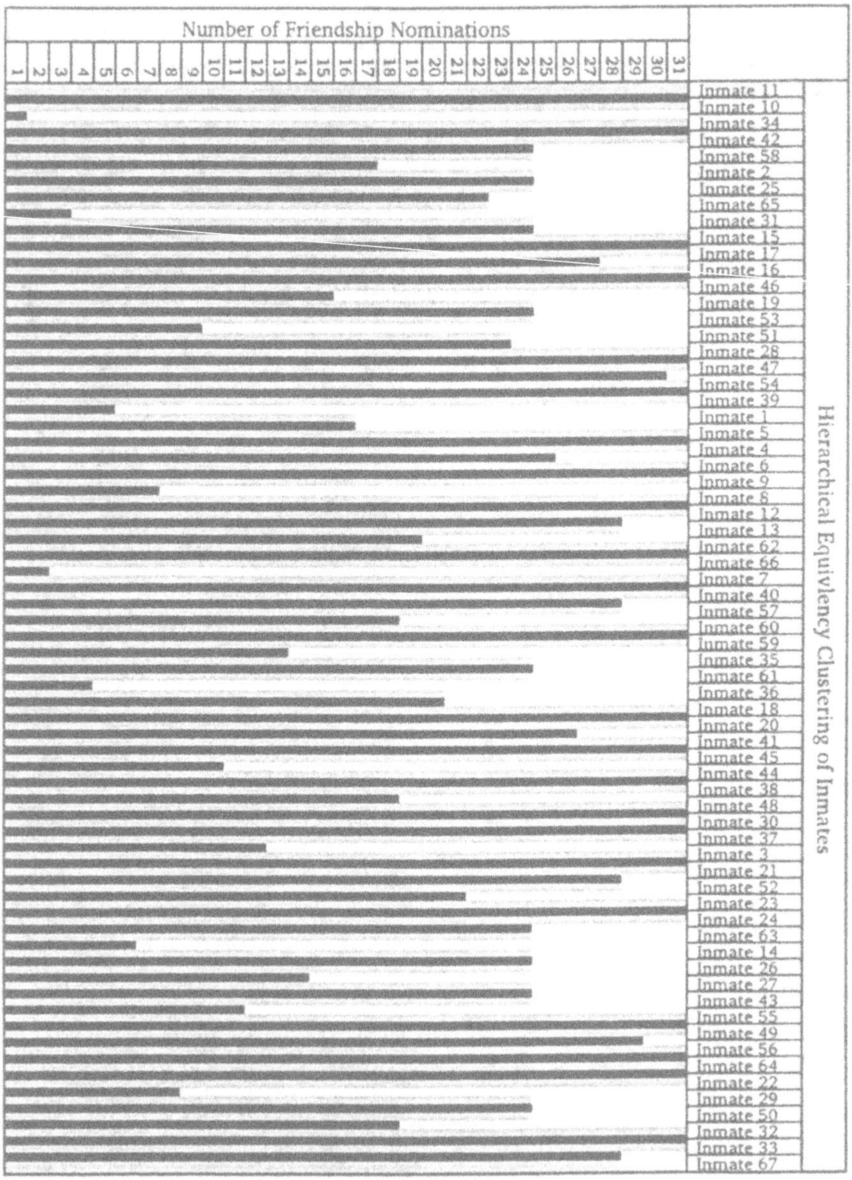

Hence, hierarchical equivalency clustering matrices can be used to represent numerous attribute edges shared between numerous nodes. For example, at the lowest level, all the inmates would share the edge of being incarcerated in the same prison. However, social network research indicates that the first thing inmates tend to ask each other is, "What are you in for?" This information may play a significant role in the development of the social networks in prison, social networks based on the attribute edges of similar crimes. Hence, the lower levels would represent fewer equivalent attribute edges of similar crimes shared between individuals. At the higher levels, smaller and smaller subgroups would appear, based on an increasing degree of equivalent attribute edges of similar crimes between individuals. Thus, the greater the degree of equivalent attribute edges, the smaller the social networks, cliques, or subgroups of broader social networks.

Complex sociograms can also be used to represent numerous attribute edges shared between numerous nodes, and software applications are under continuous development to generate an assortment of complex sociograms from the adjacency matrices. A complex graph notation system is also under continuous development to visually represent social networks. Figure 14 illustrates a number of graph notations, followed by a more detailed description of these notations.

Figure 14. Examples of graph notations for complex networks

14a. Inter-domain ties between organizational systems membership in organizational advisory boards (adapted from Krempel 1997a)

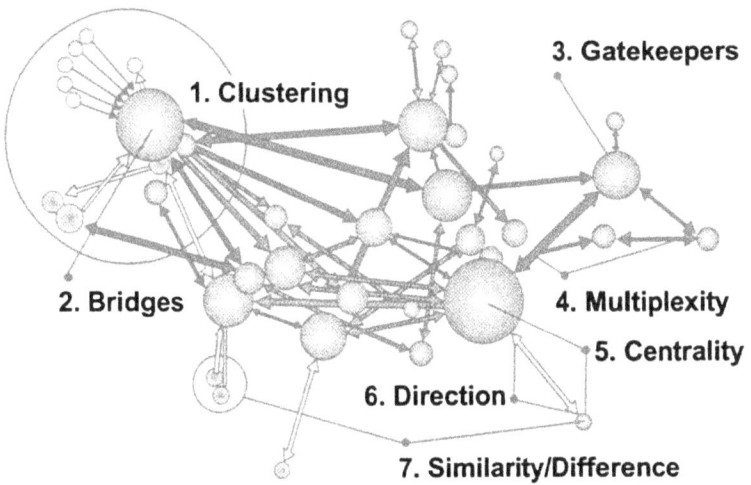

14b. World trade 1992 (adapted from Krempel 1997b)

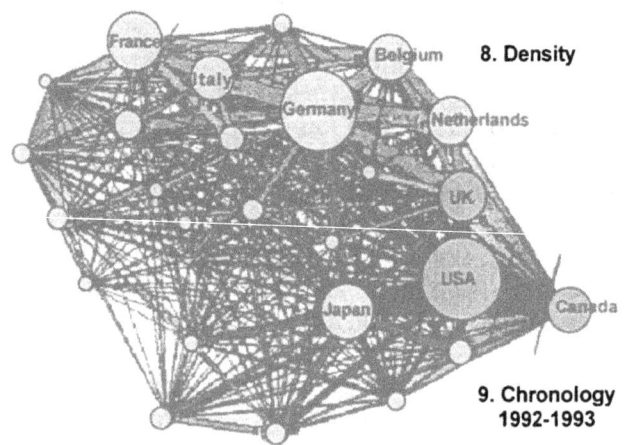

1. Clustering: groups of nodes indicating subgroups, cliques
2. Bridges: nodes that serve as paths between clusters
3. Gatekeepers: individuals that guard what comes in through the bridges between clusters
4. Multiplexity: the width of links can be used to indicate multiplexity (wide links indicating many distinct edges, and narrow links indicating fewer distinct edges), and color can also be used to indicate distinct edges in multiplexity
5. Centrality: size of nodes indicating degree or number of incoming edges (large nodes indicate many incoming edges, smaller nodes indicate fewer incoming edges)
6. Direction: arrows indicating symmetric and nonsymmetric edges
7. Similarity and difference: distance between nodes can be used to indicate similarity (the closer the nodes, the greater the similarity)
8. Density: quantity of first-order network ties in a social network, (many edges indicating a dense network, and fewer edges indicating a less dense network)
9. Chronology: color and animation can be used to indicate change in edges from distinct points in time

Social Network Analysis   147

In open unbound systems, research can be centered around ego, producing *ego-centered* or *ego-anchored* social networks as examples of social networks in the larger system, as in figure 15. Social network analysis is currently using the ego-centered network approach to determine the size of uncountable populations such as disaster victims in locations where written records are not available.

Figure 15. An ego-centered network of a "Junior Scientist" (Krempel 1997c)

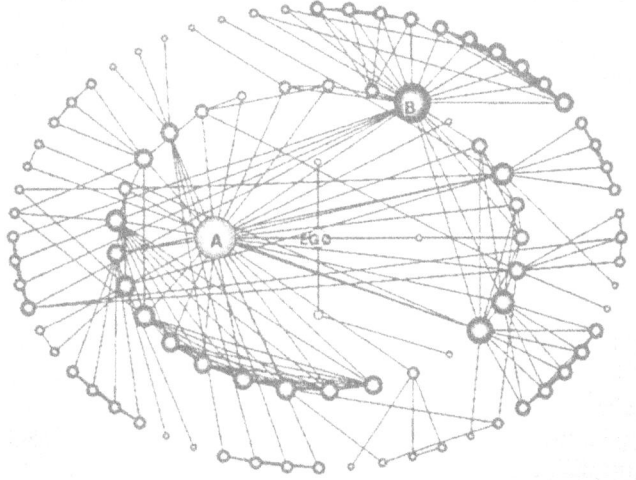

As noted earlier, a variety of attribute edges have been studied in relation to the structure of social networks. In social anthropology, features like kinship, age, sex, exchange, income, education, and mobility have been studied as social network edges. In social psychology, studies have examined various features of mental health as attribute edges in social networks, features such as social support, codependence, and gossip. Also, some consideration has been given to the provision of therapy within social networks. In education, studies have examined features like learning performance as an attribute edge in social networks. The developments in learning networks have been a significant area of recent focus in the literature on organization and management. Organizations have also given considerable attention to such factors as decision consultation and the flow of information in organizations to help develop understanding of the social network structure of an organization and the impact of these social network structures on the effectiveness of the organizations.

In review, according to Borgatti (1994) social network analysis would suggest that the atomic view of society is wrong. Hierarchical equivalency clustering provides a more precise view of society than does a simple set of structural functional class categories. Social network analysis also suggests that rather than being determined by a structural functional set of categories, individuals, linked in social networks, with constraints and opportunities, determine the structure of their society.

Review of sociolinguistic research that entails social network analysis

This section provides a review of the rather varied and limited sociolinguistic research that entails social network analysis (Graham 1996). The seventeenth annual conference of the International Network for Social Network Analysis (1997) was a milestone, as it marked the first social network analysis conference to include a language segment on the agenda. Hopefully, this will lead to additional examples of systematic social network analysis in sociolinguistic research.

Gauchat. The research of Gauchat (1905) in a small village in Switzerland is often viewed as one of the first examples of sociolinguistic research. It is also unique in that the research was repeated by Hermann (1929) twenty-four years later to test Gauchat's findings. Together these studies provide one of the earliest examples, and one of the few examples, of real-time comparative sociolinguistic studies. Gauchat studied *le patois* 'provincial dialect' in the isolated village of Charmey, selected because its 1,247 inhabitants were "relatively pure" or immobile. Traditional dialectology might have viewed this village as a perfect source context for collecting an ideal example of *le patois*. Gauchat, however, examined the villagers looking for possible linguistic diversity. He examined speakers of distinct sex, ages, and background, suggesting that these distinctions would reveal linguistic distinction. This approach broke with that of traditional dialectology, providing the possibility of a social dimension to linguistic variation.

Gauchat collected linguistic data along with interviews to supplement and verify the data provided by his subjects. He collected variation examples on the levels of phonology, syntax, morphology, and vocabulary. Gauchat notes his surprise at the degree of linguistic diversity in a relatively pure village. His research indicates a correlation between phonetic variation and the social variable of age. The research also indicates a correlation between phonetic variation and the social variable of contact with speakers of *le patois* in other villages.

Labov. Labov's research appears to have provided much of the impetus that led to the current level of developments in the field of sociolinguistics. Labov (1966) disputed Hubbell's (1950) claim that the pronunciation of English in New York City was a mass of free variation. Hubbell suggested that the pronunciation of a very large number of New Yorkers exhibits a pattern that might most accurately be described as the complete absence of pattern. Hubbell subscribed to an ideal view of language, and thus attempted to minimize the diffused linguistic variation in New York. Labov attempted to find a pattern for Hubbell's example of free variation in the pronunciation of phonemes such as /r/ in New York. He analyzed phonological linguistic variants of phonemes as the dependent variables, with the stylistic and social class environments serving as the independent variables, producing weighted index scores for each environment. Labov contended that a stylistic and social correlation would reveal that Hubbell's free variation is actually socially and stylistically motivated.

Labov used recorded interviews with 157 adults and 58 children, a random controlled selection of individuals who had not moved for two years. He also controlled the sample to assure representatives from all social classes, age levels, and ethnic groups. The interview involved reading minimal pairs, word lists, and texts. Labov's research revealed a correlation between linguistic variation and the stylistic and social class environments. His quantitative approach provided for patterns to emerge from the data, proving that Hubbell's assessment of free variation was not an accurate assessment of linguistic variation in New York. Hence, Labov contributed to the field of sociolinguistics by supporting Gauchat's findings of a social dimension to linguistic variation. However, Labov also made a significant contribution by providing a quantitative, set theory approach to conceptualizing the patterns of this social dimension in linguistic variation.

Labov also provides research examples in other contexts such as New York department stores, Martha's Vineyard in Massachusetts, and inner-city gang communities, using other linguistic features as the dependent variables, including copula variation in Black Vernacular English. His study (1972) in the gang communities in the inner city also set the stage for the examination of linguistic variation in relation to the concept of social networks.

Pellowe. Pellowe's unpublished papers provide the groundwork arguments for a survey of Tyneside English. The first paper (1970a) provides a theoretical position for the survey; the second paper (1970b) provides the groundwork on criteria and sampling; and the third paper (1970c) provides the groundwork on dealing with variables in the survey. The data gathering approach is impressively thorough, involving interviews, reading word lists, recognition of dialects, and syntax judgments. The survey covers phonological, syntactic, morphosyntactic, and lexical variation.

Pellowe builds on the work of Labov in terms of taking a quantitative approach to distill the patterns of relationship between linguistic and social variation. However, relying heavily on the aid of computers, Pellowe expands on Labov to explore a Wittgensteinian relationship between linguistic and social variation. Hence, he also reacts to the structural functional view of society accepted by Labov in his early work. The Pellowe survey attempted to identify the natural social variables, the social characterizing of the individual. The survey takes a Wittgensteinian *variety cluster* approach to structure the variation data, mapping linguistic space to social space. The computer program checks for similarities and arranges speakers into groups. It then checks for diagnostics for each group. The approach has merits in that it allows the context to define the key variant diagnostics, rather than determining key variants a priori as did Labov.

The variety clusters appear to have much in common with Le Page and Tabouret-Keller's (1985) multidimensional cluster maps. They also appear to have much in common with the social network view of social structure used by Labov in his study of inner-city gangs, and by the Milroys (1978) in their study of insular neighborhoods in Belfast.

Milroys. Milroy and Milroy (1978) studied enclaves of working-class people in the neighborhoods of Ballymacarett, the Hammar, and Clonard, in the city of Belfast. They selected these neighborhoods as highly insular neighborhoods of undereducated whites. Ballymacarett and the Hammar were Protestant neighborhoods, and Clonard was a Catholic neighborhood. Most of the employed individuals were employed in the local factory, and seldom ventured out of the neighborhood. The Milroys used a social network hypothesis to gain acceptance in the social networks that were the focus of their research. They collected linguistic information in recorded interviews as examples of everyday use of language, including conversations, story telling, questions and answers, reading word lists, and minimal pairs lists.

The Milroys build on the work of Labov in terms of taking a quantitative approach to distill the patterns of relationship between linguistic and social variation. However, they reject the structural functional view of society accepted by Labov in his early work, building instead upon the social network view of social structure used by Labov in his study of inner-city gangs. They follow Labov in building a link to Boissevain and Mitchell's (1973) social network analysis in social anthropology. However, the Milroys also attempt to link their social networks to the work of Blom and Gumperz (1972) on *closed networks* and *open networks*, which leads them to the notion of high-density and low-density networks. The Milroys suggest that dense, multiplex social network ties form the bonds of a group in general consensus, and have the capacity to maintain network conventions and norms such as religion, dress, behavior, etc. Hence, linguistic conventions and norms are maintained by these dense, multiplex social networks, which are thus viewed as the mechanism maintaining the survival of nonstandard dialects. I would contend that the clusters of Pellowe and Le Page and Tabouret-Keller would have benefited structurally from the social connections provided in the Milroy's social network view of social structure.

They used these social networks to identify their research subjects. In other words, their research subjects were encountered through the network connections in the various social networks examined. This represents a significant change in the approach from the identification and selection of research subjects taken by Pellowe (1970a-b), Labov (1972), and Le Page and Tabouret-Keller (1985).

The Milroys ranked their subjects according to five criteria: (1) kinship ties with more than one household in the neighborhood, (2) the same workplace as at least two others in the neighborhood, (3) the same workplace as at least two others of the same gender, (4) regular participation in a territorially-based activity (street gangs, bingo games, football teams, etc.), and (5) voluntary association with workmates after working hours. The subjects were assigned one point for each criterion they fulfilled, resulting in a *network strength scale*. Their research reveals a correlation between linguistic variation and social networks, and linguistic variation and age/gender features in social networks.

Cheshire. Cheshire (1982) builds upon the social network view of social structure used by Labov (1972) in his study of inner-city gangs. She builds particularly on Labov's use of reciprocal naming in the identification of social networks. It seems that Cheshire was also influenced by Labov in terms of the social context she selected for her research. Cheshire studied adolescents at adventure playgrounds in working class areas of Reading, England. The playgrounds provided a central meeting place for truant school adolescents. Boys and girls met at these playgrounds for several hours during the day.

Cheshire used a reciprocal friendship naming technique, developed for sociometric studies in education, to identify the members in a social network and the position they held in a social network. Cheshire asked the boys on one playground to name the friends with whom they spent the most time. The most frequently named individuals were identified as the central members of a social network, the less named individuals as peripheral members of the social network. This process also identifies various intermediate degrees of membership in the social network through the various degrees of naming. The process also identified any distinct social network. Like the Milroys, Cheshire developed a *vernacular culture index* scale based on six criteria: (1) carrying weapons, (2) style of clothing, (3) job aspirations, (4) participation in minor criminal activities, (5) skill at fighting, and (6) swearing. An application of the scale revealed a strong correspondence between a high ranking on Cheshire's scale and the central members of the social network, as revealed in the reciprocal naming.

Cheshire visited the playgrounds two or three times a week for a period of nine months, recording conversation with no less than three adolescents at a time. The recorded data included jokes, narratives, and obscenities. Cheshire used this data to identify a number of syntactic and morphosyntactic variables, and the frequency of these variables. The research revealed a possible correlation between linguistic variation and gender, and a correlation between linguistic variation and core group status in the reciprocal naming networks.

Cheshire's approach suggests serious potential for the identification of social networks. I would argue, however, that it is difficult to interpret the actual significance of Guttman (1944) scales in social networks. I would question whether these Guttman scales have the same significance to sociolinguists and the speakers of the language under examination.

Eckert. Eckert (1988) focuses on the spread of sound change through networks of urban adolescents. She also builds upon the social network view of social structure used by Labov (1972) in his study of inner-city gangs. She claims that variation studies have tended to focus on adults, even though variation tends to spread through networks of adolescents. She notes a discontinuity in variation studies that correlate linguistic variation to age and socioeconomic status. She argues that it is difficult to categorize adolescents according to their socioeconomic status. She suggests the possibility of peer group correlation in which adolescent variation may not correspond to the parents' socioeconomic class.

Eckert's research involved recorded interviews with fifty-two students over a period of two years. She studied phonological variation in adolescent English, as a participant observer in several high schools in the Detroit area. She asserts that these phonological variables are intimately involved in the development of adolescent identity. She examined the phonological variables in the social structure of the school-based social categories of "Jocks" and "Burnouts". She suggests these categories as the two primary categories in the school and defines the difference between the two categories as those who center their activities around the program structured by the adults in school, and those who reject the program of activities structured by the adults in school. She links these social categories to the "middle class" and the "working class", respectively. She proposes that one of the differences between the Jocks and the Burnouts is their social network structure. Her data reveals a stronger correlation between the phonological variation and her proposed categories, than between the phonological variation and the categories of sex and socioeconomic class.

Eckert argues that adolescent development tends to move them away from the family, toward their own basis of identity in the broader society. She notes that adolescents tend to depend upon their "cohorts", their adolescent society, during this development process, and she thus proposes the two cohort societies of Jocks and Burnouts as the basic division in adolescent society. She suggests that sound change and spread implications are due to the differences between these two adolescent societies; Jocks seek to transcend the local community, while the Burnouts seek to integrate into the local community.

I note that Eckert starts with social categories, laying a theoretical foundation for the categories she perceives. She then attempts to identify linguistic variation in relation to the social categories she has proposed. In this respect, Eckert's approach is quite different from the other approaches to sociolinguistic research. All of the other examples start with, or develop, a linguistic variant that they attempt to use in the identification of social categories. Eckert, on the other hand, starts with hypothesized social categories, and attempts to support the hypothesis through linguistic variation studies.

Lippi-Green. Lippi-Green (1989) was also motivated to participate in the discussion of the issue of socioeconomic class. She studied social and linguistic variation in the small village of Grossdorf in western Austria. She selected this small village of 800 residents, isolated in the mountains, assuming that this context would remove the issue of socioeconomic class, rendering socioeconomic variables insignificant. She also built upon the work of the Milroy and Milroy (1978), expanding the ranking system for her subjects to develop a scale of sixteen criteria, each of which were weighted with a different number of points. This ranking system provided a finer breakdown of four essential networks: (1) kinship, (2) proximity, (3) occupation, and (4) association. The finer ranking system thus provided for the possibility of more social correlates for the linguistic variation.

Unfortunately, Lippi-Green's ranking system does not reveal any robust correlation to linguistic variation. It is possible that her ranking system may have exaggerated the distinctions in the village social structure, or that she may not have gathered an adequate sample to examine the variation possibilities in such a fine scale of social correlates. The research did, however, reveal some correlation between linguistic variation for outsiders in relation to their association network.

Lippi-Green's example raises the earlier concern with respect to Guttman (1944) scales. The example of Lippi-Green's ranking system, not revealing any robust correlation to linguistic variation, may support the caution I presented earlier in the Cheshire example. I would again argue that the use of Guttman scales, in social networks, may be difficult to interpret in terms of actual significance to the speaker.

Edwards. Edwards (1992) was also motivated by the examination of variation in a context that would minimize the potential of a socioeconomic variable. He chose to study sixty-six black residents in a Detroit inner-city neighborhood. The neighborhood was characterized by high unemployment, with over sixty percent of the households on welfare. Hence, all of the respondents were seen to be members of the same socioeconomic class.

For each subject, Edwards calculated a *vernacular culture index*, based on the response to ten questions. The questionnaires contained five physical integration statements and five attitude statements, ranked from strongly agree to strongly disagree. The answers were given points, creating a range of points for each questionnaire. This process results in the collection of the social feelings of the subjects in the language context-social data that is defined by the perceptions of the subjects. Edwards breaks with the traditional approach to social data in the use of this approach. His ranking index is similar to the scales used by others, but the process of using the perceptions of the speakers to produce the scale is quite different.

Unfortunately, like Lippi-Green, Edwards was unable to find much in the way of correlation with his vernacular culture index, but he did find a correlation between age and the use of standard English and Black English variants. He also found a correlation between mobility/association questions and the use of Standard English or Black English variants. This indicates that there may be a relation between age and network integration.

Though the vernacular culture index did not reveal much in terms of correlation with linguistic variation in the Edwards research example, I would propose that an examination of the questions asked in the determination of the ranking might provide some insights into this lack of correlation. Also, some correlation does develop with the concept of social networks in the Edwards research, indicating some sparks of potential in the approach. However, I would recommend a comparison of the Edwards scale with the Guttman scale, to examine the potential effectiveness of these two scales.

Implications for sociolinguistic research

The limited existing research indicates sufficiently that the attribute edges in social network analysis are a potentially profitable resource in sociolinguistic research, providing for the notion of a multiplex of linguistic variables as attribute edges in a social network. Distinct sets of shared linguistic variables can serve as a marker of distinct equivalent hierarchical social network clusters-sets of linguistic variables which signal or identify a particular social network or subgroup. In the Old Testament (Judges 12:5-6), the pronunciation of one word (shibboleth/sibboleth) provided all the social identity information needed to make life/death decisions, resulting in the death of 42,000 travelers. This multiplex set of shared linguistic variables is thus seen as the linguistic identity of a social network, along with multiplex sets of shared nonlinguistic variables, such as clothing, food, religion, rituals, ceremonies, and music. As modernity and mobility chip away at the distinctions in the multiplex sets of nonlinguistic variables, the linguistic variables may end up carrying a heavier load in maintaining and signaling network identity.

Application to language development assessment

The developments in social network analysis suggests that sociology has tended to view society as a feature of the nodes, and that social network analysis has sought to develop a perspective that viewed society as a feature of the edges. Correspondingly, theoretical linguistics may have tended to view language as a feature of the nodes, while sociolinguistics has attempted to develop a perspective which views language as a feature of the edges, figure 16.

Figure 16. Language

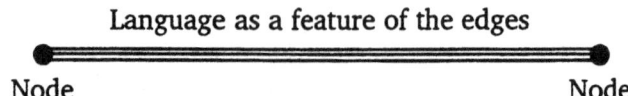

Language as a feature of the edges

In the study of pidgin and creole languages, Salikoko Mufwene (1986) has suggested the *complementary hypothesis*: the *substrate hypothesis*, and the *universalist hypothesis* are complementary in the genesis of pidgin and creole languages. Hence, a complementary hypothesis may also prove helpful for theoretical linguistics and sociolinguistics, proposing that language may be a feature of both the nodes and the edges.

In any case, in language development assessment, social network analysis may provide a meaningful framework for the study of language vitality-represented by a multiplex set of language attribute edges—with language shift represented by another multiplex set of edges, and language change by another multiplex set of edges.

Strength of weak ties

Mark Granovetter (1973), in one of the most quoted papers in social network analysis, argues that second-order ties may actually be stronger than first-order ties with regard to change, in that change and innovation generally enter a social network through the second-order network ties. Interaction between the second-order network ties of distinct social networks serves as the primary link between the first-order network ties of the distinct social networks. The second-order network ties also link the micro level (distinct social networks) to the macro level (the aggregate of distinct social network clusters which constitute the relevant social context). Hence, experimental interaction takes place on a macro level in the second-order network ties, with micro level implications in the first-order network ties of the distinct social network clusters. Granovetter refers to these as *didactic ties*, in that the learning of new concepts may enter through these second-order networks ties. Hence, the second-order network ties may have a significant impact on the diffusion of information and influence into the first-order network ties. Davis (1970) suggests that flow of information between distinct social networks is inversely proportional to the length of the path and directly proportional to the number of all the positive paths connecting the two social networks. Granovetter (1973) argues that impetus for change is not easily discerned in the strong first-order network ties. This may be due to the fact that second-order network ties are more varied than first-order network ties. It may also be due to the function of first-order network ties, in that they serve to maintain stability rather than promote awareness of change.

Hence, Granovetter stresses the power of weak ties in relations between distinct social networks. Experimentation between social networks, by individuals in the respective networks, aggregates into large-scale patterns in each network. Macro level reactions to these patterns provide feedback into the micro level as to the acceptability of the interaction between the distinct social networks. This can result in an overlap between distinct social networks. This overlap varies with the strength of the ties between the distinct social networks. Granovetter argues that the strength of ties between distinct networks is directly related to a combination of features:

1. the amount of time in contact,
2. the emotional intensity of the contact,
3. the intimacy (mutual confiding) of the contact, and
4. the reciprocal services in the contact.

Acts of identity

There are significant similarities between Granovetter's strength of weak ties, and Le Page and Tabouret-Keller's (1985) *acts of identity*. The similarities may indicate that the social network approach may qualify as a possible *multidimensional model* sought by Le Page (1983) in his research (Graham 1996). Granovetter's list of features mentioned earlier and the following list of features from the work of Le Page and Tabouret-Keller reveal significant similarities in these theories developed within their distinct disciplines. Le Page and Tabouret-Keller see the individual as creating his systems of behavior— be they social, cultural, or linguistic—in relation to the group(s) with which he wishes to identify to the extent that:

1. he is able to identify those groups (similar to Granovetter's first feature),
2. he has sufficient access to them and the ability to analyze their systems (similar to Granovetter's first feature),
3. his motivation is adequate (similar to Granovetter's second feature),
4. he is still young enough to change his behavior (similar to Granovetter's second feature), and
5. society provides him with feedback indicating what chance he has of success in his proposed identity (similar to Granovetter's third feature).

Factors which influence his behavior include

1. common economic, political, or defense interests (similar to Granovetter's fourth feature),
2. mutual linguistic intelligibility (similar to Granovetter's third feature),
3. religious beliefs (similar to Granovetter's second feature),
4. family ties (similar to Granovetter's second feature),
5. shared upbringing (similar to Granovetter's second feature), and
6. shared location (similar to Granovetter's first feature).

The model of speaking and listening which accompanies the hypothesis is one of speakers projecting (Le Page 1980) an image (in a cinematic sense) of themselves in relation to their universe, and getting feedback from others as to the extent to which their images coincide-and then either collectively focusing, or allowing theses images to remain diffused.

A graphic presentation of Le Page and Tabouret-Keller's acts of identity, figure 17, may help to communicate the concepts and their potential in the study of sociolinguistic trends in the second-order network ties.

Figure 17. Graphic presentation of the acts of identity

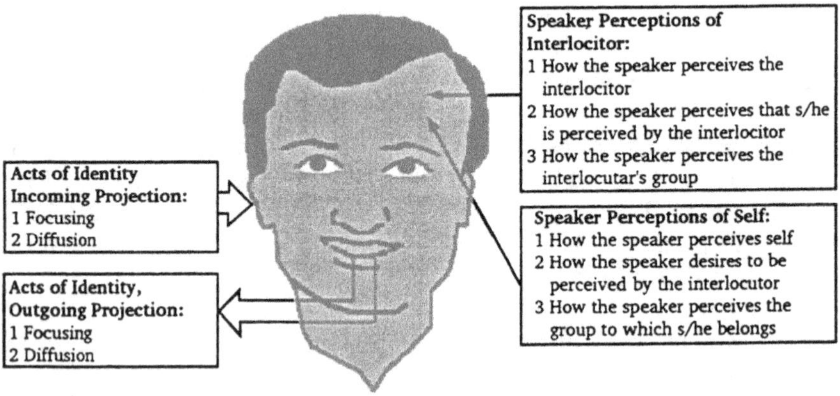

Speaker Perceptions of Interlocitor:
1 How the speaker perceives the interlocitor
2 How the speaker perceives that s/he is perceived by the interlocitor
3 How the speaker perceives the interlocutar's group

Acts of Identity Incoming Projection:
1 Focusing
2 Diffusion

Acts of Identity, Outgoing Projection:
1 Focusing
2 Diffusion

Speaker Perceptions of Self:
1 How the speaker perceives self
2 How the speaker desires to be perceived by the interlocutor
3 How the speaker perceives the group to which s/he belongs

The concept of *projection* provides a tangible link between the acts of identity and Granovetter's concept of strength in the second-order network ties. The acts of identity concepts of *focusing* and *diffusion* exhibit significant equivalence with Granovetter's concept of *experimentation*. As individuals experiment with other social networks they will respond by focusing or diffusing with the particular social network.

The development of language development assessment which builds on the similarities between the acts of identity and social network analysis in Granovetter's second-order network ties could prove very helpful in monitoring and predicting language vitality, language shift, and language change. Building on this similarity, language development assessment could examine focusing and diffusing data with respect to sociolinguistic attribute edges in the second-order network ties. The development of such an approach to variation would be less prescriptive, providing for context internal identification of sociolinguistic features. The approach would locate the assumptions about the language and social constructs in the minds of the individuals in context, rather than in the minds of those conducting the research.

Implications for language assessment

Traditional language assessment efforts have tended toward linguistically-oriented language development assessment, focusing initially on linguistic relationships through lexical and phonological comparisons, then moving on to examine the degree of intercomprehension between what could be dubbed *emic linguistic entities*. These entities are derived from the lexical and phonological comparisons, which are based on internal organizational comparison criteria of linguistic relationships. Sociological data is collected to provide some basic social correlates for the derived emic linguistic entities, but most of the social data tends to relate to the question of language development viability for the derived emic linguistic entities. The intercomprehension data and some bilingualism testing data that is also collected are largely applied to the notion of economizing on the emic linguistic entities that will be selected for language development, as the resources for language development are largely presumed to be external to the local context and, therefore, limited.

SIL, for example, has tended to manage language development assessment by training short-term personnel to identify emic linguistic entities, which are subsequently inventoried in the *Ethnologue: Languages of the World* (Grimes 1996). This relegates most of the sociolinguistically oriented research to long-term language development personnel that are assigned to the linguistic entities identified by the short-term language assessment personnel. Since the long-term language development personnel do not receive as much sociolinguistic training as the short-term language assessment personnel, it should come as no surprise that the long-term language development personnel do not tend to provide the much-needed ongoing sociolinguistic research for language development.

This failure to adequately recognize the significance of social networks may result in inadequate sociolinguistic data that may be required for consideration in the process of responsible language development. An alternative approach would provide for a long-term commitment to sociolinguistic language development assessment from the very outset. In this paradigm, sociolinguistic personnel would be assigned first as long-term personnel to a geographic area or language complex. They would be responsible for continuous long-term sociolinguistic analysis. This long-term, sociolinguistic approach to language development assessment may also open the door a bit wider to monitoring and predicting language vitality, shift, and change. This framework may also provide a role for language development assessment which builds on the similarities between the acts of identity and social network analysis in Granovetter's second-order network ties, used as a chronological tool for monitoring language vitality, shift, and change within social networks.

Recognizing that language development may not be as much a feature of the nodes as it is a feature of the links, the long-term sociolinguist's responsibilities could also include the development of collegial working relationships with others in the local context concerned with language development. The short-term language development assessment personnel would then do short-term assessment projects within the long-term sociolinguistic analysis. The language development personnel would also be viewed as relatively short-term personnel assigned to do defined linguistic analysis projects, defined literature development projects, defined translation projects, and defined applied linguistic projects within the global long-term language development planning for the particular area or language complex-planning that would develop through a social networking of all concerned.

The initial cost of social network analysis may be perceived as high, but the long-term pay-off may also be high. Also, building on the recommendation of Stephen Schooling (1990), social network analysis could be readily applied in a number of ways in the present approach towards language assessment.

Gathering. Some of the data currently collected in traditional language development assessment—such as questions on sociolinguistic questionnaires—could be processed from a social network perspective, providing some potential for network predictions. The nomination method of gathering network data might prove helpful as a characteristic extension of existing sociolinguistic data gathering efforts. The phono/lexical data could also be processed from a social network perspective as potential indicators of networks. Some participants at the seventeenth annual conference of the International Network for Social Network Analysis suggested textual analysis as a potential predictor of networks. Also, ego-centered data gathering and snowball data gathering techniques might prove helpful for gathering data in unbounded systems.

Organizing. Adjacency matrices may provide a very effective means of organizing data. They can be organized using regular spreadsheet and database software. There are also several software programs available for social network analysis that help organize adjacency matrices.

Processing. The software programs available in the field of social network analysis are very effective in processing data. A majority of the papers presented at the seventeenth annual conference of the International Network for Social Network Analysis were related to the formulas used by the software to process the data. There were a number of physicists working on the development of formulas for the physics of human interaction. Most of these software packages provide for the processing and testing of the data, using a variety of formulas which have been developed within the field, some with a greater degree of acceptance than others.

Representing. The hierarchical equivalency clustering matrix provides an interesting and helpful representation of data. However, a number of software packages in the field of social network analysis also provide a very effective means of representing the graph theory notations of the social network data. Some of these packages will provide a revolving three dimensional color representation of a complex of social networks, and other packages will even provide animated representation of chronological data, animating the changes in social networks over time or the movement between networks. Some companies will license their software only to organizations that hire them as consultants to examine issues in the organization such as the flow of information through the prescribed organizational structure, in relation to the social network structure of the organization. These packages tend to be very expensive, especially when the cost includes the consultation service. However, there are other more affordable packages available in the field ranging from $100 to $800.

Correlating. The data-gathered, organized, processed, and represented should provide for numerous network predictions. These predicted networks could be based on distinct data-for example, role-based networks, perception-based networks, action-based networks, influence-based networks, distance-based networks, phono/lexical-based networks, morpho/syntax-based networks, semantics-based networks, or psycholinguistic-based networks. Correlation between the predicted networks could serve as a gauge of the accuracy of the network predictions.

Interpreting. Networks predicted from phono/lexical data may be helpful in examining the possibility of phono/lexical identity networks, or the possibility of language shift and change over time. Networks predicted from textual analysis data may be helpful in examining the possibility of morpho/syntax, syntax, semantic, and psycholinguistic identity networks. The degree of equivalency in hierarchical clustering between these predicted networks, along with the networks predicted from role-based data, perception-based data, action-based data, influence-based data, distance-based data, etc., could be interpreted as a prediction of the macro social network system. However, the prediction of the macro social network system would require an investment of time in an area to determine the accuracy of network prediction.

Summary

Traditional approaches to language assessment may have a tendency, in a short-term language development assessment strategy, to perceive emic linguistic entities, and peg them in space and time. In this process, there may be an inclination to view language contact situations through notions such as language vitality, language shift, bilingualism, diglossia, or code switching, since such terms tend to support the notion of separate language integrity maintenance for the various languages held simultaneously in contact in the mind of a speaker. Hence, there may be an inherent tendency to overlook the notion of language change as a result of languages in contact in the minds of individuals. Traditional language assessment may tend to overlook the notion of an amalgam language resulting from languages in contact in the minds of individuals. It may also tend to overlook the notion of an innate knowledge of language engaged in the development of a purposeful communication alloy for individuals linked in multilingual social networks. This results in a Sapir-Whorf hypothesis tendency to view individuals as determined by these emic linguistic entities, rather than viewing these individuals as the determiners of communication systems that meet the needs of their everyday existence in their social networks. This tendency may result in language development decisions and initiatives that are, for the most part, controlled by the interests and perspectives of the language developers (Graham 1995). However, in complex language contact situations especially, it may not be appropriate or feasible to make long-term language development decisions or advance language development initiatives in this manner. Hence, it may be more productive to approach language development assessment in a manner that would fix the assumptions about language, and its social constructs, in the minds of the individuals in the given language context.

Complex linguistic contact situations may compel a language development strategy based primarily on co-patterned variation between linguistic network and social network phenomena. Thus, social network analysis may warrant some consideration in the design and implementation of a language development assessment strategy, as well as a structure for language development planning in language contact situations, facilitating the assessment of language vitality, shift, *and change* within the framework of social networks. Finally, network analysis might also prove helpful in providing a structure for the analysis and social networking of all the agencies and individuals that are involved, or interested, in language development within a given language development context.

References

Bavelas, Alex. 1948. A mathematical model for group structure. Applied Anthropology 7:16-30.
Blom, Jan-Petter, and John J. Gumperz. 1972. Social meaning in linguistic structures: Code switching in Norway. In John Gumperz and Dell Hymes (eds.), Directions in sociolinguistics, 407-34. New York: Holt.
Boissevain, Jeremy, and Clyde Mitchell, eds. 1973. Network analysis: Studies in human interaction. The Hague: Mouton.
Borgatti, Steve. 1994. Social network analysis overview. Paper presented at the seventeenth annual conference of the International Network for Social Network Analysis, San Diego, Calif.: 13-16 February 1994.
———, Martin G. Everett, and Linton C. Freeman. 1996. UCINET IV Version 1.64. Natick, Mass.: Analytic Technologies.
Cheshire, Jenny. 1982. Variation in an English dialect: A sociolinguistic study. Cambridge: Cambridge University Press.
Davis, James A. 1970. Clustering and hierarchy in interpersonal relations. American Sociological Review 35:843-52.
Durkheim, Emile. 1964. The division of labor in society. New York: Free Press.

Eckert, Penelope. 1988. Adolescent social structure and the spread of linguistic change. Language in Society 17:183-207.
Edwards, Walter. 1992. Sociolinguistic behavior in a Detroit inner-city black neighborhood. Language in Society 21:93-115.
Fass, Craig, Mike Ginelli, and Brian Turtle. 1996. Six degrees of Kevin Bacon. New York: Plume.
Gauchat, Louis. 1905. L'unité phonétique dans le patois d'une commune. Aus romanischen Sprachen und Literaturen. Festschrift Heinrich Morf zur Feier seiner fünfundzwanzigjährigen Lehrtätigkeit von seinen Schülern dargebracht, 175-232. Halle a.d. S., M. Niemeyer.
Graham, Steve. 1995. A case study: Language development strategies among the Diola people of southern Sénégal. Notes On Literature in Use and Language Programs 43:3-22.
———. 1996. A review of sociolinguistic research methodologies for the creole language context. Masters dissertation. University of York, UK.
Granovetter, Mark. 1973. The strength of weak ties. American Journal of Sociology 78:1360-80.
Grimes, Barbara F., ed. 1996. Ethnologue: Languages of the world, 13th ed. Dallas: Summer Institute of Linguistics.
Gurae, John. 1990. The six degrees of separation. New York, N.Y.: Random House.
Guttman, Louis. 1944. A basis for scaling qualitative data. American Sociological Review 9:139-50.
Harary, Frank, and Robert Z. Norman. 1953. Graph theory as a mathematical model in social science. Ann Arbor, Mich.: Institute of Social Research.
Hermann, M. E. 1929. Lautveränderungen in der Individualsprache einer Mundart. Nachrichten der Gesellschaft der Wissenschaften zu Göttingen. Philosophisch-historische Klasse 11:195-214.
Hubbell, Allan. F. 1950. The pronunciation of English in New York City. New York: Kings Crown Press.
Kapferer, Bruce. 1969. Norms and the manipulation of relationships in a work context. In Mitchell 1969:181-244.
Kerbo, Harold R. 1983. Social stratification and inequality. New York: McGraw-Hill.
Krempel, Lothar. 1997a. Inter-domain ties between organizational systems membership in organizational advisory boards. In Lothar Krempel (ed.), A gallery of social structures. Köln, Germany: Network Visualization, http://www.mpi-fg-koeln.mpg.de/~lk/netvis.html.
———. 1997b. World trade 1992. In Lothar Krempel (ed.), A gallery of social structures. Köln, Germany: Network Visualization, http://www.mpi-fg-koeln.mpg.de/~lk/netvis.html.

———. 1997c. An ego-centered network of a "Junior Scientist." In Lothar Krempel (ed.), A gallery of social structures. Köln, Germany: Network Visualization, http://www.mpi-fg-koeln.mpg.de/~lk/netvis.html.
Labov, William. 1966. The linguistic variable as a structural unit. Washington Linguistic Review 3:4-22.
———. 1972. Language in the inner city: Studies in the Black English Vernacular. Philadelphia: University of Pennsylvania Press.
Le Page, R. B. 1980. 'Projection, focussing, diffusion', or steps toward a sociolinguistic theory of language, illustrated from the sociolinguistic survey of multilingual communities, Stage I: Cayo Distric, Belize and II: St. Lucia. York Papers in Linguistics 9.
———. 1983. The need for a Multidimensional Model. York, UK: University of York. Photo Copy Collection.
———, and Andrée Tabouret-Keller. 1985. Acts of identity: Creole-based approaches to language and ethnicity. London: Cambridge University Press.
Lewin, Kurt. 1936. Principles of topological psychology. New York: McGraw-Hill.
Lippi-Green, Rosina L. 1989. Social network integration and language change in progress in a rural Alpine village. Language in Society 18:213-34.
Macaulay, Ronald K. S. 1976. Social class and language in Glasgow. Language in Society 5:173-88.
MacRae, Duncan Jr. 1960. Direct factor analysis of sociometric data. Sociometry 23:360-71.
Milroy, James, and Lesley Milroy. 1978. Belfast: Change and variation in an urban vernacular. In Peter Trudgill (ed.), Sociolinguistic patterns in British English, 19-36. London: Edward Arnold.
Mitchell, Clyde, ed. 1969. Social networks in urban situations. Manchester: Manchester University Press.
———. 1986. Network procedures. The Quality of Urban Life 74.
Moreno, Jacob. 1934. Who shall survive? New York: Beacon Press.
Mufwene, Salikoko S. 1986. The universalist and the substrate hypotheses complement one another. In Pieter Muysken and Norval Smith (eds.), Substrata versus universals in creole genesis, 129-62. Amsterdam: John Benjamins.
Pellowe, John. 1970a. Establishing speech varieties of conurbations: 1. Theoretical position. Newcastle upon Tyne: University of Newcastle upon Tyne. ms.
———. 1970b. Establishing speech varieties of conurbations: 2. Criteria and sampling. Newcastle upon Tyne: University of Newcastle upon Tyne. ms.

———. 1970c. Establishing speech varieties of conurbations: 3. Varieties as constructs. Newcastle upon Tyne: University of Newcastle upon Tyne. ms.

Sampson, Samuel F. 1969. Crisis in a cloister. Ph.D. dissertation. Cornell University, Ithaca, N.Y.

Schooling, Stephen. 1990. Language maintenance in Melaneasia: Sociolinguistics and social networks in New Caledonia. Summer Institute of Linguistics and the University of Texas at Arlington Publications in Linguistics 91. Dallas.

Wasserman, Stanley, and Katherine Faust. 1994. Social network analysis: Methods and applications. Cambridge: Cambridge University Press.

Modifying Language Beliefs: A Role for Mother-Tongue Advocates?

Carolyn P. Miller

Introduction

In the early sixties my husband and I moved into a village in the northwest corner of what was then South Vietnam to study the language and culture of the Bru people.[1] Maintenance of the Bru language at that time was not even a concern. Cut off from the Vietnamese by economic, social, and geographic barriers, the Bru, for the most part, knew very little Vietnamese and continued, despite the social dislocation of war, to live in self-sustaining communities. Hardly any Bru could read and write. Schools were few and generally without teachers. The Bru had never seen their language in writing, although they believed that, in the beginning of time, God had given to every people their language in written form. Unfortunately, they told us, the Bru had fallen on hard times and had cooked and eaten the animal skin on which it was written. That is why they had

---

[1] The Bru language is part of a language continuum which extends from highland areas of what is now central Vietnam across southern Laos and into northeast Thailand. The Bru-So continuum comprises a group of closely related languages and dialects and is known in its different locations and varieties as Van Kieu, Mangkong, Galler, Tri, Bru, So, Kataang, and Kha. Population figures for Vietnam are estimated to be 50,000 (Grimes 1996), for Laos 145,000 (unofficial Lao sources) and for Thailand 55,000 (Smalley 1994).

only a spoken language; it was in their stomach, but they no longer had a written language.

In the late seventies, we moved to Borneo and after a few years of language survey work, we moved into a Kadazan village in Sabah, Malaysia.[2] In many ways, life in the village was much as we had experienced it in Vietnam. Water buffalo brushed up against the posts of our house at night, shaking us awake. And a picturesque suspension bridge led across the river a few meters from our house. But the house had piped water, and the international phone system was introduced into the village while we were there. Our next-door neighbor commuted every day to his work as a plumber at the Queen Elizabeth Hospital in the city of Kota Kinabalu. The Kadazan-Dusun people had with great effort over the past twenty years successfully entered the mainstream of national life. Education had become more available. Basic literacy was no longer in Kadazan and English; all education was in the national language, Bahasa Malaysia. But with more urbanization, intermarriage, upward mobility, and education in the national language, people were expressing concern about the loss of the Kadazan-Dusun language and of traditional values. Community leaders and educators were concerned about large numbers of young people who could no longer use the Kadazan-Dusun language. A Kadazan school principal complained that children were coming to school without an adequate understanding of either Standard Malay or Kadazan. A Kadazan priest said there were young people in his parish with whom he could not discuss spiritual truth in any language because neither Kadazan or Malay were sufficiently understood. One political leader was quoted as saying, "Our future generation will be Kadazan-Dusun in name only, without a real identity if they speak only an 'alien' language" (*Borneo Bulletin* 1988).

In the nineties we returned to the area of the Bru-So, this time in northeast Thailand. We visited scattered areas of Bru-So villages and talked to them about issues of identity, language use, and language attitudes. We received letters and occasional visits from Bru friends in Laos and Vietnam. It was apparent that language maintenance had become a major question in all but the most remote areas. Residents of about half of the villages we visited in Thailand expressed the belief that in another generation their language would cease to be spoken in the village. Most viewed

---

[2] The Kadazan-Dusun language continuum is located in Sabah, Malaysia and constitutes one of the largest groups within that state. It comprises a group of dialects which include Minokok, Sugut Kadazan, Garo, Kimaragang, Tebilung, and other regionally distinct varieties of the language (Banker and Banker 1984). The group population was estimated by the 1970 census to be 183,454, though just who was included in this figure is unclear (Banker and Banker 1984). Other closely related language groups such as Rungus, Lotud, Tatana', Bisaya, etc., while linguistically distinct, are considered culturally to belong to the Kadazan-Dusun group.

this as unfortunate and representing the loss of the "inheritance from our ancestors".

In three of the Bru-So villages we visited in Northeast Thailand, speakers of the language were shifting to Lao and/or Thai. The reason they gave for the shift usually involved a question not just of language but of identity. "People are always disparaging of us and look down on us," said one. "This makes us not want to continue to use our language." Another said it was a good thing "that our group and language will die out, so that we can all be members of the Thai ethnic group and Thai people" (Miller 1994:92–3). In other villages where the language was being maintained for home use, speakers reported that they were embarrassed to speak it in front of Lao or Thai speakers.

A year or so ago I was asked by Mahidol University in Bangkok, Thailand, to present a paper at a forum of the Pan Asiatic Linguistics conference which they were sponsoring. The forum topic was "typologies and universals", and I was asked to present "something sociolinguistic" on this topic. Given my interest in the subject of language maintenance and shift, I decided to do some research into typologies of language maintenance. I wanted to apply these to the two "at risk" language continua with which we had been personally involved over the past thirty years (Miller 1996).

Factors affecting language maintenance or shift

I found to my surprise (and chagrin) that typologies were many! Numerous authors have grappled with *factors, variables, intervening variables,* and *contextual variables* associated with language shift. Some of these, such as *size*, are widely recognized to be important but are difficult to quantify in terms of the number of speakers needed to ensure survival of a vernacular language. Others are seen as more directly linked to language and culture maintenance.

Following are some of the factors commonly recognized to have major impact on language maintenance and shift. I have chosen to group them according to the model presented by Giles, Bourhis, and Taylor. In their 1977 article, they discuss ways of determining the objective *ethnolinguistic vitality* of societies. They define vitality as "that which makes a group likely to behave as a distinctive and active collective entity in intergroup situations" (Giles, Bourhis, and Taylor 1977:308). Their three categories of variables—status factors, demographic factors, and institutional support factors—are further expanded. *Status factors* include economic status, social status, socio-historical prestige, and status of the language both within and outside the community. *Demographic factors* include number of members, distribution, concentration, proportion, birthrate, and patterns of immigration and emigration. *Institutional support factors* involve the extent to which the group receives support for the language in both formal and informal institutions such as home, school, government, church, business, and so forth.

Demographic factors

Nature of contact situation. Superordinate groups are less likely to shift than subordinate ones, and for subordinate groups, those which are indigenous to their area (having established social institutions) are more likely to maintain their language than those which have migrated to the area (Lieberson, Dalto, and Marsden 1981). Furthermore, those who have become subordinate through annexation or colonization will not shift as quickly as those who have become subordinate through migration (Paulston 1994, Tabouret-Keller 1968).

Distribution of speakers. Groups whose members are adjoining and cohesive in their spatial arrangement are more apt to maintain their language than are those which are nonadjoining or noncohesive (Edwards 1992, Fishman 1991).

Immigration and emigration patterns. Groups with little out- or in-migration are more likely to maintain their language (Paulston 1994).

Marriage patterns. Groups practicing endogamy (particularly with arranged marriages) are more likely to maintain their language than those with strong tendencies toward exogamy (Paulston 1994).

Status and development factors

Language status. Languages with high status are more likely to be maintained than those with low status (Tabouret-Keller 1968). Status is enhanced in the following situations:

1. *Outsider evaluation of the language.* Majority language speakers have respect for the vernacular language (Smolicz 1987).
2. *Internal regard for the language.* Insiders perceive their language to be a "core value" of their culture (Smolicz 1992).
3. *Language development.* A language has a written form and a recognized standard (Fishman 1980).

Economic status. Where speakers of a vernacular are of equal economic status with speakers of the majority language or where knowledge of their language has direct economic value, the language is more likely to be maintained (Paulston 1994).

Social status. Where members of a language community have achieved a level of social acceptance equal to members of the majority culture, they are more likely to value language maintenance. "Being a member of a disparaged low-status group can take its toll on the collective will of members to survive or maintain themselves as a distinctive linguistic community in the intergroup structure" (Harwood, Giles, and Bourhis 1994:170).

Sociohistorical status. Where a language is perceived to have classical or religious significance, it is more likely to be maintained (Paulston 1994; Harwood, Giles, and Bourhis 1994).

Institutional support and control factors

Government policy. Where government policies are pluralist rather than incorporationist or assimilationist, the language is more likely to be maintained (Schermerhorn 1970). If the vernacular language community agrees with the government policy, the policy will be more effective. This may have either a negative or positive effect on language maintenance, depending on government policy (Schermerhorn 1970).

Language use factors. The following language use factors favor the maintenance of the vernacular language:

1. *Mass media.* The language is used in radio, television, or print media (Fishman 1980).
2. *Education.* The language is used in school either as a medium of instruction or as a subject of study (Fishman 1980).
3. *Government services.* The language can be used in government offices, clinics, etc., to request service.
4. *Industry.* The language can be used in the workplace.
5. *Religion.* The language is used for group religious functions (Paulston 1994).
6. *Culture.* The group maintains control of cultural functions and conducts these in their own language.
7. *Politics.* Political activity (campaign speeches, government policy speeches, etc.) is carried on in the language.

Evaluation of factors affecting maintenance of Kadazan-Dusun and Bru-So

In applying the above factors to the Kadazan-Dusun and Bru-So language continua, the picture was not encouraging, especially for the Bru-So. In the face of increasing language contact, the aggressive spread of the larger national languages, and signs of language loss (decay) in phonology, syntax, and lexicon, it was hard to see how they could avoid the continuing downward spiral to language death.

Demographically, both groups claim an area to which they are indigenous, but the cohesion of these areas has been eroded by emigration and immigration, either due to economic factors (for the Kadazan-Dusun) or the disruption of conflict (for the Bru-So). Exogamy is becoming increasingly frequent.

Although neither language has sociohistorical status, Kadazan-Dusun has a longer history of language development and greater prestige on the state level. Bru-So claims little prestige in any of the three countries where it is located and has had only minimal development in any of the three national scripts.

Language diversity in Malaysia and Vietnam, while not encouraged, is at least permitted. In Laos and Thailand policies are clearly assimilative. Because of greater educational and economic advantages, Kadazan-Dusun speakers are influential in government and educational circles and able to promote use of the language in some public media. Bru-So are generally educationally and economically disadvantaged and unable to exert influence on any level above the village.

At the same time, both from a study of the literature and from personal experience, it is encouraging to note that the spiral is not inevitable. People make choices on an individual, family, community, and societal basis. Not every group responds to the same situations in the same way. There are examples of other cultures and languages which have integrated, developed, and joined the wider society and nation without losing their sense of groupness or devaluing their cultural and linguistic identity. These demonstrate that ephemeral quality referred to by Paulston as "ethnic pride or ethnic stubbornness" (1994:16), which causes them to persist in maintaining their language and culture against all odds.

For the Kadazan-Dusun, and to a lesser extent for the Bru-So, speakers there are some indications that the importance of the language as a "core value" of the society is increasingly being recognized. A Kadazan-Dusun leader reflecting on the declining use of the language said, "If the Dusun language is lost, this means the loss of the Dusun identity which forms the basis, the source and the spiritual repository for Dusun culture" (Tombung 1988:6). A Bru-So village leader in Northeast Thailand echoed the same feeling when, in our hearing, he asked the question, "If we lose our language, who are we?" Both groups have reacted positively to efforts to develop their languages.

It is also encouraging that the use of the vernacular, although eroded in some cases, is still fairly strong in intergenerational home use. In a survey of Kadazan-Dusun parents, 44 percent reported Kadazan-Dusun to be the language of use in the home, 35 percent use both Kadazan-Dusun and Malay, and 9 percent use Kadazan-Dusun, Malay, and English. Only 9 percent reported no use of Kadazan-Dusun in the home (Lasimbang, Miller, and Otigil 1992). When evaluating their children's ability in Kadazan-Dusun and Malay, however, 69 percent said their children spoke Malay "well" or "very well", while only 62 percent said their children spoke Kadazan-Dusun at that level. Also, 40 percent said their children spoke both languages equally well, 35 percent said their children were better in Malay than Kadazan-Dusun, and 25 percent that their children were better in Kadazan-Dusun than Malay. So, although Kadazan-Dusun is still fairly widely used in the home, Malay is making strong inroads into this domain.

A Bru-So friend living in Laos reports that in many areas of Laos, the home language is shifting to Lao, but it is not known how extensive this is. In Thailand, home maintenance of the Bru language is strong in twelve of the eighteen villages we visited. Two villages reported both the vernacular and Lao to be used in the home, and four reported a shift to Lao in the home domain.

So, while bilingualism is clearly the norm for both Kadazan-Dusun and Bru-So communities, in areas from which data is available, the vernacular language continues to be used at home either almost exclusively or occasionally.

Subjective vitality

Bourhis, Giles, and Rosenthal extended the 1977 ethnolinguistic vitality model to include the *perception* of the majority and vernacular language communities regarding the position of both languages. They state that "a group's subjective assessment of its vitality may be as important in determining inter-ethnic behaviours as the group's 'objective' vitality" (1981:147). To try to discover this "subjective" vitality, they constructed a questionnaire to elicit the "impressions" of a language community about the relationship between a vernacular language and the language of the majority. They tested this model with Greek and Anglo communities in Australia. Others took the instrument and adapted and used it elsewhere.

Testing has shown that although there are some "perceptual distortions in favor of ingroup vitality" (Harwood, Giles, and Bourhis 1994:172), overall "studies have demonstrated that people's subjective perceptions are fairly accurate when compared to more objective assessments of the vitality context" (1994:181–82).

Allard and Landry (1992:192), after extensive testing in Canada, concluded that ethnolinguistic vitality (EV) beliefs "reflect with a considerable degree of validity the EV of majority and minority ethnolinguistic groups which are in contact. Also, a high degree of relationship exists between EV beliefs and first and second language use." While ethnolinguistic vitality beliefs are formed by the contacts individuals have within their ethnolinguistic networks, for individuals within a vernacular language community, these beliefs lead to choices concerning "the composition of one's ethnolinguistic networks, and to choices concerning language use in one's linguistic networks" (1992:192) in a form of reciprocal determinism.

A person's network of linguistic contacts in both the first and second language determines his competence in these languages as well as his beliefs, attitudes, and values about language. "Language aptitudes and competencies," Allard and Landry affirm, "and the cognitive-affective disposition toward ethnolinguistic aspects will have an impact on language learning and behaviour and, ultimately, on language maintenance and loss" (1992:173, 175).

Language beliefs

Allard and Landry (1992) distinguish between four types of language beliefs: general, personal, normative, and goal beliefs. All of these must be evaluated in determining ethnolinguistic vitality. To consider only general beliefs, they say, does not lead to an accurate understanding of the position of languages in contact.

General and normative beliefs are considered *non-self* beliefs, while personal and goal beliefs are *self* beliefs. In places where general, normative, personal, and goal beliefs are positive, language maintenance is likely to continue.

General beliefs. General beliefs involve an objective evaluation of the situation regarding the position of the languages in question. These may be about either the present situation (X speakers are more numerous than Y speakers in this area) or the future (X speakers will control most of this region's industries and businesses in the future). They also include beliefs about the behavior of friends and role models (my friends usually attend social events where the X language is spoken).

General beliefs are held about facts which are perceived to exist between language communities. These include assessment of demographic factors such as relative size, educational profile, economic advantages, and so forth.

Normative beliefs. Normative beliefs affirm what ought to be the situation in terms of the relative position of these languages. They express what each ethnic group ought to be able to expect (in this area, government services should be provided to X speakers in their mother tongue).

Personal beliefs. Personal beliefs involve questions of valorization, belongingness, and personal efficacy in regard to language. Valorization reflects the degree of importance placed on access to the resources identified by the ethnolinguistic vitality factors (it's important to me that I be able to pursue my education in X). Belongingness refers to the feelings of the individual concerning belonging to an ethnolinguistic group (when I reflect on the choices I make about friends, I feel as if I were very much an X person). Personal efficacy beliefs reflect the extent to which the person believes he can achieve personal goals based on ethnolinguistic vitality factors (I can attain my career goals while working in X language).

Goal beliefs. Goal beliefs involve the group member's desire and aspiration regarding the languages. This may involve the intention to change behavior in some way regarding language competence or use (I want to learn to speak X better).

Changing language beliefs

"Because self beliefs are more intimately related to the personal experiences of the individual and because they are presumed to be more instrumental in determining behavioural intentions, it is also hypothesized that self beliefs will be more strongly related to language use than non-self beliefs" (Allard and Landry 1992:179). Therefore, we should, it would seem, be more concerned about changing self beliefs than changing other beliefs.

Here are four of the negative beliefs we encountered among the Kadazan-Dusun and Bru-So.

Our language is inferior to the national language

One commonly held belief by both Kadazan-Dusun and Bru-So communities was that their language was in some way inferior to the national language or languages of wider communication. Our Kadazan teacher, who was also a teacher at the local grade school, told us one day about a discussion she had held with the other teachers in which they insisted that Kadazan had no grammar. She had watched us arrange the incredibly complex forms of verbs into paradigms and opined that perhaps Kadazan *did* have grammar. But her fellow teachers would have none of it.

It was a fascinating process to work with Kadazan staff of the dictionary project on the incredibly complex morphophonemic variation and morphology of the Kadazan-Dusun language and watch their respect for the symmetry and adequacy of their language grow. They had never realized the very fine range of semantic distinction they could make with slight changes of focus affixation.

Bru people were routinely told that they were ignorant and their language useless. Bru village literacy teachers we were training in Vietnam were completely undone by the scornful question of a local official as to whether they thought it was going to be possible to do university study in the Bru language. Later, at a workshop in Thailand where we were discussing ways to write the language in Thai script, one of the participants confessed, "I never thought it was possible to study our language and to write it."

For the Bru-So speakers, it was the complex sound system of their language, straining the resources of Vietnamese, Lao, and Thai orthographic inventories, which caused them to be aware that their language was "special". And as they began to learn to express ideas in the language, they found to their joy that they could write anything they wanted to.

If children learn the vernacular, they will not be able to learn the national language well

Kadazan parents who wanted to do well by their children frequently tried to switch and speak only Malay with them, from the time they began to learn to speak, thinking that they were doing them a favor. Feeling that their children's brains could only hold a limited amount of information, they were afraid that the children would be hindered in learning Malay if their parents spoke to them in Kadazan and caused them to learn that language first.

Modifying Language Beliefs: A Role for Mother-Tongue Advocates? 177

When I was asked to present a paper on the subject of language maintenance to a gathering of Kadazan-Dusun community leaders, I cited a number of studies which stressed the advantages of additive bilingualism. One such study showed that children who continued to have their home language reinforced while adding a second language performed better in all subjects (including knowledge of the second language) than children who were encouraged to switch from their home language to the second language. This was encouraging to Kadazan parents who feared they would be placing an unmanageable load on their children by encouraging them to learn both Kadazan and Malay simultaneously.

Maintaining the language is divisive and nonpatriotic

Efforts to encourage shift to the dominant language of a country are often motivated by a genuine concern on the part of the dominant group to promote unity and facilitate good communication within a country. An early French Minister of Education is quoted as saying, "For the unity of France the Breton language must die" (Walker 1984:116). But in many cases this desire is voiced without understanding of the effect of the shift on members of these vernacular groups. According to Smolicz, the attempt to "homogenize" a society may unbalance the process of tradition adaptation and retard, rather than enhance, social resilience. He feels that the pressure placed on Australian Aboriginal societies, for example, "combined with the denigration of their languages and cultures and the questioning of their intrinsic worth, has resulted in the alienation of some Aborigines both from western and from their own traditions" (Smolicz 1992:278).

Even for the vernacular community, the desire to support a national language and culture is often seen as a patriotic duty and felt somehow to be in conflict with maintenance of their own language and culture. Both groups can be helped by being introduced to examples of societies where healthy respect for each other's language and culture has led to stable bilingualism and racial harmony.

Maintaining the language is too costly

For a government or an education ministry struggling to prepare curricula and produce materials in the national language, the cost of encouraging and supporting literature and education in vernacular languages is often perceived as too great a burden. Generally, vernacular languages cannot count on strong governmental support or support from the dominant language communities.

As Paulston points out, "While moral decency dictates the language rights of minority groups, it does not necessarily follow that the state is under any obligation to economically support such rights..." (1994:40). Increasingly, in recent years the Kadazan-Dusun community has demonstrated the willingness to shoulder this burden. The recent formation of a language institute and a language foundation within the Kadazan-Dusun community with goals for literature production and language promotion is evidence of this. But for the Bru-So community few such resources exist, and the leadership and financial capability to undertake this task seem a long way off.

Denison (1988), when asked to help with language maintenance efforts for a small group in Italy, struggling with the implications of this, "Now I find myself hauled down from my ivory tower and conscripted into a local action group...They require, in less than no time at all, a standard orthography, a dictionary, a grammar and texts for school use." Unable to justify this tremendous output of labor unless some compelling social benefit were to be gained, he considered the various options open to the community. He finally decided that the historical continuity of the group provided this justification and stated, "This can most realistically and enrichingly be understood within a compound ethnicity, containing other linguistic and cultural strands, too, but linked with a clear determination not to surrender, in particular, the historical minority linguistic tradition which is not infrequently the chief identifying characteristic of members of the sub-group vis-à-vis non-members and toward each other" (1988:7).

Activities which can promote change of belief concerning the vernacular

While decision making remains the responsibility of national and local groups, we have seen some areas where sympathetic outsiders can have a role in presenting options or in correcting negative beliefs about vernacular language development and use.

Language study

The greatest compliment which can be paid to a language is to learn it. The impact of outsiders learning a vernacular language can be tremendous. When we began to construct language lessons for learning Kadazan, one

Kadazan man offered to help us so that his son could learn the language. He had come to greatly regret his decision to teach his son only Malay and English. Later, the Kadazan Cultural Association published the lessons in Kadazan and English and the state museum published them in Kadazan and Malay. We were told that Kadazan school children checked them out of the library to learn English! But a group of non-Kadazan spouses and friends of Kadazan people used them to begin a class to learn to speak the language.

We were not the only outsiders who had expressed interest in the Bru language as spoken in Dong Luang, Mukdahan, Thailand. Some of the linguistic students from Mahidol University had also gone to the area to study the language as a basis for their master's theses. When asked to tell about his area on tape, our language assistant said,

> We were undeveloped, they say. We carried things in back-baskets and were dependent on others for help before...We still are not very advanced, we Bru. Now we have come here in order to tell the foreigners. They want to know about our Bru language because they want to translate it into their language, which is something good. Now we Bru are not any longer neglected. Every other country is interested in learning about this Bru Dong Luang language. What does *mpai* mean? What does *maheq* mean? What does *nyin nyin* mean? What does *bieq* mean? What does *ap* mean? We must tell them these things so that they will share them with foreign countries to read and study, so that all other countries will know that this Bru group still exists in Thailand in the areas of Sakon, Mukdahan and Nakhon Phanom. (Miller 1996).

Dr. Suwilai Premsrirat took a group of Mahidol students to do a period of study in a Thavung village in northeast Thailand. In order to collect natural text, she asked a number of the villagers to tell on tape about their happiest experience. One woman in this tiny threatened language community said, "The happiest thing which has happened to me is having these young people come to learn my language" (Suwilai 1995).

Language development

Two men from a Bru-So community in Sakon Nakhon province came to work with us to develop an initial trial orthography for their language. It was something they had never attempted, but they entered into the project with a will. When they returned home after an initial period of work, they carefully gathered up not only the texts and materials they had written, but all the scrap paper we had used to test different combinations. Later when they made a second visit, one of the men reported that his daughter had taken the texts and small books we had prepared together to the Thai high school she was attending. When a crowd gathered around to see the materials, she told them proudly, "It's our language. We have a written language, you know."

We have found that preparing materials in the national language and a language of wider communication as well as in the vernacular confers special status on the vernacular. Lao and Thai speakers would sometimes ask for help from the Bru-So authors to try to pronounce the Bru-So words in the trilingual thesaurus or phrase book. Even the Thai owner of a photocopy shop where some of the materials were copied asked if he could make an extra copy of a trilingual picture book, "so my children can study the So language."

A great deal of prestige also accrues to a language with the introduction of a dictionary in that language. It was heartening to us to see the community effort of the Kadazan-Dusun people that went into the production of a very extensive dictionary which included morphological and lexical information in two dialects of the language as well as glosses in Bahasa Malaysia and English. A dictionary of one of the Bru-So varieties spoken in Thailand was published by Chulalongkorn University (Thongkum and Puengpa 1980). A dictionary of the Bru language in Vietnam has recently been compiled by Prof. Vuong Huu Le of the University of Hue (1997).

Use of the language for cultural events—music, drama, seminars, and so forth.

Use of the language at major cultural events such as the Harvest Festival among the Kadazan helps to reinforce its importance to the culture. At the launching of the Kadazan dictionary, featured on the program were a riddle-telling contest by some of the older members of the community and a story-telling display by a noted raconteur.

SIL ethnomusicologists Todd and Mary Saurman are recording and analyzing Hmong traditional music at the request of that community so that they can adapt and compose songs in their own musical style for church services. Recently, they encountered opposition from a Hmong man who is convinced that the way ahead for the Hmong people is to give up their language and culture and adapt completely to Thai. In the course of conversation, however, he shared his frustration in trying to teach the Hmong people and told of the inability of the older people to understand apart from their traditional ways of learning—one of which was through music.

In trying to explain to him why they were doing what they were doing, Todd and Mary echoed back to him his own words which indicated the extremely high value of Hmong music within the community. His eyes widened, Mary reported, "as he heard his own words coming back to him in these new thoughts. His heart opened, too. He really listened hard to what we were saying. He gave us the best support for what we're doing in the area of Hmong music" (Saurman, personal correspondence).

Because the Bru-So groups in Thailand are small and isolated from each other (some not knowing of the existence of the others), we decided to bring together speakers of the six languages we had worked with in our research project. We sponsored a seminar to discuss problems in writing these closely related languages in Thai script and to prepare health booklets on a topic of concern throughout the area. We also invited members of the Thai academic community, as well as SIL members working in other related languages. The seminar was a huge success. Most of the participants had not been aware that their language group was so large or extensive. When the project was completed and the materials distributed, one participant asked sadly, "Does this mean there won't be any more seminars?"

In order to raise awareness of the problem of language shift, the Kadazan-Dusun Cultural Association produced T-shirts with their logo on the front and the statement on the back in Kadazan-Dusun, "If you lose your language, you lose your culture."

Encouragement of leadership

One factor which may be seen to either reflect or influence the will of a group to maintain their language is the attitude of leadership. While it would be difficult to establish causality for this variable, yet it seems true that where leaders promote and encourage language use and language pride, the language is more likely to be maintained (Wardhaugh 1987). In the village where the headman told us it was better for the language to be lost, no one under the age of thirty or forty could even give us a word list. Yet in another village in a neighboring province, language use remains strong. Announcements are made over the loudspeaker in Bru. A sign in Bru notifies visitors that when the sun rises over Thailand it rises first over that village. On our first visit to the village, the village headman called the village together over the loudspeaker, telling them (in Bru) that foreigners had arrived who could speak their language. It was one of very few villages where the vernacular language was used on the government loudspeaker. A large crowd gathered to contribute to the word list elicitation, demonstrating both pride and expertise in the language. Yet this village is one of only two villages in Thailand which speak that dialect, and no other Bru-So villages are found in the entire province. We told a young man from the village that some Bru villages had told us it was better to give up the language. He asked us why they thought this. I replied, "Because people tell them that the language is useless. It isn't even written and its speakers are ignorant." His reply was, "Well, they tell us the same thing, but we don't want to give up our language."

Among the Kadazan, leadership at a high level is encouraging the maintenance of the language. Datuk Joseph Pairin Kitingan, who in the early '80s was recognized as the *huguan siou* or titular head of the Kadazan-Dusun people and holds the position of President of the Kadazan-Dusun Cultural Association wrote in the Foreword to the recently published dictionary of the language (Kitingan 1995):

Atagak o boros, atagak o koubasanan,
Atagak o koubasanan, atagak o kointutunan;
Atagak o boros, atagak o pirotian,
Atagak o pirotian, atagak o piunungan, pisododungan om pibabasan;
Atagak o pibabasan, atagak o piobpinaian,
Atagak o piobpinaian, kopitongkiad o rikoton do rusodon.

'Lose your language and you'll lose your culture,
Lose your culture and you'll lose your identity;
Lose your language and you'll lose mutual understanding,
Lose your mutual understanding and you'll lose harmony, mutual support, and peace;
Lose your peace and you'll lose your brotherhood,
Lose your brotherhood and you'll lose your mutual destiny.'

Those of us with access to outside literature about language maintenance efforts can strengthen the hands of leadership in vernacular language communities by making information available to them which will help to dispel fears about using and promoting the language. When we were living in Sabah, I overheard a Kadazan leader quoting some of the facts and figures from a paper I had presented at a national seminar concerning the use of vernacular languages at the village level. "Studies show ..." he was saying, and I was gratified that I had helped give him ammunition to counter disparagement toward use of the vernacular language.

Encouragement of parents

Because of the concern that parents were not encouraging their children to learn and use the Kadazan-Dusun language, a survey was conducted with the help of Kadazan elementary teachers to find out what the language use situation was in Kadazan homes. At the same time, the teachers participated in a workshop to produce children's literature in Kadazan. Though some of them had never before tried to write in their own language, they produced twelve small volumes ranging from a picture dictionary to folk stories to health and science stories. When we suggested including Malay and English translations in the back of the book, one of the teachers who was also a mother, objected. "I know my kids," she said, "they'll just turn to the back of the book and read the Malay. It's better to put in only the Kadazan, so they will be forced to read in that language." Eventually, a compromise was reached in which only some of the books included translations.

The children's books were included in school libraries and sold at cost by the cultural association and the local Jaycees. Parents were contacted after the books had been available for a period of time to see which of them were being read and which were most popular.

Linguistic training for vernacular speakers

It may be possible to provide opportunities training for people from vernacular groups to enable them to carry out the many tasks related to language development. At the Kadazan-Dusun Standardization Symposium in 1989, one of the Kadazan-Dusun leaders made a strong appeal for training in linguistics for some of their own people so that they could carry out this work (Topin 1989).

Several have taken up such studies. Some of them have become the technical support for a Kadazan-Dusun language foundation recently formed to address concerns about vernacular language production and promotion within the state of Sabah.

Education of national language speakers

Not only is it important to change negative language beliefs on the part of the vernacular community; language beliefs of majority language speakers and officials also often need to be addressed.

In many cases these beliefs are based on lack of information about the aspirations of the vernacular groups within their borders. When we visited provincial and district offices in northeast Thailand to explain the survey and language development project we were undertaking, we were told by one official, "Researchers often come here and carry out projects, but we are never given the results of this research." Because of this, we asked Thai colleagues at Mahidol University to translate the survey report into Thai. We went back to every province and district where we had obtained information to present copies of the report. The report contained concerns expressed by the vernacular language people regarding maintaining and developing their languages. We also gave each district head copies of the trilingual picture books, thesauruses, and phrase books which had been produced by vernacular language speakers in that district. In each case, officials expressed appreciation and seemed impressed by the work of the vernacular language speakers from their area.

Often majority language speakers and language planners have never considered the possible consequences of cultural and linguistic assimilation for a vernacular group. Those who tend to view "culture" as costumes, dances, and handicrafts need to realize that, as Smolicz has said, "languages constitute the core values of many, probably most cultures. If these are lost or destroyed, the cultures become residual and intellectually de-activated. In this way, they become reduced to mere fragments that can then be regarded as sub-cultural variants upon the majority culture" (1987:393). Smolicz goes on to say, "the concept of languages as core values in many ethnic cultures helps to mark out the boundary at which assimilation must stop if meaningful and stable multiculturalism is the desired outcome. In this sense languages can be regarded as the 'cultural markers' of minority existence and the indispensable prerequisites for cultural pluralism in ethnically heterogeneous societies" (1987:394).

Conclusion

Allard and Landry (1992:192–93) stress the importance of ethnolinguistic vitality (EV) beliefs.

> We believe that this conceptualization of EV in terms of beliefs has important implications for education in both formal and informal contexts. In ethnolinguistic minorities, both the family and the school have an important role to play in the formation of beliefs which will favor first language learning and maintenance. These beliefs can be nurtured, if we seek to promote an additive form of bilingualism, while also nurturing beliefs conducive to second language learning. It may be

difficult to modify the structural variables that are the basis for the objective EV of a community at the sociological level, but it may be possible, through effective educational programs to change the subjective EV of both minority and majority group individuals. Minority group individuals, when schooled in their first language, can acquire strong personal beliefs that may foster language maintenance even in low EV conditions. (1992:192-93)

Most of us, as outsiders, play no direct role in either the decisions made by members of majority language groups regarding language planning and language policies or the decisions made by vernacular groups about the development and maintenance of their language. But we can sometimes have a role in helping people become aware of options and the consequences of decisions made in other places and by other groups. This allows them to make decisions based on knowledge rather than ignorance and on confidence rather than fear. And sometimes we can even help them develop the tools they need to implement their decisions.

References

Allard, Réal, and Rodrigue Landry. 1992. Ethnolinguistic vitality beliefs and language maintenance and loss. In Fase, Jaspaert, and Kroon 1992:171-95.

Banker, John, and and Elizabeth Banker. 1984. The Kadazan/Dusun language. In Julie K. King and John Wayne King (eds.), Languages of Sabah: A survey report, 297-324. Canberra: Australian National University.

Borneo Bulletin. 1988. Preserve your own language. Borneo Bulletin, 21 May 1988, 36/21. Kuala Belait: Brunei Darussalam.

Bourhis, Richard Yvon, Howard Giles, and Doreen Rosenthal. 1981. Notes on the construction of a "Subjective Vitality Questionnaire" for ethnolinguistic groups. Journal of Multilingual and Multicultural Development 2:145-50.

Denison, N. 1988. Twixt the Scylla of total assimilation and the Charybdis of suicidal purism. Paper presented at the Seventh Sociolinguistics Symposium, York, England.

Edwards, John. 1992. Sociopolitical aspects of language maintenance and loss: Towards a typology of minority language situations. In Fase, Jaspaert, and Kroon 1992:37-54.

Fase, Willem, Koen Jaspaert, and Sjaak Kroon, eds. 1992. Maintenance and loss of minority languages. Amsterdam: John Benjamins.

Fishman, Joshua A. 1980. Minority language maintenance and the ethnic mother tongue school. Modern Language Journal 64:167–72.

———. 1991. Reversing language shift: Theoretical and empirical foundations of assistance to threatened languages. Clevedon: Multilingual Matters.

Giles, Howard, Richard Y. Bourhis, and Donald Taylor. 1977. Towards a theory of language in ethnic group relations. In Howard Giles (ed.), Language, ethnicity, and intergroup relations, 307–48. London: Academic Press.

Grimes, Barbara F. 1996. Ethnologue: Languages of the world, thirteenth edition. Dallas: Summer Institute of Linguistics.

Harwood, Jake, Howard Giles, and Richard Y. Bourhis. 1994. The genesis of vitality theory: Historical patterns and discoursal dimensions. In Rodrigue Landry and Réal Allard (eds.), Ethnolinguistic vitality, International Journal of the Sociology of Language 108:167–206.

Kitingan, Joseph Pairin. 1995. Kadazan-Dusun Malay English dictionary. Kota Kinabalu, Sabah: Kadazan-Dusun Cultural Association.

Lasimbang, Rita, Carolyn Miller, and Francis Otigil. 1992. Language competence and use among Coastal Kadazan children: A survey report. In Fase, Jaspaert, and Kroon 1992:333–55.

Lieberson, Stanley, Guy Dalto, and Mary Ellen (Johnston) Marsden. 1981. The course of mother tongue diversity in nations. In Anwar S. Dil (ed.), Language diversity and language contact: Essays by Stanley Lieberson, 48–82. Stanford, Calif.: Stanford University Press.

Miller, Carolyn P. 1994. Perceptions of ethnolinguistic identity, language shift and language use in Mon-Khmer language communities of Northeast Thailand. Mon-Khmer Studies 23:83–101.

———. 1996. Application of typologies for language maintenance and loss to Southeast Asian linguistic minorities: The case of the Bru-So and Kadazan-Dusun language continua. Pan-Asiatic Linguistics: Proceedings of the Fourth International Symposium on Languages and Linguistics. vol. 5. Salaya, Thailand: Mahidol University. Institute of Language and Culture for Rural Development,

Paulston, Christina Bratt. 1994. Linguistic minorities in multilingual settings: Implications for language policies. Amsterdam: John Benjamins.

Schermerhorn, Richard A. 1970. Comparative ethnic relations. New York: Random House.

Smalley, William A. 1994. Linguistic diversity and national unity: Language ecology in Thailand. Chicago, Ill: The University of Chicago Press.

Smolicz, Jerzy J. 1987. National language policies in Australia and the Philippines: A comparative perspective. In Asmah Haji Omar (ed.), National language and communication in multilingual societies, 382–418. Kuala Lumpur: Dewan Bahasa dan Pustaka.

———. 1992. Minority languages as core values of ethnic cultures: A study of maintenance and erosion of Polish, Welsh, and Chinese languages in Australia. In Fase, Jaspaert, and Kroon 1992:27–305.

Suwilai Premsrirat. 1995. On language maintenance and language shift in minority languages of Thailand: A case study of So (Thavung). Paper presented at the International Symposium on Language Endangerment in Tokyo, Japan.

Tabouret-Keller, Andrée. 1968. Social factors of language maintenance and language shift. In Joshua A. Fishman, Charles A. Ferguson, and Jyotirindra Das Gupta (eds.), Language problems of developing nations, 107–18. New York: Wiley.

Thongkum, Theraphan L., and See Puengpa. 1980. A Bruu-Thai-English dictionary. Bangkok: Chulalongkorn University.

Tombung, Raymond Boin. 1988. Kebudayaan Dusun Sebagai Landasan Identiti: Tren dan Potensi masa Hadapan. Paper presented at the conference of the United Sabah Dusun Association, Kota Kinabalu, July 1988.

Topin, Benedict. 1989. Problems and aspirations of the Sabahan communities on preservation, development and standardization of their language dialect and opportunities to standardize the native dialects of Sabah. Paper presented at the Symposium on the Standardization of the Kadazan Dialects, Kundasang, Sabah, Malaysia.

Walker, A. G. H. 1984. Applied sociology of language: Vernacular language and education. In Peter Trudgill (ed.), Applied Sociolinguistics, 159–202. London: Academic Press

Vuong Huu Le. 1997. A Bru-Vietnamese-English dictionary. Hue: Nha Xuat Ban Thuan Hoa.

Wardhaugh, Ronald. 1987. Languages in competition: Dominance, diversity, and decline. Qxford: Basil Blackwell.

———. 1992. An introduction to sociolinguistics. Oxford: Basil Blackwell.

Assessing Motivations: Techniques for Researching the Motivations behind Language Choice

Mark E. Karan and Jürg Stalder

Introduction

Karan (this volume) applied a new language shift model to language vitality assessments. His *perceived benefit model* of language shift allows projections of language vitality based on the language-related motivational structures present in communities. Motivations influencing language choice—either communicative, economic, social, or religious—provide the data necessary for language vitality assessments.

Karan concluded his paper by saying, "At present, we need survey tools to gather data on the present language use motivational structures in a community, tools which allow the data to show the motivational variation within the community" (this volume, p. 75) This present paper discusses various methods for collecting this language use motivational structure data, and presents a "how to" approach for collecting data on these communicative, economic, social, and religious language-related motivations.

We need to show the motivational variation within a community because variation in language use motivations (LMs), such as across generations, or based on social class factors, can profitably be used to gain valid insights into present and future language shift. Differing motivational patterns in different subsections of a community can signal the direction of change in motivational, and thus, language use patterns.

Karan states,

> New methods are needed to make assessments of language-related motivational structures in order to determine which language-related motivations are active in the differing subsections of a speech community. We need further development of survey methodology, designed to reveal present language-related motivational patterns. These tools must be designed to enable discovery of all the different types of LMS and also must be able to have some way of distinguishing the magnitude or strength of an individual motivation, perhaps with a type of high, medium, or low motivation ranking.
>
> It is necessary that these developments in survey methodology take into consideration all areas and types of motivations, and that they assess the motivations of a broad spectrum of the society. Motivational data are needed from a representative sampling of the community, with care taken to record relevant social factors of the individual subjects in the sampling.
>
> We need to record these factors of the individual subjects so that studies of the variation in the motivational structures of the community can be made, such as variations across gender lines, based on educational factors, or correlated with the innovators of linguistic change. (Karan: p. 71)

What then is called for, and what this paper attempts to provide, is a methodology which

1. gathers data on the differing language use motivations present in a community,
2. gathers this data from individuals, as the model is based on individuals' motivations,
3. gathers this data from a sample of the community which represents the population as well as possible,
4. gathers this data in such a way that motivational variation across sub-sections of the community can be studied,
5. gathers this data from a large number of subjects, so that motivational variation studies can be done, and
6. provides tools which are not too difficult to use.

Data gathering and sampling techniques

Since the model calls for individuals' motivations, the data-gathering tool should first be one which deals with individuals and not with groups. The group interview technique in sociolinguistic research, thus, is not applicable. A group consensus is not adequate. The data gathering for language-use motivational data must be done by testing or interviewing individuals.

Interview techniques

Next, in order to determine the optimal data-gathering technique, it is necessary to choose whether to use individual questionnaire techniques or some other method to gain access to each individual's LMs. For our research, we decided that individual interviews, using questionnaires, would be able to provide information about the different areas of motivation, that they could be done easily, and that they would in most cases provide accurate information concerning the motivations. Henerson, Morris, and Fitz-Gibbon (1978) address self-report in the area of attitude research in their book *How to Measure Attitudes*, where *attitude* is broadly defined as "all the objectives we want to measure that have to do with affect, feelings, values, or beliefs" (1978:13). They ask, "Should we assume that we can accept a person's statements about his own attitude as the best indicator of the attitude? In some instances, yes, particularly when we can see no reason for him to hide anything" (1978:12). They maintain that:

> When you use self-report procedures, you assume that the people whose attitudes you are assessing have the self-awareness to recognize their own beliefs and feelings and the ability to articulate them. You also assume that they have no reason to lie about their attitudes.
>
> Self-report procedures represent the most direct type of attitude assessment and should probably be employed unless you have reason to believe that the people whose attitudes you are investigating are unable or unwilling to provide the necessary information...
>
> IF the people whose attitudes you are investigating are able to understand the questions and have sufficient self-awareness to provide you with the necessary information, and IF they are likely to answer honestly and not deliberately falsify their responses...use SELF-REPORT PROCEDURES. (1978:21, 39)

We did think that it would be important to verify the motivations data that we gathered through these self-report interviews. For this we developed certain "guised" techniques.

In 1967, Lambert introduced a technique for assessing language-related attitudes called the *matched guise* technique. In this technique, people are asked to evaluate the speakers of certain recorded sections of speech for qualities such as kindness, intelligence, ambition, sincerity, etc. What the subjects do not know is that more than one of the sections of speech were recorded by the same person, but recorded in a different language or dialect (a different guise). Differences between the evaluations of the same speaker in the different guises (different languages or dialects) reveals attitudes toward the languages or dialects in question. Based on this, we define a "guised" technique as one where the subjects think they are evaluating something other than what they are actually evaluating.

Thus, in our individual interviews, as well as using direct questions concerning different areas of LM, we also employed certain guised techniques to verify this self-report information.

It is also very important that the tool developed to assess LMs be one that is easy and quick to apply. There is a need to test large numbers of subjects in order to have access to the societal variation in LM patterns. For this tool to be practical, it must be easily applicable, allowing an individual to be tested in just a few minutes. Often, the value of a larger sample of individuals far outweighs the added "accuracy" of a tool that is more comprehensive but much more difficult to apply because of the larger amount of time needed for each subject.

Sampling method

A very good sampling technique for a motivation assessment tool is a systematic sampling. Systematic sampling has "precision equivalent to a simple random sample and will be mechanically easier to draw" (Fowler 1984:23). A systematic sampling selects every nth member of a population, where the n is determined by the size of the desired sample and the size of the community. For instance, if the population's size is 200,000 and the desired sample is 200, n will be 1000. With this method, the starting point is not the first person on the list, it is rather the person on the list corresponding to a randomly drawn number between *1* and n. The shortcoming of this method is that it requires a complete list of the population, as does simple random sampling (numbering the population and then, with a random number generator, getting the numbers which select the members of the sample).

There are sampling methods which maintain many of the advantages of simple random sampling and systematic sampling, but which do not require a complete list of the population. These methods are very commonly used because, especially in the context of the developing world, complete lists of the population are rare.

One such method is called *area probability sampling* by Fowler and *multistage cluster sampling* by de Vaus.

> The basic approach is to divide the total target land area into exhaustive, mutually exclusive subareas with identifiable boundaries. A sample of subareas is drawn. A list then is made of housing units in selected subareas, and a sample of listed units is drawn. As a final stage, all people in selected housing units may be included in the sample, or they may be listed and sampled as well. (Fowler 1984:28)

> The basic procedure is first to draw a sample of areas. Initially, large areas are selected and then progressively smaller areas within the larger ones are sampled. Eventually we end up with a sample of households and use a method of selecting individuals from the selected households. (de Vaus 1990:67)

These multistage methods must assure that the first selection of areas is large enough to avoid distortion of results by the random choice of certain areas which would not reflect the total population. For instance, if the first stage were to select 2 districts of the 23 districts in a population center, and the 2 districts that were randomly chosen were the upper class areas, the results of the survey would not be reflective of the population. If 6 of the 23 districts were among the first selection, this type of distortion would be much less likely.

A variation of these multistage methods has proven to be very useful in sociolinguistic surveys among villages or small towns. In cases where the target area includes many different villages and towns, the first stage in the multistage method would be selecting certain villages or towns. Where the target area is just one town or village, the first stage of the above proposed method is dropped. All of the sections of the town or the village are selected. A list of all of the households in the town or village is made, following geographic distribution, and then a systematic sampling is used to choose every nth household. At that point, every member of the selected households (or a sampling of those in the selected households) are interviewed and tested. This method not only does not need a list of the population, it also does not need the presence or knowledge of district type divisions in the population center.

We recommend the use of a multistage method: For larger geographic areas, first select, randomly or systematically, certain population centers or divisions, then for each center or division, systematically select certain households, and then test or sample each selected household. For smaller areas, towns, or villages, just systematically select certain households and then test or sample each selected household.

There are cases in real-life survey situations where certain information is needed, and the resources to gather this information are not fully available. In these cases, certain expediencies can and are used to get general impressions of the needed information. An example of this is perhaps where a survey team is able to be in a village for only one afternoon, and they would need to have an idea of the language use motivational structure of the village. In such cases, inferior sampling methods might be used.

One such method is a stratified quota type of system, where the researchers, based on general knowledge of the makeup of the community, attempt to include in a somewhat haphazard sampling of the community a certain number of people from the different subsections of the population: a certain number of men, women, educated, uneducated, upper-class, lower-class, etc. This type of system is inferior, because it has the strong potential of attracting subjects who either see themselves, or are seen by the community, as being "stronger" in the linguistic realm, thus distorting the results. Attempting to find a certain number of subjects in a particular class (e.g., urban, middle-aged, uneducated men), when the community has become aware of the general area of the research, will often result in the researcher "falling into contact" with those in the community who not only match the particular class being sought, but also are more comfortable with the area of research. When such expediencies are used, the possibilities of the data being distorted are present. Nevertheless, certain cases might call for certain expediencies; but in these cases, the reservations as to the quality of data collected should be noted.

Data-gathering tool

This section presents one specific data-gathering tool which fits the specifications already given. It uses an acceptable sampling method. It assesses individuals' motivations. It is easy to administer. It collects data that can be used to see the variation of motivations in the community Also, it is applicable for collecting data for all motivation areas: communication, economy,

Assessing Motivations: Techniques for Researching

prestige, solidarity, and religion. The tool largely depends on direct, individual questioning and is verified by some guised questions.

The main part of this tool is a short questionnaire, to be administered in a speech community. The questionnaire has a part for recording certain social category facts about the subject. Each subject is asked their name, age, gender, educational level, occupation, and residence history. This personal data is collected after the subject has been asked the eleven short questions on the questionnaire. The first question asks what languages are used in the speech community. The following questions, in five sets of two, ask what languages people are motivated to use in order to gain an advantage in one of the motivational areas, and then ask about the strength of the motivation. An example of one of these pairs of questions (this one concerning economic motivations) is:

What languages are important for getting money?

How important: very important or a bit important?

The second question is asked for each language mentioned as a response to the first question. The list of questions is included as appendix 1. A sample response recording form is included as appendix 2. On the response form, the test administrator lists the languages mentioned, and then puts a *2* in the appropriate box for each "very important" response, and a *1* for the "somewhat important" response.

This type of coding, where numbers are assigned to degrees of motivation, is very common in the social sciences. Often, instead of this three-value scale (not important, somewhat important, very important), a five-value scale is used, as in figure 1.

Figure 1. A five-value scale

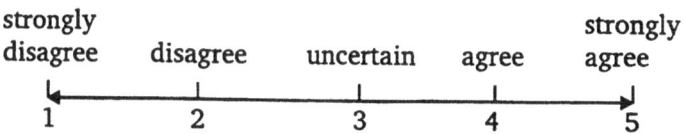

When numbers are assigned to this type of motivation information, it must be realized that the data are still ordinal. They are not interval data. The categories can be ranked, but the difference between the categories cannot be specified numerically. The assigning of values to the categories is done to give a comparative profile of motivations. A motivation assigned a value of 2 is not twice as strong as a motivation assigned a value of 1, thus the data are ordinal. This has important implications as to the type of statistical measures which can and cannot be rightly applied to the data. For descriptive statistics, "those which summarise patterns in the responses of people in a sample" (de Vaus 1986:102), cross-tabulations and rank correlation, such as Kendall's *tau* and Spearman's *rho* would be appropriate. Pearson's *r* or regression statistics would not be appropriate. For appropriate inferential statistics, those which "provide an idea about whether the patterns described in the sample are likely to apply in the population from which the sample is drawn" (de Vaus 1986:102–3), tests for significance of *tau* or *rho*, but not of *r*, would be appropriate.

After a number of subjects have been questioned, a pattern starts to emerge. Normally, the answers to the questions reveal varying degrees of different types of motivations toward the use of the different languages in the community. When a pattern is evident, guised questions can be asked of the subsequent subjects to verify the pattern. The guised questions to be used in such a situation could, for example, request the subject to pick between two imaginary, though described people, hypothetically choosing one as a future spouse for a sibling, or as someone who would be elected to be mayor, or as someone who would be most likely to succeed. The descriptions of the candidates for the choice would include that one controls a language that the other does not. Through this, the value of controlling this language for a particular field of motivation could be verified.

Some examples of guised type questions which could be used are:

If you had to choose between the following two men as a husband for your little sister, who would you choose? Why?

1. Joe who walks to his job as a store manager, or Pete who rides his motorcycle to his job as a gas station attendant.
2. Chris who speaks Ewondo and French, or Paul who speaks French and Pidgin.
3. Tim who has a moped but who only speaks Ewondo, or Mike who only has a bicycle but who speaks French as well as Ewondo.

Guised questions of this type would make individual interviews longer, but are seen as necessary to complement the self-report data with a type of data that was not based on direct questioning. In some cases, the answers to the interview questions might reflect a commonly accepted understanding about language motivations, rather than the true state of motivations. The guised questions would help reveal such a situation.

In a particular test situation, if the use of the guised questions does not reveal any discrepancies between the people's declared motivations and the "real" motivations, their use could be discontinued to ease the test application. If the direct questions were giving the same answers as the guised questions, the use of the direct questions alone would be indicated. If the guised questions did reveal some discrepancies between the people's declared and real motivations, use of this direct question interview method would be contraindicated, or at the minimum, only used with the understanding that the method is amassing a commonly accepted understanding about the motivations, and not real motivations data (see figure 2). In this case, insights into the real motivation patterns would be gained through the answers to the guised questions. This would call for an expansion of the use of guised questions in this situation.

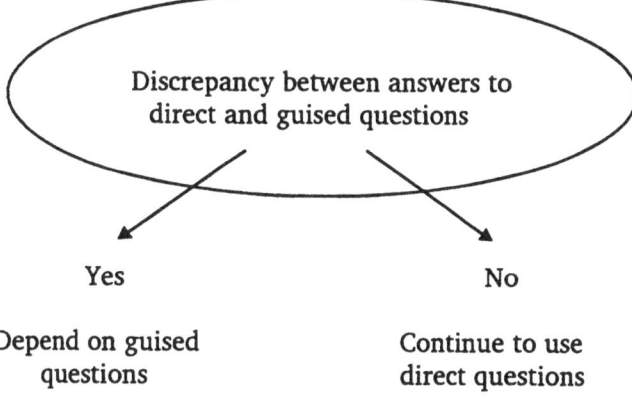

Figure 2. Expanded use of direct and guised questions

Treatment and presentation of data

Once the subjects in the sample have been interviewed, the data is treated and presented in two main ways: (1) a global presentation of the motivations, and (2) a presentation of the data which enables comparisons between the motivational patterns of different subsections of the community.

Global presentation

With the global presentation of the data, for each motivation of each language, the scores of all the subjects are added together and then divided by the number of subjects, giving an average score for each type of motivation for each language for the entire sample.

A preliminary testing of only 15 subjects was done in Yaoundé, basically with the goal of evaluating the questions on the questionnaire. Not only did the questions work well, the data on this preliminary testing revealed interesting results which plausibly appear to reflect the language use motivations situation. For this limited sample of only 15 subjects, the group average of the different motivations for each language is presented in table 1, where the sum of the *0, 1, 2* responses was divided by the number of subjects. Thus, these numbers combine strength of response by individuals with how many individuals responded to a particular category of motivation for a language.

Table 1. Group average of motivations for each language

	Communication	Economy	Prestige	Solidarity	Religion
French	1.9	1.9	1.8	1.5	0.3
English	0.4	0.7	1.2	0.1	0.3
Local	0.7	0.9	0.6	1.2	0.5
Pidgin	0.1	0.2	0.0	0.0	0.0

The graphic display of the same data (figure 3) presents these motivation patterns in an easily accessible form.

Figure 3. Group average of motivations for each language

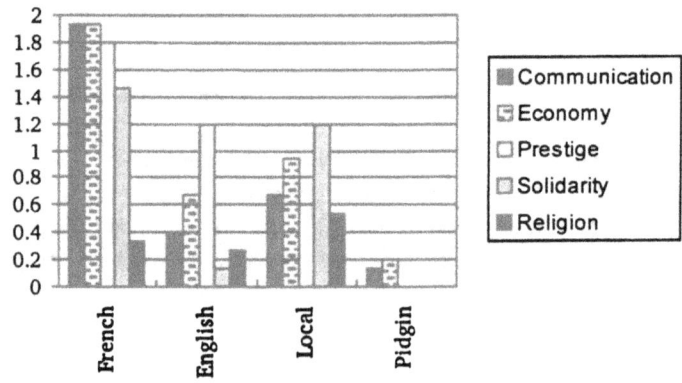

Through this graph, the validity of this measure, this system, and these data are demonstrated by different observations. The high-prestige motivation for the use of English is a phenomenon known in many cultures. The high-solidarity motivation for the use of the local language is a normal pattern. The high motivations to use French in this culture are well known. In this particular bilingual situation, French is used as the language of wider communication, while the numerous local languages such as Ewondo are used only with those having the same mother tongue. The relatively low religious motivations for all of the languages reflect a norm in many cultures, where no one particular language is motivated by a desire to please God or spirits. The use of Pidgin in the Yaoundé context is largely limited to commerce and some communication between groups from the west of the country.

In general, we were astonished by the concise and seemingly accurate profile of language use motivations presented in this graph. LM data is accessible, and LM data is extremely useful.

This average score for each type of motivation for each language combines the frequency of responses with the strength of the responses. This average is a composite of the number of subjects who indicated the type of motivation in question with the strength of the indications for that type of motivation (2 or 1 for very or somewhat important). For those who do not want to combine these two different effects—the strength and the frequency of the responses—a table could be prepared which would substitute for the above table and graph. This new table would state the number of 2s, 1s and 0s for each type of motivation for each language. Thus, for example, communicative motivations to learn and use French (table 2), instead of being simply reflected by the average of 1.9 (14 times 2 plus 1 times 1 divided by 15), would be represented by 14 2s and 1 1.

Table 2. Strength of motivations to learn and use each language

Total subjects	Communication		Economy		Prestige		Solidarity		Religion	
15	2s	1s	2s	1s	2s	1s	2s	1s	2s	1s
French	14	1	14	1	13	1	10	2	2	1
English	2	2	4	2	8	2	0	2	2	0
Local	2	6	5	4	4	1	7	4	3	2
Pidgin	0	2	1	1	0	0	0	0	0	0

0 = not important; 1 = somewhat important; 2 = very important

In the discussion of the comparison of the motivational patterns for the different subsections of the community given in the next section, this same type of table could be used to replace the tables and charts which use the averaging method. This type of table is possibly preferred by some because it is a more transparent presentation of the raw data.

Comparisons of motivational patterns

The second part of the data treatment and presentation is one which enables comparisons between the motivational patterns of different subsections of the community. As mentioned above, these differences can be very useful in demonstrating the direction of present language shift patterns, and through this they can be useful in projecting future language shift patterns.

This data treatment and presentation can be done in many different ways, some "higher tech" and some "lower tech". A high-tech way of treating and presenting the data would be to use analysis of variation (ANOVA) statistics to reveal which social factors have what type of effect on the various responses. A very low-tech way of treating and presenting the data would be to repeatedly divide the data into two parts, distinguished each time by a social factor (e.g., gender) and compare the motivation results of the two parts.

The procedure that we would suggest is somewhat "medium tech" and is very useful. The results of the motivational questions are charted out in such a way as to enable comparison of differing patterns of language use motivations in different subsections of the community. An example of this is suggested in table 3. For each language, the data is separated into age, gender, rural/urban, and social class categories. The presentation of the data in this format facilitates comparisons between the motivational patterns of young and old, male and female, urban and rural, and upper class and lower class. Each cell of this table would be filled either by the average score of the responses or by the number of 2s and 1s and the overall number of subjects for each particular social category.

Assessing Motivations: Techniques for Researching

Table 3. A comparison of motivations and social categories

		Young										Old									
		Female					Male					Female					Male				
		C	E	P	S	R	C	E	P	S	R	C	E	P	S	R	C	E	P	S	R
urban	upper																				
	lower																				
rural	upper																				
	lower																				

In this particular case, the categories of upper and lower class are the result of collapsing the categories of occupation and educational level into the category of social class. This type of combination of factors, if done following normal societal patterns, can be very useful in that it allows a more concise presentation of the data, enabling the comparison between the relevant subsections of the community.

Along with the examination of the data presented in such tables, different graphs can be made to give a more visual presentation of the differences in motivational patterns between different subsections of the population. As an example of the technique, and only as such, figures 4 and 5 are presented. They are good only as examples because they are based on an inadequate sampling of a population (the sampling mentioned earlier which was designed to evaluate certain questions in the questionnaire). These charts give an example of the motivational pattern diversity between younger and older members of the population for the local language and for English.

Figure 4. Motivations of younger and older people for using the local language

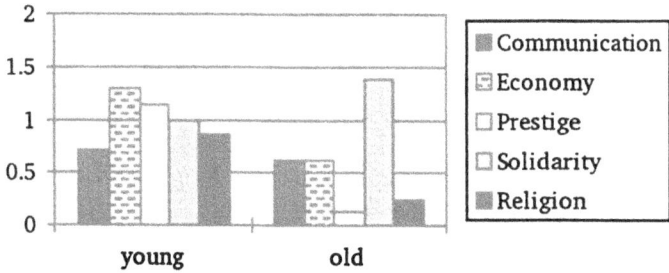

Figure 5. Motivations of younger and older people for using English

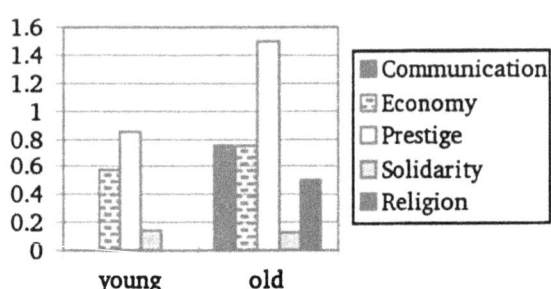

Such a graphic or table-based presentation of the data will reveal differences in the language use motivational patterns between subsections of the community. These differences can then be used to gain understanding of present and future language shift patterns.

Interpretation of data

Differences between the motivational patterns for the different languages in a community can give vast amounts of insight into the social role of the languages. An understanding of the different facets of the motivational structure of a language discloses, in a way no other study can, the function and importance of the language in that community.

Language use data provides information on what language is spoken where and to whom. Motivation data provides information on the rationale and significance of the language use patterns.

The differences between the subgroups in their motivation patterns then goes much further in shedding light on the direction of change in the language use patterns of a community. Based on the understanding that those who are the normal innovators of change in a community will also be the innovators of language use pattern change, projections of future language use motivation patterns can be drawn from the study of the patterns of those in the forefront of innovation. Thus, motivational studies can provide not only insights into current language shift patterns, but also insights into potential language shift in the future.

As an example of this, we recently learned that in Paoua, in the Central African Republic, young women are motivated to use and are actually using Sango more than the other subsections of the population. Sango is the prestigious language of wider communication in the area. Based on the knowledge that young women are often in the forefront of linguistic change in very similar cultures, we can interpret the difference between the motivations of the young women and those of the rest of the population to signal that future motivations for the whole community will most probably have a larger place reserved for Sango.

Conclusions

The consideration of motives plus opportunity can be profitable in language use questions. If people are motivated to learn and use a particular language, and if the society presents them with the opportunity to do so, the most likely result will be that those people will learn and use the language. This, then, would increase the level of opportunity in a society to learn and use that language. The added number of people who use the language in question would also normally cause an increase in motivation for others in the community to learn and use that language.

Thus, language motivation data is not as useful by itself as it is in combination with language use data—motive plus opportunity. In the same light, language use data, by itself, is not as useful as when combined with language motivation data. This, however, has been our unfortunate status quo: attempting to study language maintenance, language shift, and language vitality questions without collecting data on motivations. This unfortunate status quo should definitely be changed. Language motivation data are much too useful to continue to ignore.

The tool introduced in this paper for gathering motivation data has a lot of potential. We recommend its further development and use. It is easy to apply, reasonably accurate, and does provide data that reveals the variation present in the community.

The true value of this paper, however, is not in presenting one model of assessing language use motivations, useful though it may be, but rather in demonstrating that language use motivation data are accessible and are very useful in understanding and dealing with language shift and viability issues.

APPENDICES

Appendix 1: Questions

1. What are the languages used here in _____?
2. What languages are important for communicating with people?
   How important: very important or a bit important?
3. What languages are important for getting money?
   How important: very important or a bit important?
4. What languages are important if you want to better yourself, to be important, to have a lot of prestige?
   How important: very important or a bit important?
5. What languages are important if you want to be one of the group, one of the large family, one of the intimate neighborhood group?
   How important: very important or a bit important?
6. What languages are important if you want to please God or the Spirits?
   How important: very important or a bit important?

Appendix 2: Sample Response Recording Form

Response Recording Form
Name: Location:
Age: Sex: Educational Level:
Occupation:
Residence History:

	Communication	Economy	Prestige	Solidarity	Religion
L1					
L2					
L3					
L4					

0 or blank = not important; *1* = somewhat important; *2* = very important

References

de Vaus, D. A. 1986. Surveys in social research. London: George Allen and Unwin.
Fowler, Floyd J., Jr. 1984. Survey research methods. Newbury Park, Calif.: Sage.
Henerson, Marylene E., Lynn Lyons Morris, and Carol Taylor Fitz-Gibbon. 1978. How to measure attitudes. Newbury Park, Calif.: Sage.
Lambert, Wallace. E. 1967. A social psychology of bilingualism. Journal of Social Issues 23(2):91–109. Also in J. B. Pride and Janet Holmes (eds.), 1972, Sociolinguistics: Selected readings, 336–49. Harmondsworth: Penguin Books.

SIL International
Publications in Sociolinguistics

Recent Publications

3. **Assessing ethnolinguistic vitality: Theory and practice,** by Gloria Kindell and M. Paul Lewis, eds., 2000.
2. **The early days of sociolinguistics: Memories and reflections,** by Christina Bratt Paulston and G. Richard Tucker, eds., 1997.
1. **North Sulawesi language survey,** by Scott Merrifield and Martinus Selsa, 1996.

For further information or a full listing of SIL publications contact:

International Academic Bookstore
SIL International
7500 W. Camp Wisdom Road
Dallas TX 75236-5699

Voice: 972-708-7404
Fax: 972-708-7433
Email: academic_books@sil.org
Internet: http://www.sil.org

www.ingramcontent.com/pod-product-compliance
Lightning Source LLC
Chambersburg PA
CBHW051522230426
43668CB00012B/1710